Mobile L

How should we understand the personal and social impacts of complex mobility systems? What are the costs of mobile lives? Can lifestyles based around intensive travel, transport and tourism be maintained in the twenty-first century? What are the possibilities of developing post-carbon lifestyles?

In this provocative study of 'life on the move', Anthony Elliott and John Urry explore how complex mobility systems are transforming everyday, ordinary lives. The authors develop their arguments through an analysis of various sectors of mobile lives: networks, new digital technologies, consumerism, the lifestyles of 'globals' and intimate relationships at-a-distance. Elliott and Urry introduce a range of new concepts – *miniaturized mobilities, affect storage, network capital, meetingness, neighbourhood lives, portable personhood, ambient place, globals* – to capture the specific ways in which mobility systems intersect with mobile lives.

This book represents a novel approach in 'post-carbon' social theory. It will be essential reading for advanced undergraduate students, post-graduates and teachers in sociology, social theory, politics, geography, international relations, cultural studies, economics and business studies.

Anthony Elliott is Chair of Sociology at Flinders University, Australia, and Visiting Research Professor at the Open University, UK. His recent books include *Contemporary Social Theory: An Introduction* (2009), *The New Individualism 2nd Edition* (with Charles Lemert, 2009), *The Routledge Companion to Social Theory* (editor, 2010) and *Globalization: A Reader* (co-editor, 2010) – all published by Routledge.

John Urry is Distinguished Professor of Sociology at Lancaster University, UK, where he is Director of the Centre for Mobilities Research. His recent books include *Mobile Technologies of the City* (co-editor, Routledge, 2006), *Mobilities* (Polity, 2007), *Aeromobilities* (co-editor, 2009), *After the Car* (co-author, Polity, 2009) and *Mobile Methods* (co-editor, 2010).

International Library of Sociology

Founded by Karl Mannheim
Editor: John Urry, *Lancaster University*

Mobile Lives

Anthony Elliott and John Urry

Routledge
Taylor & Francis Group

LONDON AND NEW YORK

First published 2010
by Routledge
2 Park Square, Milton Park, Abingdon, Oxon OX14 4RN

Simultaneously published in the USA and Canada
by Routledge
711 Third Avenue, New York, NY 10017

Routledge is an imprint of the Taylor & Francis Group, an informa business

© 2010 Anthony Elliott and John Urry

Typeset in Times New Roman by
Florence Production Ltd, Stoodleigh, Devon

British Library Cataloguing in Publication Data
A catalogue record for this book is available from the British Library

Library of Congress Cataloging in Publication Data
Elliott, Anthony.
    Mobile lives: self, excess and nature/by Anthony Elliott and
John Urry.
        p. cm.
    1. Transportation – Social aspects.   2. Civilization, Modern.
    3. Information technology – Social aspects.   4. Sociology –
Philosophy.   5. Social sciences – Philosophy.   I. Urry, John.
    II. Title.
    HE147.5.E45 2010
    303.48'32 – dc22   2009050207

ISBN10: 0–415–48020–5 (hbk)
ISBN10: 0–415–48022–1 (pbk)
ISBN10: 0–203–88704–2 (ebk)

ISBN13: 978–0–415–48020–8 (hbk)
ISBN13: 978–0–415–48022–2 (pbk)
ISBN13: 978–0–203–88704–2 (ebk)

Contents

Figures

All images © Ross Harley, reproduced with permission

Preface

Consider the following irony. People today are 'on the move', and arguably as never before. Massive social changes – globalization, mobile technologies, intensive consumerism and climate change – are implicated in the ever-increasing movement of people, things, capital, information and ideas around the globe. It is estimated that people today travel 23 billion kilometres each year. By 2050 it is predicted that, if resource constraints do not intervene, this will increase fourfold to 106 billion kilometres each year.[1] Travel and tourism make up the largest industry in the world, worth in excess of $7 trillion annually. The number of international flight arrivals nears one billion. People today are travelling further, faster and (for some at least) more frequently. While many choose to travel, others are forced to be 'on the move'. Asylum seekers, refugees and forced migration also proliferate. Add to this a rapid explosion in communicative and virtual mobilities, with more mobile phones than landline phones and over one billion internet users, and it is clear that a golden age of mobility has truly arrived – bringing with it dizzying possibilities and terrifying risks. Meanwhile, some social scientists warn of the dangers of declaring that there really is any 'epochal social change' taking place here; there is business as usual.

How might we account for such denial? Why is it that, in a globalizing world based on accelerating mobilities, issues concerning transformations of movement are mostly neglected by mainstream social science? This and other difficult questions surrounding issues of movement are asked and answered in the 'mobilities paradigm' – which is a systematic sociology of mobility transformations, as detailed in John Urry's *Mobilities*.

Mobile Lives raises many *new* questions about the intersections of institutional mobility systems and transformed, everyday, ordinary lives. The argument of the book is that changes in how people live their lives today are both affected by and reflect the broader changes of global mobility processes. Or, more specifically, the increasing mobilization of the world – accelerating carbon-based movements of people, goods, services, ideas and information – affects the ways in which lives are lived, experienced and understood. This book thus expands the 'mobilities paradigm' through its focus on mobile *lives*. Our conjecture is that, in the face of a new global narrative of mobilities, the self-fashioning of lives is now recast and transformed. *Mobile Lives* connects the sociological analysis of different forms of travel, transport, tourism and communications with the multiple and sometimes novel ways in which identities are constituted, performed and organized across various spaces and through times.

To live a mobile life is, to be sure, a mixed blessing. Experimentation and danger, possibility and risk, jostle uneasily in the making of mobile lives. Especially in 'fast-lane' mobile lives and mobility systems, the proliferation of novelty and peril looms large. On an institutional level, fast-track mobile lives (the privileged, gated worlds of those we call 'globals') involve endless organizational remodelling, corporate downsizing, just-in-time production, carbon crises and electronic offshoring. On an individual level, today's acceleration of mobile lives has come to signify, among other practices, cosmetic surgery, cyber-therapy, speed dating and multiple careers. Various descriptors have emerged in contemporary social theory to illuminate such processes, trends and lifestyles. 'Individualization', 'reflexive self-identity' and 'liquid life' are some of the terms used to capture the flows, fluidities and dispersals of the contemporary mobile world. Elsewhere, one of us has identified the emergence of a 'new individualism' as both a set of institutional processes and novel kinds of identity-formation. The analytical focus here, concerns increasing speed of movement, the demand for instant change and the desire for continual self-reinvention. Yet none of these approaches in social theory addresses adequately, or specifically, the concrete practices that facilitate forms of personal, social and political life as increasingly 'mobilized'.

To develop an account of mobile lives as situated in relation to extensive and hugely contested mobility systems requires a new approach in social theory. Building upon the ideas set out by one of us in *Mobilities*, we show how the mobilities paradigm can be extended to the analysis and critique of self-identity and ordinary, daily life. Our specific focus is the mobility of self and how complex mobility processes profoundly structure, and are restructured by, people's ordinary lives. In developing this focus, we introduce new concepts – *miniaturized mobilities, affect storage, network capital, meetingness, neighbourhood lives, portable personhood, ambient place, globals* – in order to capture the specific ways in which mobility systems intersect with mobile lives.

Throughout the book, we use many sources in mapping mobile lives – from specialist journals to trade books, from social statistics to social theory. One resource upon which we draw extensively requires some brief clarification: narratives drawn from in-depth interviews conducted with people from various walks of life – all of them both navigating and experimenting with the thrills and spills of mobile worlds.[2] We deploy this narrative approach, not only because it offers a distinct way into the telling of mobile lives, but also because it provides profound insights into the complex interplay between mobile lives and mobility systems. Our approach thus grants a special place to the investigation of the subjective or lived experience as a means of better comprehending the import of complex and hugely contested mobility processes. As with previous books written by one of us in this idiom – namely *The New Individualism* and *Making The Cut* – we take the liberty of speaking for the people who have been interviewed through fictionalized narratives. One reason for this is the protection of individual identities, in order to guarantee anonymity. Another reason is that this approach facilitates the compressing of several voices into one, or the condensation of narratives into a complex story.

The aim throughout is to distil what is going on in people's contradictory experiences of their mobile worlds, and to illuminate concretely the textures of mobile lives in the twenty-first century. We also consider the preconditions that have made such strange experiences contingently possible and that, as we examine towards the end of this book, could come to a shuddering slowdown or even reverse. We consider thus, not so much postmodern futures, but rather post-carbon futures and their implications for the continued growth, range and impact of mobile lives. This book, then, is partly about post-carbonism. It is perhaps one of the first examples of 'post-carbon' social theory.

Acknowledgements

This book evolved over several years. Appropriately enough for a volume examining mobile lives, the book was written in various parts of the world (and sometimes when travelling between them): Adelaide, Lancaster, London, Dublin, Tokyo, Singapore, New York, Helsinki, Shanghai and Hong Kong. Thus, in terms of our own mobile lives, the reader will discern that we have spent time in London and Tokyo and not Baghdad or Lagos – although we try to remain mindful of how such geopolitical mobilities may influence the arguments in what follows.

Most of the book was written with the aid of that virtual mobility known as email, although regular face-to-face meetings and fast travel were, we believe, essential to the research too. We were fortunate enough to be able to rehearse its arguments in a masterclass at the South Australian State Library in 2009. We are grateful to the members of that group and, in particular, Ross Harley, Gillian Fuller and Greg Noble. We are very grateful for Ros Harley's images of mobile lives made possible by his own mobile, digitized life. Other colleagues and friends who have offered helpful comments and suggestions, and whom we wish to thank here, include Kay Axhausen, Zygmunt Bauman, Monika Büscher, Javier Caletrio, Daniel Chaffee, Saolo Cwerner, Kingsley Dennis, Pennie Drinkall, Bianca Freire-Medeiros, Paul du Gay, Nicola Geraghty, Tony Giddens, Kevin Hannam, Eric Hsu, Sven Kesselring, Jonas Larsen, Charles Lemert, Glenn Lyons, Mimi Sheller, Bron Szerszynski, Bryan Turner, David Tyfield, Sylvia Walby and Laura Watts. Gerhard Boomgaarden made many substantial suggestions, and we appreciate his support of the project throughout. Thanks also to Louise Smith for her copy-editing. Finally, our thanks to Daniel Mendelson, who did a marvellous job providing research assistance.

Anthony Elliott, Adelaide
John Urry, Lancaster

Figure 1.1 Baggage collection, Xian Xianyang International Airport, 2007

1 Mobile lives

A step too far?

Yet other contrivances might be invented for transporting people from one place to another, submarine, subterranean, aerial and spatial, as well as new methods of disseminating speech and thought; but, since the people travelling from one place to another are neither willing nor able to commit anything but evil, the thoughts and words being spread will incite men to nothing but evil.

Leo Tolstoy[1]

A mobile life

Simone is a British-based academic, originally from Brazil, who travels a great deal for her work.[2] Like many academics living in expensive cities of the West, her job involves her in continuous renegotiation of her professional and personal commitments, and perhaps nowhere more so than when it comes to travelling. Consider one of her recent trips to the US, where she attended a conference. Flying into JFK airport, Simone went through a drill she had undertaken many times since major changes to airport security following the New York terror bombings of September 11: biometric ID, fingerprinting, passport check and close scrutiny of her reasons for travelling to Manhattan, especially given her ambiguous racial characteristics and her husband's Iranian background. Clearing customs, Simone reached for her BlackBerry to check incoming emails, and afterwards phoned a friend who had already arrived in New York earlier that day. An academic of international renown, Simone travelled to New York, not only to deliver a keynote address to an academic conference, but also to act as a consultant for a private recruitment company operating throughout the Middle East. After her journey to Manhattan by taxi, Simone checked into a hotel she had booked the previous week from Berlin (while attending another conference) and flicked on the Chinese-made TV in her room, seeking updates on the increasingly turbulent international weather. As it happens, she has a string of other professional commitments in the coming weeks, which will involve further travel and probable delays.

Travel is itself an ambivalent category in Simone's life. On the one hand, she finds travel exhilarating, liberating and the source of new opportunities both for networking and for indulging herself in places of excess, especially being able to shop without limit. On the other hand, her regular international travel seems to bring new burdens. She is concerned about the amount of time she is spending away from both her husband and six-year-old daughter. Sitting down to coffee and launching her Apple laptop, she scans through the academic paper she will read tomorrow at the conference. Unable to concentrate, she picks up the phone and dials London, hoping to reach her husband and above all to talk with her daughter before she goes to bed. But she has not brought the correct adapter to recharge the battery of her mobile. Frustrated, Simone is able to activate iTunes on her laptop and selects a song that vividly evokes emotions she feels for her family. As she listens to the music, and now in a calmer state of mind, she returns to thinking about her conference presentation. All of this has taken a couple of hours to unfold since clearing customs and the suspicious security guards at JFK. The city is New York, but it could as easily be Dublin, Durban or Dubai. Indeed, Simone has travelled to all of these in the last couple of years, as her hurried (and harried) professional life transports her through various major cities of the planet, networking and shopping as she goes.

What does Simone's fast-paced, consuming life tell us about the changing social world in the first decade of the twenty-first century? Partly it shows the importance of the fast modes of movement that have developed in recent times, often at the expense of slow modes such as walking and cycling. While in 1800 people in the US travelled fifty metres a day, principally by foot, horse and carriage, they now travel fifty kilometres a day, principally by car and air.[3]

This growth in fast travel stems from various interdependent processes: the growth of automobility throughout the world, with over 650 million cars roaming the world's highways, increasingly in the world's two most populous societies of China and India; the rapid growth of cheap air travel based on new budget business models; the resurgence of rail transport, especially through high-speed trains across Europe and Japan; the development of new kinds of globally significant themed leisure environ-ment that have to be visited from afar; the increased 'miles', both flown and travelled, by manufactured goods, components and foodstuffs on the world's 90,000 ships; and the greater distances travelled by work colleagues, members of leisure organizations, families and friends in order to sustain 'distanciated' patterns of everyday life.[4] Carbon use within transport accounts for fourteen per cent of total greenhouse emissions, is the second fastest growing source of such emissions, and is expected to double by 2050.[5] It is not so much money that makes the world go round but cheap plentiful oil and its resulting carbon emissions.

Forms of life in the 'rich north' (such as Simone's) have thus been 'mobilized'. Social practices have developed and become 'necessary', presupposing large increases in the speed of travel (by humans) and in the distances covered (by both goods and humans). Simone's professional work reflects how it has become almost impossible to undertake the routine 'practices' of business and professional life without regular train journeys, flights, taxi rides, tourist buses, email, text, phoning, skyping and so on. The practices are mobilized.

Moreover this hurried, and what Linder termed 'harried', life criss-crossing the globe presses in deeply upon the self, on its everyday routines, scripts of selfhood and textures of emotion.[6] This explosion of fast mobilities is fundamentally significant to the transformed nature of occupations, personal identity and life-strategies. There are various transformations involved here that we now elaborate.

First, an individual's engagement with this expanding mobile world is not simply about the 'use' of particular forms of movement. Rather, the rise of an intensively mobile society reshapes the self – its everyday activities, interpersonal relations with others, as well as connections with the wider world. In this age of advanced globalization, we witness *portable personhood*. Identity becomes not merely 'bent' towards novel forms of transportation and travel but fundamentally recast in terms of capacities for movement. Put another way, the globalization of mobility extends into the core of the self. Mobility – especially the demands that issues of movement place upon people – has been a feature of most societies. One can note pre-industrial mobility systems of horse riding, coach travel, shipping and especially walking. In conditions of advanced globalization, by contrast, software-driven, digitized systems of mobility – from air traffic control systems to mobile telephony – exert new demands upon the self and its capacities for psychic reorganization. This is clear, not only from the dynamism of Simone's incessant travel, but also from her traversing new communicational and virtual mobility systems. One central consequence of this is that identity in the 'rich north' of the world is significantly constituted as, and inscribed in the scripts of, a *mobile life*. And this is true, not only of those actually doing the travelling, but also those who are receiving visitors, being 'hosts', paid or unpaid, to those who are incoming from near and especially those travelling in from afar.[7]

Second, Simone's schedule of international travel indicates that the trend towards individualized mobility routinely implicates personal life in a complex web of social, cultural and economic networks that can span the globe, or at least certain nodes across parts of the globe. This engenders what has been described as the 'small-world' experience. Those meeting in distant places can discover that they are in fact connected through a relatively short set of intermediaries. As many people predictably state: 'It's a small world, isn't it?' This notion is sometimes couched in terms of 'six degrees of separation' between any two people on the planet, with much lower degrees of separation between those who are closely networked, as with Simone.[8]

Third, owing to the transnational spread of various fast 'mobility systems' (from the car system to air travel, from networked computers to mobile phones), people seem to define aspects of their self-identity, as well as schedules of self- and life-strategies, through reference to de-synchronized, post-traditional or 'detraditionalized' social settings, where such schedules are rarely shared.[9] Life 'on the move' is the kind of life in which the capacity to be 'elsewhere' at a different time from others is central. Email, SMS texting, MP3 audio, personal DVD recorders, internet telephonic services and so on enable people to seek escape from the constraints of pre-existing traditions or traditional forms of cultural life, under more fluid patterns and practices. Such mobile lives demand flexibility, adaptability, reflexivity – to be ready for the unexpected, to embrace novelty, as even one's significant others are doing different things and at different times. People's experiences are de-synchronized from each other, so that systems and people have to be available 'just-in-time'.[10]

Fourth, this means that peoples' lives involve enticing possibilities – something Simone grasps well as she moves up her profession, although she believes she has already met a glass ceiling as she is not quite in the 'right' male (mobile) networks for global advancement. But it is also a world of new threats. A life 'on the move' is one with unwanted sexual advances, the uncertainties of delayed and unpredictable journeys, and regular separation from family and neighbours. There are, of course, various virtual mobilities (mobile telephony, email and so on) to repair the journeys or to keep in touch; but these are only so good as long as they work, which they quite often do not.

Fifth, Simone's mobilities presuppose many other people whose lives can be relatively immobilized. These include check-in clerks, hotel room and aircraft cleaners, the repairers of mobile phone masts, those making her fashionable clothes in South East Asian sweatshops, baggage handlers, her daughter, security guards on Iraqi pipelines and the conference organization teams, who are all on hand around the world in order to make Simone's mobile, 'just-in-time' life on the move just about feasible. They are, in a way, 'immobilized' by the movement of others (some of the dark aspects of 'immobilization' are analysed in Chapter 5).

Sixth, the reshaping of the self through engagement with increasingly complex, computerized systems turns life towards the short-term, the episodic, bits of scattered information, slices of sociality. Life 'on the move' appears to unfold faster and faster in the early days of the twenty-first century, as people become more reliant upon interdependent, digitized systems. Through the use of what we term *miniaturized mobilities* (mobiles, laptops, iPods), people track the twists and turns of social life inherited and co-created with others. Through 'do-it-yourself' scheduling and rescheduling, people are forced to plan courses of action and forge plans with others that comprise complex interplays of connection *and* disconnection.[11] In realizing such DIY lifestyles, today's digitized systems of mobility open the self to new forms of 'openness' and self-disclosure – reconstituting Being, as Heidegger says. If *Dasein* or Being is 'referentially dependent' on the social things around it (as Heidegger argued), then a world of accelerated mobilities cannot leave the self fundamentally unchanged. On the contrary, we should see that the emergence of complex, global mobility systems involves the creation of new forms of mobile life, new kinds of daily experience and new forms of social interaction. People of course carry on doing many of the things that they have always done. But the rise of mobile worlds also spawns radical experiments in mobile life. Life 'on the move' is one in which 'networking' and the 'networked' self-undertake routine, repetitive operations of connecting and disconnecting, logging on and off. With this in mind, we can reinterpret Heidegger's description of Being-in-the-world in terms of getting 'wrapped up' within mobile systems.[12] In a mobile society, our ways of Being-in-the-world tend towards the individualized, privatized collecting of experiences, places, events, trips, acquaintances, data and files. As a general phenomenon, the social things in which people become 'wrapped up' centre more and more upon what elsewhere we refer to as 'instantaneous time', or what Rosa and Scheuerman term 'acceleration'.[13] Thus, the task of holding self and one's social network together is increasingly reconstituted around instantaneous computer clicks of 'search', 'erase', 'delete', 'cut-and-paste' and 'cancel'.

This theme goes to the core of *Mobile Lives*. Our argument is that 'disorganized capitalism' in the rich north of the world, with its dominance of finance, outsourcing, short-term contracts and just-in-time deliveries, has parallel consequences for personal and social lives. This is even registered in the dominance of short-term thinking or the emotional weight of multi-tasking and multiple careers.[14] Just as financial flows facilitate the virtually instantaneous transfer of capital around the globe, as well as the buying, selling and accumulation of mobile resources across the territorial boundaries of nation states, so too globalism ushers in an individualized order of flexible, liquid and increasingly mobile and uncertain lives, at least for some citizens in some parts of the contemporary world.

Others, of course, have mobility thrust upon them, as the number of refugees, asylum seekers and slaves also hit record levels in the early twenty-first century. Such migrants will experience many short-term, semi-legal employments, relationships and uncertainties as they dangerously travel across borders, in containers and backs of lorries, always on the lookout for state and private security. And much of the time, refugees are immobilized within refugee camps located outside cities. As Homi Bhabha argues: 'for the displaced or the dispossessed, the migrant or the refugee, no distance is more awesome than the few feet across borders.'[15]

Seventh, the increasing reliance on miniaturized mobilities serves to facilitate the development of what we call affect storage and retrieval. Consider, again, Simone's inability to reach her family on the phone. How did she respond to this? She called up iTunes on her laptop, and selected a Brazilian song that evoked strong memories of home and family in London. People have, of course, 'used' music to evoke memory in many different social settings and historical contexts. The arrival of miniaturized mobilities, such as MP3 players, iPods and mobile phone audio, alters the social contexts in which people can access music, photos, videos and text. A central argument here is that the social impact of mobile lives can be grasped only if we dispense with the received wisdom that people mainly use new information technologies to transmit information from sender to receiver, the communications model of 'inputs' and 'outputs'. Our argument is that the use of various miniaturized mobilities involves transformations in self-experience through the storage and subsequent retrieval of affects and emotions in the object world of generalized media communications. Drawing from the psychoanalytic research, we explore in Chapter 2 how miniaturized mobilities enable people to deposit affects, moods and dispositions into techno-objects – storing such emotional and aesthetic aspects of self-experience until they are 'withdrawn' for future forms of symbolic elaboration and interpersonal communication.[16] In a fundamental way, the affect storage and retrieval organized through various kinds of mobile life generate new modes of identity that are less tied to fixed localities, regular patterns or dwelt-in cultural traditions.

Finally, people's lives, whether they know it or not and whether they hanker for freedom or security, are being redrafted as they deposit bits of scattered information as *traces* of themselves across various mobility systems. From Simone's biometric ID information stored on US immigration's computational database to her credit card details lodged with her Manhattan hotel, traces of the self are deposited in space and time, all of which can be, in principle at least, retrieved for review or regulation or disciplining at a moment's notice. Many recent developments regarding the collection of personal information onto databases concern the field of travel, information and telecommunications, and the ways in which relevant databases have come to be exploited commercially and through new modes of governmentality. In examining the social consequences of the mobilization of interdependent systems, we examine a range of institutions producing and reproducing new opportunities for gathering and recording information about the self, and how such information 'feeds' upon itself to facilitate the further mobilization and circulation of people, goods and information. This becomes especially significant as the different databases get hooked up to each other, and those scattered traces of the self are reconnected, like a ghost in the machine. There is increasingly less that is simply 'private', except of course for the super-rich able to evade the paparazzi.

Various themes of a mobile world and people's mobile lives can be gleaned from the vignette of Simone's travels 'around the world in eighty hours'. There is little doubt that she leads a privileged life, but there are aspects of her self-experience that are increasingly prevalent for many people throughout the world, who find movement is thrust upon them as a kind of 'burden'. As we demonstrate, mobility is central, not only to the ongoing effort of social scientists to understand the social world – its institutions, processes and socialities – but also to the daunting task of engaging with the texture and composition of people's everyday lives. The paradigm of mobilities, we suggest, is becoming increasingly central to contemporary identity formation and re-formation.

This chapter examines some major changes relating to the conditions and consequences of people's lives in the rich north arising from issues of movement and the rise of fast mobilities (as opposed to walking, horse riding and cycling). We argue that the most consequential feature of accelerated mobilities for people's lives is the recasting of identity in terms of flexibility, adaptability and instant transformation. In the age of intensive travel and communications media, many people are or may be, or their acquaintances are, 'on the move'. From budget airline travel to 'sun, sand and shopping' tourism, from mobile phones to teleworking, from blogging on the internet to videoconferencing, many lives in the rich north are being transformed by multiple mobility systems, which are intensive *and* extensive, through physical, interpersonal, imaginative and virtual transformations.

In introducing and contextualizing such mobile lives, the chapter reviews the mobilities paradigm – its theories and main findings. This discussion of the intersections between mobile worlds and mobile lives serves as the conceptual backcloth for new ways of thinking about how people's mobile lives are assembled. We conclude this chapter by outlining the arguments to be developed throughout the book, arguments that indicate how the restructuring of the private and public spheres as a consequence of mobilities is producing new possibilities and pleasures, as well as growing burdens for many, with various awesome conflicts over whether this mobile life on planet earth is actually sustainable into the medium term for the still rapidly growing world population.[17]

On the move

Freedom of movement, as represented in popular media, politics and the public sphere, is the ideology and utopia of the twenty-first century. The UN and the EU both enshrine rights to movement in their constitutions. More than knowledge, more than celebrity, more than economic success itself, it is the infinity of promised and assumed opportunities arising from movement that counts most. Mobility now provides the overarching narrative, depicting the relation of each life 'on the move' to the micro electronics, software-operated communications and mobility systems. And the story it tells is mesmerizing, split as it is between intoxicating possibility and menacing darkness. Intoxicating because the rise of an extensive and intensive mobile society has provided one powerful answer to the existential question of where are our lives supposed to be going? That answer has come in the form of 'going elsewhere', being somewhere else. Yet the idea of fulfilling one's personal dreams and professional ambitions through trying to be elsewhere – jumping, as it were, a series of hurdles in order to reach some final destination – has proven to be the flip side of something darker and more menacing. The emptiness of this vision and its costs for personal lives, for those excluded, and for the planet have meant that the experience of a fulfilling life remains a distant chimera.

In the globalized swirl of mobile systems and technologies, people characterized by 'networked individualism' are linked together by complex systems of scheduling, monitoring, surveillance and regulation.[18] As the dream of open, fluid and free travel and movement becomes constrained by tightly regulated and locked-in systems of surveillance and securitization, in relationship to wars on terror and global warming, so increasingly that freedom of movement becomes unequally distributed. As a result, writes Zygmunt Bauman, 'Mobility climbs to the rank of the uppermost among coveted values – and the freedom to move, perpetually a scarce and unequally distributed commodity, fast becomes the main stratifying factor of our late modern or postmodern time.'[19]

What is the lure of mobile life? There is the well-known myth surrounding mobility and the successful life that runs like this: it's not what you know, it's who you know. Thus, the more you move, travel around, meeting others and making and sustaining contacts, the more successful you can reasonably hope to become, in both professional and personal terms. Although there may be some truth to this myth, other elements turn out to be dubious. People may hanker after the celebrity-inspired, jet-setting lifestyle, but many of those who in fact lead such lifestyles suffer high levels of anxiety, emotional disconnection and depression. People may perceive – arguably rightly – that those who are highly mobile have the power to escape all sorts of formal responsibilities and organizational duties, especially taxation. However, research again suggests that many mobile lives that are both intensive and extensive generate no greater levels of well-being. We investigate and discuss various limitations to the myth of mobility and the good life throughout this book.

However, we will stay with the link Bauman identifies between new mobilities (corporeal, imaginative and virtual) and emerging structures of social stratification and inequality. In a previous work, the ways in which mobilities generate social, financial, emotional and practical benefits were fleshed out with reference to the notion of 'network capital'.[20] The significance of this stems from the emerging 'mobility complex', a new field of economy, society and resources that has been spreading around the globe and moving out from the rich north. Large-scale mobilities are not new, but what is new is the development of this 'mobility complex'. This involves a number of interdependent components that, in their totality, have the effect of remaking consumption, pleasure, work, friendship and family life. The components of this complex or field are as follows: the contemporary scale of movement around the world; the diversity of especially fast mobility systems now in play; the especial significance of the self-expanding automobility system and its risks; the elaborate interconnections between physical movement and communications; the development of mobility domains that bypass national societies, especially shipping, aeromobilities and future space travel; the significance of movement across borders to contemporary governmentality; the development of places of leisure that mostly have to be travelled to from afar; the development of a language of mobility; the capacity to compare, contrast and collect places from around the world; and the increased importance of multiple mobilities for people's social and emotional lives.

Such a mobility field or complex changes the nature of power relations. All mobilities lead to rich and complex social worlds: the position an individual occupies within the institutional parameters of today's multiple mobilities generates new kinds of power for realizing ambition and interests, new possibilities and risks for embodied experiences of movement, as well as new ways for engaging with culture, taste and social contestation.

The social transformations arising from such mobilities can be analysed in terms of the notions of cultural and economic capital, as well as symbolic power – as set out by Pierre Bourdieu.[21] For, just as people have sought to distinguish themselves culturally and economically through either educational advancement or high levels of personal consumption, so the 'multiplying' mobile forms of life – actual, imaginative and virtual – now serve as key resources for the accumulation of recognition, respect and prestige. A life 'on the move' is viewed as a fundamental indicator of achieving 'the good life'. Indeed, we might say that multiple mobilities have become the drivers of symbolic power, bodily habituses and pleasure-seeking lifestyles.

However, in addition to Bourdieu's analysis of cultural and economic capital and the symbolic power to which they give rise, there is another form of power that stems from the extension and elaboration of the mobility field. This type of power arises from what we term 'network capital', and in a previous work one of us detailed its productivities and specificities. Network capital is a fundamental aspect of current social processes and lies at the core of generating novel experiences in distant places and with others at-a-distance.

There are eight core elements to the constitution and reproduction of network capital:

1   an array of appropriate documents, visas, money, qualifications that enable safe movement of one's body from one place, city, country to another;
2   others (workmates, friends and family members) at-a-distance who offer invitations, hospitality and meetings, so that places and networks are maintained through intermittent visits and communications;
3   movement capacities in relationship to the environment: to walk distances within different environments; to be able to see and board different means of mobility; to be able to carry or move baggage; to

have readable timetabled information; to be able to access computerized information; to arrange and rearrange connections and meetings; the ability, competence and interest to use mobile phones, text messaging, email, the internet, Skype etc.;

4   location-free information and contact points: fixed or moving sites where information and communications can arrive, be stored and retrieved, including real/electronic diaries, address books, answerphones, secretaries, offices, answering services, emails, websites, mobile phones;

5   communication devices: to make and remake arrangements, especially on the move and in conjunction with others who may also be on the move;

6   appropriate, safe and secure meeting places, both en route and at the destination(s), including office, club space, hotel, home, public spaces, street corner, café, interspaces, which ensure that the body is not exposed to physical or emotional violence;

7   access to car, road space, fuel, lifts, aircraft, trains, ships, taxis, buses, trams, minbuses, email account, internet, telephone and so on;

8   time and other resources to manage and coordinate 1–7, especially when there is a system failure, as will intermittently happen.[22]

Network capital can be distinguished from cultural or economic capital (in Bourdieu's sense). Whereas the latter were, for the most part, built up by individuals, network capital is largely subjectless, communications-driven and information-based. People with very high levels of network capital – as we see in Chapter 4 – experience high levels of geographical mobility (and can demand the extensive movement of others, as will be seen in the darker implications of Chapter 5), have extensive institutional contacts, and are 'at home' in, and moving across, many diverse settings. What especially matters is information – its production, transmission, circulation and, above all, sharing. To have high network capital is to join a field of expanding networks, or what Wellman and his collaborators term 'connected lives'.[23]

The term 'mobile lives' suggests an increasingly complex, detraditionalized patterning to personal life. People with substantial network capital learn to live with the making of personal and social worlds 'on the move', fashioned on shifting ground. One key issue people face is how to make the complexities of social life work within the social context of the needs and desires of others – family, friends, work colleagues – who are all also in a sense 'networked'. Making social life 'work' especially involves the *scheduling and rescheduling* of events, meetings, dates, trips,

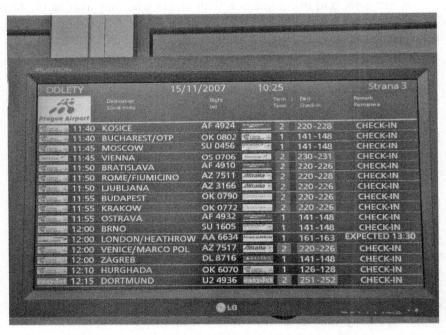

Figure 1.2 Announcement board, Prague International Airport, 2007

videoconferences and holidays. Such scheduling is desynchronized from certain traditional settings of neighbourhood. There are these do-it-yourself, individualized time–space patterns, in and through which some people in the richer third of the world can cover more ground, consume abundantly and live more varied lives, but need to be on the go performing their 'coordination of life'. This individualization is derived from Beck's analysis of do-it-yourself identity-building and of the social constitution of a desynchronized individualism.[24]

The process of self-choosing and self-invention is meant to be premised upon the 'identity' of specific, unique individuals. Yet the idea of the self-legislating, unique individual is a notion that has been undermined in three important ways. First, the tropes of decentring, splitting, multiplicity and fragmentation within much contemporary social theory problematize the notion of the 'whole' individual self. Second, the neo-liberal turn in economic, political and social life, which we discuss in Chapters 6 and 7 in particular, so elevates the individual as consumer that it is often hard to conceive of the individual apart from their consumer purchases, brands and experiences. And third, people's everyday experiences involve an astonishing dependence upon complex 'systems' of collective coordination and specialized forms of technological expertise, especially, as we see in this book, of physical movement and communications. The production of daily life, as Paul Valéry memorably argued, involves various processes other than those of individual doing or decision-making.[25]

The 'splitting' of identity between individual creation and system dependency, activity and passivity, subjective and objective, is especially evident. To put the matter starkly: there is a paradox about mobile lives. The paradox is that, while we examine the intensive and extensive dimensions (real, imagined, virtual) of people's movements and travel in order to unearth the novel textures of individual life, today few social forms are more predictable, routine and uniform than those of the mobile denizens of this global age. People use the internet, travel daily by car or train, catch international flights, send text messages on mobiles, search global electronic databases and accept just-in-time delivered goods from around the world to their front door. The social structure of human agency and individual life is substantially and increasingly constituted through systems of movement.

The view during the Enlightenment presumed a primacy of head over heels, mind over body, and of humans as separate from, and productive of, society and culture.[26] But this assembling of mobile life is not the product of *human* agency. Mobile lives are rather the outcome of complex con-figurations of relationality, affect, desire, socialities, systems, states, regional organizations and global institutions. In that sense, the analysis of mobilities is part of the critique of such a humanism that posits a disembodied *cogito* and, especially, human subjects able to think and act in some ways independent of their material worlds. This book presumes that the rather limited powers of 'humans' are almost always augmented by various material worlds, of clothing, tools, objects, shoes, paths, machines, buildings and so on.

In reworking Gilles Deleuze's analysis of the social, Manuel DeLanda details the idea of 'assemblages' for analysis of the person, lived experience, organizations, social movements, regions and territorial states in the wider context of the global capitalist economy.[27] Assemblages are relational complexes that continually oscillate in their fusing of properties or identities of the component elements of systems, and thus can be cast as an emergent actualization moving through space–time and concretized in historically specific processes. This Deleuzian emphasis on tendencies and potentialities indicates that lived experiences – when cast within the framework of mobile lives – are not to be understood in terms of individual subjectivity, for DeLanda's treatment of the person, in the words of Clough *et al.*: 'emerges from relations of exteriority rather than resulting from an inner source of being constituted through linguistically based categories as the "speaking subject".'[28] The 'assemblage of self' is thus the condition of possibility of the person, woven out of an ongoing interplay of cognitions, affects, emotional capacities, socialities and diverse processes of socialization. DeLanda rightly emphasizes that, in theorizing the formation and re-formation of assemblages of the person, the critical task lies in connecting the generation of an individual's capacities for sensation, affect and desire to inter-human and cultural assemblages, which in turn can be connected to broader organizational, technological and institutional processes of contemporary sociality. We draw, in a partial and implicit fashion, from DeLanda's account of assemblages throughout this book in order to develop new concepts for the critique of mobile lives.

One example, introduced in the next chapter, is the idea of *affect deposits, storage and retrieval* through *miniaturized mobilities*. While the detail is explored in Chapter 2, briefly this refers to how new digital technologies interweave with forms of mobile lives and specifically in connection with the 'containment' of emotional anxiety. Understanding such an assemblage, we try to show, involves grasping how technologies and persons are interwoven in the production and transformation of intermittently mobile lives.

Moreover, what the study of mobile assemblages emphasizes is that the objects are highly varied, providing different affordances especially enabling or presupposing movement. Objects can thus be distinguished in terms of whether they are *fixed* in place (railway track, hotel); temporarily *stationary* (car in garage, engine in engine shed); *portable* (book, car transporter); *corporeally interwoven* (Walkman, watch); *prosthetic* (heart pacemaker, mobile phone); *constitutive* of a mobility system (car, plane); or consist of *code* (washing machine, spreadsheets). Such a classification of 'objects' brings out huge variations in their ready-to-handedness, but in all cases humans are nothing without such objects organized into various systems. The systems come first and serve to augment the otherwise rather puny powers of individual human subjects. Those subjects are brought together and serve to develop extraordinary powers only because of the assemblages that implicate them, and especially those that move them, or their ideas, or information or various objects.

The mobilities paradigm

We have so far talked rather generally about increasing mobility and how this characterizes the contemporary world. In this section, we turn to what is increasingly referred to as the mobilities paradigm for rethinking the social sciences. This consists of a number of interrelated claims that we now set out.[29]

First, all social relationships should be seen as involving diverse 'connections' that are more or less 'at-a-distance', more or less fast, more or less intense and more or less involving physical movement. Historically, the social sciences have overly focused upon geographically propinquitous communities based on more or less face-to-face social interactions with those who are currently co-present. But many connections with peoples and social groupings are not based only upon propinquity. There are multiple forms of 'imagined presence' occurring through objects, people, information and images travelling, carrying connections across, and into, multiple other social spaces. Social life involves continual processes of shifting between being present with others (at work, home, leisure and so on) and being distant from others. And yet, when there is absence, there may be imagined presence, as we have already noted about the present period. All societies deal with distance, but they do so through different sets of interdependent processes, and these include various 'discourses' relating to movement.

Second, these processes stem from five interdependent 'mobilities' that produce social life organized across distance and that form (and re-form) its contours. These mobilities are:

- the *corporeal* travel of people for work, leisure, family life, pleasure, migration and escape, organized in terms of contrasting time–space modalities (from daily commuting to once-in-a-lifetime exile);

- the physical movement of *objects* to producers, consumers and retailers, as well as the sending and receiving of presents and souvenirs;
- the *imaginative* travel effected through the images of places and peoples appearing on, and moving across, multiple print and visual media;
- *virtual* travel, often in real time and thus transcending geographical and social distance;
- the *communicative* travel through person-to-person messages via messages, texts, letters, telegraph, telephone, fax and mobile.

This paradigm emphasizes the complex assemblage between these different mobilities that make and contingently maintain social connections across varied and multiple distances. It emphasizes the interconnections between these five mobilities, as well as the discourses that may prioritize one or other such mobility (such as the belief that business has to be done 'face-to-face').

Third, physical travel involves lumpy, fragile, aged, gendered, racialized bodies. Such bodies encounter other bodies, objects and the physical world multi-sensuously. Travel always involves *corporeal* movement and forms of pleasure and pain. Such bodies perform themselves in-between direct sensation of the 'other' and various 'sensescapes'. Bodies are not fixed and given, but involve performances, especially to fold notions of movement, nature, taste and desire into and through the body. Bodies navigate backwards and forwards between directly sensing the external world as they move bodily in and through it and experiencing discursively mediated sensescapes that signify social taste and distinction, ideology and meaning. The body especially senses as it *moves*. Important here is that sense of movement, the 'mechanics of space', of touch, such as feet on the pavement or the mountain path, hands on a rock face or the steering wheel. There are thus various assemblages of humans, objects, technologies and scripts that contingently produce durability and stability of mobility. Such hybrid assemblages roam countrysides and cities, remaking landscapes and townscapes through their movement.

Fourth, on occasions and for specific periods, face-to-face connections are made. People physically travel to connect face-to-face, but this face-to-faceness needs explanation. There are five processes that generate face-to-faceness. These are: legal, economic and familial obligations to attend a relatively formal meeting; social obligations to meet and to converse, often involving strong expectations of presence and attention of the participants; obligations to be co-present with others to sign contracts, to work on or with objects, written or visual texts; obligations to be in and experience a place 'directly' on occasions through movement through it and touch; and obligations to experience a 'live' event that happens at a specific moment and place. These obligations can be very powerful and generate what Durkheim termed 'effervescence'.[30] Such feelings of intense affect can generate a compulsion to travel, often at specific moments along particular routes.

Fifth, there are at least thirteen different kinds of social practice of contemporary mobility, each involving specific sets of network capital. These different assemblages of humans, objects, technologies and scripts involve different social practices that are examined below. These social practices are:

- business and professional travel;
- discovery travel by students, au pairs and other young people on their 'overseas experience', where this can constitute a 'rite of passage' and involve going overseas to civilizational centres;
- medical travel to spas, hospitals, dentists, opticians and so on;
- military mobility of armies, tanks, helicopters, aircraft, rockets, spyplanes, satellites and so on;
- pilgrimage travel, which can involve some of the largest co-present gatherings in the contemporary world (Mecca);
- post-employment travel and the forming of transnational lifestyles within 'retirement';
- refugee, asylum and homeless migration;
- service worker travel around the world and especially to global cities;
- the 'trailing travel' of children, partners, other relatives and domestic servants;
- travel and migration across key nodes within a diaspora, such as that of tens of millions of overseas Chinese;
- tourist travel to visit places and events;
- visiting friends and relatives, currently the fastest growing category of travel;
- work-dependent travel, especially commuting.

Sixth, 'distance' generates massive problems for the sovereignty of modern states which, from the eighteenth century onwards, have sought to 'govern' their populations. Such governmentality involves, not just a territory with fixed populations, but mobile populations moving in, across and beyond 'territory'. The 'apparatuses of security' involve dealing with the 'population', but any such population is at-a-distance, on the move and needing to be statistically measured, plotted and trackable. Such a 'mobile population' is hard to monitor and govern. The security of states increasingly involves complex control systems of recording, measuring and assessing populations that are intermittently moving, beginning with the system of the humble passport but now involving many elements of a 'digital order' and of temporary camps. Imposing systems of reason on the rapidly moving, the restless and the furtive is especially problematic, as discourses of movement carry much weight in the contemporary historical moment.

Seventh, while social science typically treats social life as purified, as a social realm independent of the worlds of 'nature' and 'objects', this viewpoint is challenged here. We have seen that what constitutes social life is fundamentally heterogeneous, and part of that heterogeneity consists of various material objects (including 'nature' and 'technologies') that directly or indirectly move or block the movement of objects, people and information. In order to concretize the turn of social science towards incorporating the object world, it is necessary to examine the many ways in which objects and people are assembled and reassembled through time–space. Objects themselves travel across distance; there are objects that enable people to travel forming complex hybrids; there are objects that move other objects; there are objects that move that may mean that people do not move; there are objects and people that move together; there are objects that can be reminders of past movement; and there are objects that possess value that people travel often great distances to see for themselves. So the entities that combine together to produce and perform social practices are highly heterogeneous.

Eighth, crucial to analysing these relationships is the concept of 'affordance'. People do not encounter a set of objective 'things' in the environment that they may or may not visually perceive.[31] Rather, different surfaces and different objects, relative to the particular human organism and its technologies, provide affordances. These are objective *and* subjective, both part of the environment and of the organism. Given certain past and present social relations, then, particular 'objects' in the environment afford possibilities and resistances, given that humans are sensuous, corporeal, technologically extended and *mobile* beings. Examples of such affordances are: a path that draws people to walk along it; a straight road that affords speeding; a mountain that reveals a clear way of climbing it; a wood that is a repository of childhood adventures; and a museum that facilitates 'touching' of the displays by the visually impaired who are moving through it.

Ninth, the focus on objects combining with humans into various coupled relationships also implies the significance of often carbon-based systems that distribute people, activities and objects in and through time–space and are key in the metabolic relationship of human societies with nature. The human 'mastery' of nature has been most effectively achieved through movement over, under and across it. In the modern world, automobility is by far the most powerful of such mobility systems, while other such systems include the pedestrian system, the rail system, the ship system and aeromobility.[32] Historically, most societies have been characterized by one major mobility-system that is in an evolving and adaptive relationship with that society's economy. Such mobility systems are also in adaptive and co-evolving relationships with each other, so that some such systems expand and multiply, whereas others may, over time, shrink in terms of their range and impact. Further, the richer the society, the greater the range of mobility systems that will be present, and the more complex the intersections between such systems. These mobility systems have the effect of producing substantial inequalities between places and between people in terms of their location and access to these mobility-systems, what we referred to as network capital. We might say that unforced 'movement' is power, that is, to be able to move (or to be able voluntarily to stay still) is a major source of advantage and conceptually independent of economic and cultural advantage.

Tenth, mobility systems are organized around the processes that circulate people, objects and information at various spatial ranges and speeds. In any society, there will tend to be a dominant process of circulation. The key issue is not the objects that are involved in movement (such as vehicles or telephones or computers), but the structured routeways through which people, objects and information are circulated. Such routeways in a society include the networks of bridleways, footpaths, cycle tracks, railways, telephone lines, public roads, networked computers and hub airports. The more that a society is organized around the value of 'circulation', the greater the significance of network capital within the range of capitals available within a society.

Eleventh, these various mobility systems and routeways linger over time. There is often a powerful spatial fixity of such systems. New systems have to find their place physically, socially, economically and discursively within what physicists term a 'fitness landscape' in which there are already physical structures, social practices and economic entities overcoming distance and structuring mobility in multiple locked-in forms. Some of these sedimented systems are organized over very large spatial scales, with their spatial fixing being national or international. Systems are organized through time, and this entails a path-dependency of such systems. The last decade or so has seen the establishment of two new mobility systems, 'networked computers' and 'mobile telephony', which are ushering in new environments, social practices, economic entities and discourses, as we explore in the following chapters.

Twelfth, mobility systems are based on increasingly expert forms of knowledge. This can be seen in the shifts in corporeal movement from slow modes such as walking and cycling to fast modes based on arcane technologies that require exceptional technical expertise. Such mobility systems tend to be based upon computer software that increasingly drives, monitors, regulates and, in cases, repairs the system in question. The way that computers have entered the car is a good example of a progressive 'expertization' of systems that makes cars less easy to understand, let alone repair, by the mere driver, whereas in many developing societies cars remain repairable, with a complex recycling of parts.[33] If the systems go wrong, which of course they do, they are mostly unrepairable. Moreover, as people move around developing their individual life projects, especially in the 'north', so they extend their personal networks and appear to exert increased 'agency'. But, as they exert such 'agency', so much about them gets left behind in traces on computers central to almost all mobility-systems. These reconfigure humans as bits of scattered informational traces resulting from various 'systems', of which most are unaware. Thus individuals increasingly exist beyond their private bodies and leave traces in informational space. The self comes to be spread out or made mobile as a series of traces. The self, we can thus say, is itself 'mobilized' and 'immobilized' as traces.

Finally, interdependent systems of 'immobile' material worlds, and especially exceptionally immobile platforms (transmitters, roads, garages, stations, aerials, airports, docks) structure mobility experiences. The *complex* character of such systems stems from their multiple fixities or moorings, often on a substantial physical scale. Thus 'mobile machines', such as mobile phones, cars, boats, aircraft, trains and computer connections, all presume overlapping and varied time–space immobilities. There is no linear increase in fluidity without extensive systems of immobility. There are several of these systems, co-evolving and interdependent, which extend and reorganize mobilities in the contemporary era. This involves the bending of time and space and the generation of dynamic system characteristics. Systems of material worlds produce *new* moments of unintended co-presence. The 'gates' designed to prevent networks from colliding are less sustainable, eliminating the invisibilities that kept networks apart. Some of these new material worlds produce increasingly exciting *and* equally dangerous flows across otherwise impenetrable distances.

So, in this book, we seek to apply these thirteen components of the new mobilities paradigm to our understanding of mobile lives. We believe that these components result in a rather different kind of social science. It is not just that travel and communications are systematically studied and analysed. A mobilities paradigm is not just substantively different, in that it remedies the neglect and omissions of various movements of people, ideas and so on. It is transformative of social science, authorising an alternative theoretical and methodological landscape. It enables the 'social world' to be understood as a wide array of economic, social and political practices, infrastructures and ideologies that all involve, entail or curtail various kinds of movement of people, or ideas, or information or objects. And, in so doing, this paradigm brings to the fore theories, methods and exemplars of research that have been mostly subterranean, out of sight. We use the term mobilities to refer to the rather broad project of establishing and developing a movement-driven social science.

The argument of the book

This book is concerned with how people's lives are being reorganized as works of mobility, as *mobile lives*. Throughout, we try to identify some structuring features at the core of the digitized, interdependent systems that intersect with the constantly changing worlds of mobile people trying to navigate their territories and form their lives. In the rest of this chapter, we summarize some of the main arguments.

Having set out a framework for the analysis of mobile lives in this opening chapter, the next chapter critically examines the personal and social impacts of digital technologies upon everyday mobile lives. The chapter introduces a range of new concepts and ideas in examining the relations between digital technologies and mobile lives, and examines in depth the 'internalization' of new technologies into the mobile rhythms of daily life. Mobile phones, personal laptops, iPods, BlackBerries and Bluetooth wireless connectivity are increasingly central to both working life and leisure time. To capture the relations between such complex systems and everyday life, we introduce the term *miniaturized mobilities*. Corporeally interwoven with the body and augmenting the mobile capacities of individual subjects in physical, communicative and virtual forms, miniaturized mobilities – from iPhones to laptops – facilitate digital lives that are increasingly structured around deposits, storage and retrievals of affect. The investment of affect into virtual objects – Facebook, Second Life, Skype – comprises part of a 'containment of anxiety', which comes to the fore in conditions of complex mobilities and a digital life.

Chapter 3 brings together material from the two previous chapters to examine the importance of networked relationships within people's lives. Research is drawn upon to detail how both work and leisure lives are networked and some of the dilemmas and burdens that this induces. Such lives in particular depend upon what we call network capital. Such capital has become hugely important and is to be seen as different from both economic and symbolic capital. And, as it has come to be more significant, so it comes to produce greater inequalities. Much of the chapter thus details the many ways in which experiences of mobility are unequal by class, gender, age, ethnicity and capacity.

In the following three chapters, we move the discussion onto a consideration of how complex mobility processes are restructuring particular fields of social life – namely, the 'fast lane' mobilities of the ultra-rich or global elite; the fluid sexualities of contemporary intimacy; and the excess consumption bred by global capitalist mobilities. Chapter 4 looks specifically at the impacts of globalization and transnationalism upon global elites working in the 'new economy' – namely, executives very high in network capital in media, hi-tech and finance sectors. The chapter examines in detail what we term the mobile lives of 'globals'. The mobile worlds of globals are made up of ever-changing, frenetic networking; in a certain sense, globals are 'pioneers' of mobile lives. We chart various lifestyles and life-strategies of globals, setting such intensively mobile lives within complex mobility processes more generally. We develop the argument that the 'thick texture' of the lifestyles of globals is cemented in various new mobile strategies, which range from *detached engagement* to *distance from neighbourhood* to the *chronic mapping of escape routes*.

In Chapter 5, we develop the argument that the advent of complex and intensive mobile lives has significantly contributed to the emergence of some new forms of intimacy and sexual relationships in the contemporary world. Examining the changing forms of intimate relationships today – from commuter marriages to distance relationships to 'living-apart-togethers' – we concentrate on fundamental transformations of private and public life. Drawing on a range of contemporary social theories that interpret social changes affecting intimacy, sexualities and interpersonal relationships, we focus on the dynamics of what we term *portable personhood*: the psychological *bridging* of spatial fragmentation between self and others that unfolds in conditions of intensive mobilities. What it is like to live in a world of fast, intensive mobilities – at least as far as intimate relationships are concerned – depends to a significant extent on people's emotional capacities to maintain and negotiate both their public and their private, family lives while moving back and forth between jobs and residences. In exploring these issues, we take into account feminist contributions to recent debates and reflect on the complex intertwining of mobilities and immobilities in the production of intimate life more generally, especially for those drawn into the global sex and trafficking industries.

Following on from this, Chapter 6 investigates some of the extraordinary new spaces of excess that this contemporary capitalism ushers into existence, places in which globals in particular can apparently consume to their heart's content. Such sites of excess consumption enable the self to be fashioned as people desire – the internationalization of a consumer culture held in thrall to instant gratification, continual self-reinvention, superficiality and addictive, short-term 'highs'. Our aim is to mobilize the study of consumer culture, focusing on how mobile lives are entangled with the purchase, use and display of multiple goods and services that are obtained in places distant from local neighbourhoods. We argue that places of excess consumption are fantasized, travelled to, stayed in, experienced through credit card purchases, and subsequently remembered and talked about in the presence of others. In the rich north especially, mobile populations escape from the constraints of local neighbourhoods, consuming goods, services and experiences in themed and designed environments.

In the final chapter, we return to some of the contradictions of mobilities and, in particular, trace their significance within the emerging high-carbon societies of the second half of the twentieth century. Certain patterns were laid down then, and we are reaping their consequences today. And these consequences are, not only mobile lifestyles and their personal costs, but also the energy costs of a probably unsustainable future world. Global warming and the peaking of oil may well ensure that mobile lives will not be with us forever. Within two or three decades, many of the world's current mobility systems may be rusting away in the relentless heat or washed away by repeated flooding. Much of what the late twentieth century saw as the global, borderless future may also be mothballed. The mobile order may thus come to be seen as part of the late twentieth century's energy-consuming hubris, unsustainable in the long term. We will explore, then, various visions for the future, ranging from Virgin Galactica and flying cars for all to rusting planes and derelict runways as droughts and floods ravish the land. What happens to travel will index what happens to high-carbon societies and those mobile lives, like that of Simone, that we seek to decipher in this book.

Figure 2.1 Online services, Kuala Lumpur International Airport, 2007

2 New technologies, new mobilities

As we encounter the object world we are substantially metamorphosed by the structure of objects; internally transformed by objects that leave their trace within us.

Christopher Bollas[1]

Digital mobilities

Sandra Fletcher is sophisticated and smart – a high-profile advertising executive.[2] At forty-four, she describes her life as 'full' in both professional and personal terms. The mother of three children (ranging in age from nine to fourteen), and married to a successful architect, Sandra divides her week between the family home in Leeds and the company office in London. She had felt somewhat troubled about a working arrangement that would take her away from her family three (and sometimes four) nights a week, or at least she did when first experimenting with living and working this way some years ago. But much of her worry was unfounded. Her children have adapted well to her weekly absence and appear fond of the live-in nanny whom Sandra and her husband, Michael, selected (and screened) from an agency, many of which have spring up in order to provide mobile childcare for mobile couples. She also discovered that her relationship with Michael was fine, indeed thriving, when living and working away during the week and then reuniting for 'quality time' over weekends. Taken together, these factors meant she could feel relaxed about navigating the demands of her professional and personal lives. Indeed, she looks forward to the routine departure from Leeds on Tuesday mornings, eager to embrace the exciting challenges of professional life in London.

Helping her coordinate, manage and sort through this life divided between London and Leeds are various digital technologies. For Sandra threads and rethreads her professional and personal life together through the use of such technologies. She actively embraces a digital lifestyle. An avid follower of consumer electronic technologies, mobile and wireless products, Sandra relies on mobile communications in order to keep on the move, to access information and to communicate with others. From the broadband terrain of wireless and storage technology to videoconferencing and laptop imaging, Sandra deploys digital lifestyle technologies in order to fashion a mobile, multiplex, connected life with others. In doing so, she has found a new kind of freedom: one that allows her to experience and explore other kinds of communication, information and knowledge. This has been of key importance to her professional success, to locating herself in new and ever-expanding advertising networks, and to the flourishing of her own business. But, for Sandra, the beauty of the digital lifestyle is that she gets to bring her family (or, more accurately, her emotional connection with her family) along on these virtual networks. For though she might be physically separated from family life for much of the week, the digital lifestyle of mobile communications means she is also never far away from them – or so it seems to Sandra.

Consider Sandra's weekly journey from Leeds to London, usually undertaken by car. A journey of approximately four hours (much longer than the train), this might well be 'empty time', but Sandra (like countless motorists) prizes this time as a period for both strategic business thinking and communicating with others. Viewing her car as somewhat akin to a mobile office, Sandra commences her journey by checking her voice-activated email and subsequently undertakes various business calls using her Bluetooth, hands-free mobile.[3] Along the way, she also dictates letters to her secretary on her Apple iPhone, using its 'voice memos' function. These recorded letters she often emails to her secretary while taking a coffee break on the long journey, especially if the communications are a priority and need to be sent out later in the day. When she is not working while driving to London, Sandra's car metamorphoses into a personal entertainment system. She listens to music while driving, lost in private reverie to songs that she has selected and arranged on 'track lists' on her iPod.[4]

To be sure, Sandra plays music using various technologies – internet downloads, iPod, iPhone – throughout her working week in London. A self-described pop music enthusiast, she likes listening to the latest hits (and mentions that she feels this draws her closer to some of the cultural interests of her eldest daughter, Victoria). But she also spends much time listening to past favourites – especially music current when her children were very young, and she was at home full-time. This immersion in music, especially being able to recapture memories and feeling-states from years gone by, is very important to Sandra, and is a theme we develop throughout this chapter.

The complex relations between digital technologies and identity are also manifest in Sandra's living arrangements in London. The Kensington apartment that Sandra and her husband purchased some years ago is fitted with the standard array of new technologies, which Sandra describes as her 'open communication line' to the family in Leeds. Landline, fax, email, Skype: these are the main ways in which she keeps in touch with her husband and children throughout the working week. In Sandra's case, however, such technologies are not only a medium through which to communicate with others. Importantly, they also function as a basis for self-exploration and self-experiment. For Sandra describes herself as immersed in, and sometimes consumed by, the 'film' of her life, and especially of her role as mother to her young children. She speaks of the 'thousands' of family photos she has stored on Google's Picasa, and of devoting extensive time to cataloguing these family snapshots, arranging them in folders. She also spends countless hours editing home-recorded family videos, mixing vision and sound on Apple's iMovie. Sandra comments that she finds all this engrossing, captivating, but she worries that she might be a little 'too obsessive', given the amount of time devoted to her digital life. At the emotional core of this experience, as we will subsequently examine, there lies anxiety, mourning and melancholia.

What does Sandra's mobile life tell us about the role of new digital technologies in contemporary societies? What are the social consequences of digital technologies in light of the rise of global mobilities? Do software-operated, digital, wireless technologies give rise to any specific contemporary anxieties? Do they contain anxiety, or do they help create it? In exploring these and related questions, this chapter examines how mobile lives are interwoven with digital technologies and are reshaped in the process as techno-mobilities. Throughout the chapter, we explore how mobile lives are fashioned and transformed through various technological forms – virtualities, electronic discourse – in the emotional connections people develop with themselves, others and the wider world. Today's culture of mobile lives, we argue, is substantially created in and through the deployment of various *miniaturized mobilities* – mobile phones, laptop computers, wireless connections. We introduce and contextualize the concept of *miniaturized mobilities* in the next section of this chapter, deploying it to underscore how digital technologies intricately interweave with mobile lives. Computers and databases, mobile telephony and SMS texting, the internet and email, digital broadcast and satellites, all go into performing mobile lives. Yet digital technologies also facilitate the mobilization of feelings and affect, memories and desires, dreams and anxieties. What is at stake in the deployment of communications technologies in mobile lives, we contend, is not simply an increased digitization of social relationships, but a broad and extensive change in how emotions are contained (stored, deposited, retrieved) and thus a restructuring of identity more generally.

Digital technologies and miniaturized mobilities

The dichotomies of professional/private, work/home, external/internal and presence/absence are all put into question by Sandra's mobile life. Such a digital life is inextricably intertwined with the engendering of new kinds of sociability, as Sandra's mobile connectivity serves to both expand the network capital she enjoys in advertising and rewrites experiences of her personal and family life in more fluid and negotiated ways. In order to grasp the sociological complexities of such experience, we introduce the concept of *miniaturized mobilities*. We have coined this term to capture both essential elements of communications 'on the move' and specifically how digital technologies are corporeally interwoven with self in the production of mobile lives. Miniaturized mobilities, we contend, are fundamental to the current phase of development of contemporary societies and facilitate an intensification of 'life on the move' through advances in new portable software and hardware products.

Our understanding of this miniaturization of mobile technologies dates back to 1948, when Bell Telephone Laboratories held a press conference to announce the invention of the transistor. The transistor-powered radio represented a major break with previous ways of regulating power flows in electronics through vacuum tubes, which were very bulky and immobile. Small and relatively mobile, the first transistors were roughly the size of a golf ball – though quite expensive to produce. The subsequent introduction of circuit boards reduced transistors dramatically in size, and today they are only microns across in integrated circuits. As it happens, scientists predicted in 1961 that no transistor on a chip could ever be produced smaller than 10 millionths of a metre,[5] whereas today, for example on an Intel Pentium chip, they are 100 times smaller than that. Moreover, transistors today are not only mobile but mass: it has been estimated, for example, that there are approximately 60 million transistors for every person on the planet. Whereas a single transistor used to cost up to fifty dollars, it is difficult today to even speak of a price for a single transistor, given that one can buy millions for a dollar.

Over the past thirty years or so, miniaturization has progressively increased with the expansion of new technologies. Developments in microelectronics for the portable production, consumption and transfer of music, speech and data date from the late 1970s. The Sony Walkman, unveiled to the international press initially in 1979, is perhaps the most important innovation from this period. Paul du Gay *et al.* sum up what is culturally distinctive about the Walkman in their study of this iconic Japanese product thus:

> We do various things with the Walkman . . . listening while travelling in a crowded train, on a bus or in an underground carriage; listening while waiting for something to happen or someone to turn up; listening while doing something else – going for a walk or jogging.[6]

The Walkman occupies an important place in the historical emergence of miniaturized mobilities because it represents an early instance of 'techno-blending' – the reorganization of temporal/spatial settings or contexts in human sensory experience. Doing two different things at once, and the psychic corollary of being in two different places at once, became widespread with daily use of the Walkman: 'being in a typically crowded, noisy, urban space while also being tuned in, through your headphones, to the very different, imaginary space or soundscape in your head which develops in conjunction with the music you are listening to'.

In more recent years, the emergence of portable, powerful communications-based systems – the 'mobile machines' of BlackBerry devices and iPhones, Bluetooth wireless connectivity, laptops and compact DVD players – have fast transformed the production, organization and dissemination of interpersonal communication, information-sharing and knowledge transfer. This can be seen, for example, in the revolution of private databases concerning addresses, contacts, schedules, photos and music. Whereas traditional, stationary forms of communication (letters, telegrams) were dependent upon large, bulky collections of information (office filing cabinets, family photo collections, large music libraries), today's post-traditional, digitized world of communication initiates new kinds of 'virtual object', increasingly central to mobile lives. These miniaturized systems, often carried directly on the body and thus increasingly central to the organization of self, are software-based and serve to inform various aspects of the self's communication with itself, others and the wider world. Electronic address books, hand-held iPhoto libraries, iTunes music collections, digital video libraries: these techno-systems usher in worlds that are information-rich, of considerable sensory and auditory complexity, as well as easily transportable.

As miniaturized mobilities are packaged and sold in the marketplace as smaller, sleeker and more stylish than 'last year's model', so the capacity to use such technical objects as corporeally interwoven with the body grows exponentially. Castells captures the contemporariness of this well:

> What is specific to our world is the extension and augmentation of the body and mind of human subjects in networks of interaction powered by micro-electronics-based, software-operated, communications technologies. These technologies are increasingly diffused throughout the entire realm of human activity by growing miniaturization.[7]

This twinning of lives and systems through miniaturized mobilities is also captured by Thrift's notion of 'movement-spaces', that is: 'the utterly mundane frameworks that move "subjects" and "objects" about'.[8] Miniaturized mobilities, corporeally interwoven with the body, become organized in terms of 'movement-spaces': as software-operated, digital technologies that serve to augment the mobile capacities of individuals.

But there is more at stake than just the technical and socio-spatial range of such digital technologies. Miniaturized mobilities influence social relations in more subtle ways, especially in regard to the redrafting of the self. Lay understandings of such digital technologies tend to emphasize the expanded reach of the self's communicative actions – of 'what can be done'. In doing this, lay understandings of digital lifestyles are surely correct, but this is only part of the story. The individual self does not just 'use', or activate, digital technologies in day-to-day life. On the contrary, the self – in conditions of intensive mobilities – becomes deeply 'layered' within technological networks, as well as reshaped by their influence. Indeed, as we explore in this chapter, not only are mobile lives lived against the digital backdrop of miniaturized mobilities, but such portable technical systems give specific form to the self's relations with affect, anxiety, memory and desire.

There are four central ways in which miniaturized mobilities enter into the constitution of self and of other novel social patterns, all of which are discernable from Sandra's mobile life.

First there is *mobile connectivity*, which, in constituting the person as the portal, unties the self from specific locations or places and reconfigures identity as dispersed, adrift, 'on the move'. 'Mobile phones', writes Barry Wellman, 'afford a fundamental liberation from place.'[9] If landline telephones designate a fixed location (for example, 'the office'), mobile telephony (an example *par excellence* of miniaturized mobilities) is emblematic of wireless technology, international roaming, spatial fluidity. This much is clear from Sandra's personalized, wireless world, in which – as the designer of her own networks and connections – she is able to remain in routine contact with colleagues, friends and family, no matter where she is travelling. In so doing, Sandra's life is reflective of wider social trends: not only are there now more mobile phones than landline phones, but research undertaken by Nokia suggests that approximately two-thirds of the world's population will deploy mobile connectivity by 2015.[10] This worldwide spread of powerful, interdependent, communications-based systems forms a virtual infrastructure, or what Knorr Cetina terms 'flow architectures',[11] for the routine, repetitive actions that constitute the mobile lives of many today. Such virtual backgrounds – mobile phones, ringtones, voicemail, signals, satellites – make it possible for Sandra to activate email while driving to London, transfer voice recordings to her secretary at the push of a button and video-call her family back home in Leeds. One consequence of digital communications technologies is that aspects of social life are recast as adaptable, flexible, transferable and self-organizing. New systems of mobile, virtual communications permit fast, flexible sociabilities, which in turn cut to the core of lived identities, relationships, intimacies, sexualities, careers and families. But it is not only de-spatialized, dispersed and fluid communications, activated telephonically at any moment, that come to the fore under conditions of intensive mobilities. What is equally striking is the social impact of mobile communications upon the self and its cultural coordinates. For what Sandra's digital lifestyle reveals is a world of increased negotiation between family, work and the private sphere, which in turn involves continuous and flexible coordination of arrangements, communications and face-to-face meetings with others. This leads directly to our next point.

Second, miniaturized mobilities are part and parcel of a *continuous coordination* of communications, social networks and the mobile self. We have seen already how developments in digital technologies have made possible novel relations with others at-a-distance and have desynchronized social life more generally. Research indicates, however, that all social ties at-a-distance depend upon multiple processes of coordination, negotiation and renegotiation with others. 'Renegotiation' is especially significant in the coordination of mobile networks, as people 'on the move' use new technologies to reset and reorganize times and places for meetings, events and happenings as they go about preparing to meet with others at previously agreed times. The work of Ling, for example, underscores the often impromptu nature of most mobile calls and texting.[12] Again, this can be gleaned from Sandra's mobile life – from the brief calls she makes to her office to rearrange business meetings to the texts she makes to her family upon returning to Leeds on Friday evenings, whether to advise of last-minute train delays or arrange for the collection of take out food on the way home. Such 'revisions to clock-time' enacted through mobile calls, emailing and texting suggest a deeper shift in how people experience time itself in conditions of advanced mobilities. For what the continuous coordination of communications, social networks and the mobile self spells is a transformation from punctual time to negotiated time.[13]

Third, in a world saturated with miniaturized mobilities, *strategic travel planning and communications scheduling* become of key importance. With the advent of miniaturized mobilities, travel times of one kind or another increasingly revolve around the pursuit of work, business or leisure activities while travelling. That is to say, the complex connections that exist today between transport systems and new communications technologies mean that travel time is less likely to be approached by individuals as unproductive, 'wasted' time, and more likely to be used productively for a range of both professional and personal activities.[14] Indeed, communications scheduling 'on the move' comprises a substantial amount of the individual's travel patterns in conditions of advanced mobilities. In contrast to the immobile, fixed desk of previous work environments, today's digitized, mobile workstations, made up of palmtops, laptops, PDAs, WiFi and 3G phones, mean that portable offices are increasingly commonplace throughout cars, planes and rail carriages and places of waiting en route. It is true, of course, that work and related professional activities have been undertaken by people throughout time and across a wide spectrum of traditional travel forms – from strategic military thinking on ships to routine paperwork done on trains. But contemporary communications scheduling performed in relation to travel times and travel planning is different in scope to previous types of travel communication, because of the instantaneity of new communications technologies and the global reach of digital networks. This is significant because we may also speak of reflexivity at the heart of communications-based travel planning, in relation to both the calendars of work and professional activities that individuals intend to undertake while 'on the move', and also in terms of alterations to schedules that arise from either not being able to 'get hold' of key contacts or learning of new information that demands a revision to one's work schedule. That such strategic travel planning and communications scheduling 'on the move' is commonplace depends on a vast array of technological infrastructures – for example, the 'screens' located in business class areas of planes and rail carriages or the provision of computing facilities throughout airports and railway stations.

In such travel situations, it is not only the substantive time of the journey itself that can be 'filled' with productive work or meaningful life pursuits. It is also the 'edges' of travel time – waiting in an airport terminal lounge, sitting on a delayed train – that become potentially usable in this way. It is characteristic of contemporary attitudes to work and related professional activities that people seek to undertake various productive activities – mobile telephony, SMS texting, email – while experiencing unanticipated temporal delays when travelling. Only when ready-to-hand miniaturized mobilities are more or less easily available, however, can we speak of networked communication and information as productive possibilities for people in this context. These delayed edges of travel time have been captured nicely by Lyons *et al.*, who describe the importance of 'equipped waiting'.[15] Equipped waiting, situated on the delayed edges of travel time, allows for an inhabiting of, or dwelling within, information communications networks, from which individuals can conduct business, work, romance and family negotiations.

Finally, as a result of the widespread use of miniaturized mobilities, the *technological unconscious* comes to the fore and functions as a psychosocial mechanism for the negotiation of sociabilities based upon widespread patterns of absence, lack, distance and disconnection. In underscoring the generative, creative aspects of the unconscious for both self-identity and social relations, Freud uncovered the complex, contra-dictory emotional connections between presence and absence – for example in the Oedipus complex, or the 'symbolic order' in Jacques Lacan's Freud – which constitute psychic life.[16] In classical Freudian theory, patterns of presence and absence primarily refer to significant others, such as parents, siblings, extended family and such like. With complex, network-driven systems, by contrast, we witness the emergence of various 'virtual' others and objects resulting from the revolution of digital technologies. These virtual others and objects reconstitute the background to psychic experiences of presence and absence in novel ways, through, for example, the virtual experience of otherness in Second Life. As a result, it is necessary to speak of a technological unconscious at work in the negotiation of social relations involving high degrees of absence, distance and disconnection.[17] This last theme provides a convenient transition to the next section of the chapter, which deals with the transformations of emotional containment brought about by digital, wireless technologies.

Digital life: deposits, storage and retrieval of affect

The backdrop here is the restructuring, or renegotiation, of professional and personal realms that is characteristic of mobile lives. The techno-communications systems of twenty-first-century mobilities create slices of life where people can simultaneously be 'on the move', access vast amounts of information, and communicate with others (both near and far) in real time through miniaturized mobilities. As we have seen in the case of Sandra, approaching life in terms of mobile technologies certainly has its rewarding and uplifting aspects – as the more or less constant technological communication and continual travel produce a world of rapid change and dazzling excitement. But mobile life also has some very unsettling aspects, again connected to the sheer momentum of change and often tied to novel trials and tribulations stemming from difficulties in relating professional, intimate and family lives. Mobile technologies, as Sandra's story reveals, assist in connecting, understanding and discovering meaningful aspects entailed by the various time–space dislocations of life 'on the move'. But technological intervention into, and restructuring of, mobile lives result in no straightforward victory over emotional difficulties. For, whatever the more positive aspects heralded by mobile lives (and we do not deny that they are many and varied), we emphasize that life 'on the move' is also bumpy, full of the unexpected and unpredictable, involving considerable ambivalence.

Understanding how miniaturized machines play an important role in containing many forms of anxiety helps explain why, in conditions of complex mobilities, people come to dwell within communications networks, activities and capabilities. There is an emerging literature on this subject, although we do not review it in detail.[18] 'Technological containment' may sound some-what odd or jarring, as the term 'containment' is usually associated with the sympathy or support of another person (for example, a therapist) in much psychological research. On an emotional plane, however, there are close connections between digital technologies, miniaturized mobilities and emotional containment. Think, for example, of a person talking on their mobile phone while on a train: the intimacy shared with the person to whom they are speaking may be very close (even though this other is 'at–a–distance'), while those co-present on the train merely 'fade into the background'. In 'filtering out' the presence of other people on the train, a sense of self-identity involving perhaps major transitions or tensions – for example, a marriage breakdown – might be explored in the mobile phone conversation. In such a situation, miniaturized mobilities facilitate forms of emotional containment – the opportunity to express and explore anxieties, doubts, worries or dangers.

One reason we chose to write about Sandra's story is that her experiences of digital technologies reflect the deeply ambivalent psychological dimensions that come to the fore in living mobile lives. There is, for example, little doubt that Sandra's routine use of miniaturized mobilities helps her maintain 'shared histories' of intimacy with her family. Sandra's

Figure 2.2 Departure hall, Seoul Incheon International Airport, 2007

shared history of intimacy with her family may be created and sustained through very different orderings of time and space to those processes of intimacy she was part of when living full time in Leeds as a young mother, but, nevertheless, the role of miniaturized mobilities is plainly evident in how she today integrates aspects of her family's calendar into her professional and personal lives. To that extent, Sandra's digital life is deeply dialogical, built as it is out of ongoing virtual connections with significant others. Mobile technologies thus play, not only a facilitating role in the maintenance of Sandra's close emotional bonds, but a containing one as well. She comments, for instance, that she finds it 'deeply reassuring' to know that she can have virtually instantaneous contact with family members at-a-distance through mobile telephony or electronic communications (assuming they work). Again, this is partly to do with the 'use' of such technologies; but, more than that, miniaturized mobilities offer some reassurance, some degree of emotional containment of anxiety, even when not activated. Simply knowing that her mobile is 'at hand', or that she can see and talk with her children through Skype if she wants to, is oftentimes enough to contain Sandra's anxieties about working and living away from home for extended periods. Such a focus on the 'potential' for mobility (in this case, communicative and virtual) is sometimes referred to in the literature of mobilities as 'motility'.[19]

We may also trace in Sandra's story, however, various disturbing pathologies of the self – again related to matters of containment – in her burgeoning preoccupation with these technologies. This is evident especially from her immersion in electronic family photos and videos – conducted on both Apple's iMovie and Google's Picasa. What was meant to become a 'family resource' (in which members of the family could access this virtual archive) has, in recent times, shaded over into something that Sandra worries is 'too obsessive'. Of course, many people spend large amounts of their leisure time immersed in pursuits such as photography or video editing. In the case of Sandra, however, something else appears to be at work here. She acknowledges that she feels considerable levels of guilt over being away from the family so regularly. She also seems aware of the disquieting scenario of loss more generally. But Sandra's reflexive level of self-awareness also seems to falter in this connection. She feels not on 'solid ground' when it comes to understanding the countless hours she spends organizing their electronic photo library, or editing family videos. Because she does not quite understand the emotional prompts for these activities, she says that she feels worried.

Post-Freudian developments in psychoanalytic theory, we contend, are especially helpful for grasping the state of mind that Sandra has entered through her ongoing, relentless technological explorations. Although psychoanalysis is sometimes portrayed as anti-sociological in its examination of the imaginative, unconscious forms of self-identity, it nevertheless provides a sophisticated conceptual means for exploring the self's relationship to cultural meanings and society more generally.[20] This applies, not only to social relationships, but also the self's relations with non-human objects (such as digital technologies).[21] Given the emphasis in this chapter on the theme of emotional containment in the context of mobile lives, the conceptualization of anxiety developed by the psychoanalytic tradition known as Kleinian and post-Kleinian theory is especially relevant. Kleinian psychoanalysis is fundamentally concerned with the emotional logics of primitive anxiety – both in the life of the young infant, and also throughout the life-course. Kleinianism stresses that the infant's early sense of anxiety comes from a primary destructiveness, or fear that envy and rage may result in injury to loved objects – principally the mother or primary caretaker. Anxiety in this perspective 'eats away' at the core of the self, and consequently Kleinian theory devotes great attention to the interpersonal forms in and through which anxiety may be ameliorated, contained and transformed. For it is only through the containment of anxiety, or so argue Kleinians, that basic trust in self and others can be developed and nourished.

The post-Kleinian contribution of psychoanalyst Wilfred Bion is especially important, given the attention he paid to the emotional processes by which normal anxiety can spill over into neurotic anxiety. Again, the theme of containment looms large. Bion emphasized the complex emotional processes through which an individual generates new experience as genuinely *new*.[22] Human experience, according to Bion, has to be understood in relation to the overall *processing of emotion* that an individual develops across time, rather than as something that impacts upon people only in a generalized manner. For Bion, experience generated with others has the capacity to unlock previously unknown, unthought or unpredicted aspects of emotional life. Reflective engagement with others – facilitative of the containment and transformation of unconscious anxiety – is essential to experiencing the world as new as well as to autonomous thought. The flipside, says Bion, is when people become emotionally stuck, caught in stultifying routines and endless repetition. From this angle, if an individual's emotional repertoire becomes constrained or damaged, this in turn discounts fresh experiences as new. Indeed, the emotional imprint of an individual's previous encounters – from early family relationships through childhood to maturity – is very often limiting or coercive to learning and development from fresh experiences.

One of us has elsewhere explored in detail the import of Bion's psycho-analytic approach for social theory, especially in terms of the analysis of modern communications within contemporary societies.[23] What we under-score here is that Bion's work is insightful for the critique of mobile lives because of its emphasis on both the projection outwards, and subsequent retrieval into self, of affects regarding surrounding objects, both human and inhuman. In order for experience of the world to become emotionally imprinted upon the psyche, according to Bion, the individual self must surrender itself to the here-and-now of daily happenings. This involves, in effect, a 'letting go' of consciousness of self and an immersion in sectors of pure experience. Indeed, it is only through immersion in the object world that the self can subsequently 'attach meaning to experience' in creative and open-ended ways. It is only in terms of the 'processing' of experience, the origin of the reflective self, that the individual comes to engage in that act which Bion calls 'thinking', as well as the storing of thoughts as memory. Thus, there is an essential interplay between experience and thinking, raw emotions and reflective life, which is essential to the individual's creative engagement with the self, other people and the wider world.

The psychoanalyst Christopher Bollas, influenced by Bion, has undertaken various studies that demonstrate the emotional impact of non-human objects (such as communications technologies) upon the self. In a passage from *Being a character*, Bollas makes a fundamental point about the process of object engagement:

> the processional integrity of any object – that which is inherent to any object when brought to life by an engaging subject – is used by the individual according to the laws of the dream work. When we use an object it is as if we know the terms of engagement; we know we shall 'enter into' an intermediate space, and at this point of entry we change the nature of perception, as we are now released to dream work, in which subjectivity is scattered and disseminated into the object world, transformed by that encounter, then returned to itself after the dialectic, changed in its inner contents by the history of that moment.[24]

Understanding the interweaving of self and object in this way directs our attention to the complexities of affect in the production of meaning. For Bollas, all psychic engagement with others and the world involves a kind of 'holding' of the trace of the object itself. It is as if part of the object itself becomes deeply lodged in the self. All individuals, according to Bollas, inhabit highly condensed psychic textures of the object world. Or, to put it slightly differently, it is as if the unconscious communications that arise between people in their use of everyday objects are somehow deeply inscribed within these structures of interaction, preserved in the object world for future forms of self-reference, self-experiencing and self-understanding. 'As we encounter the object world', writes Bollas, 'we are substantially metamorphosed by the structure of objects; internally transformed by objects that leave their trace within us'.

What is meant by the term 'trace' in this context? And how, exactly, can the self use an object (either human or non-human) in such a way that the latter comes to act as a kind of emotional container for the former? According to Bollas, the trace of any object lodged deep within the self has its roots in a web of affects, splittings, projective identifications, part–object relatedness and omnipotent thinking. Such psychic processes mark a structural boundary for the 'self-holding' of affective states, preserved, as it were, for future forms of thinking and symbolic elaboration. All object-use is emotionally tensional, involving an unconscious oscillation between love and hate, excitement and guilt. Seeking to capture the experiential dimensions of emotional containment, Bollas contends that certain objects are like 'psychic keys' for particular individuals, in that they enable an opening out of unconscious experience, a symbolic context for the elaboration of selves. Hence, Bollas speaks of the *transformational* aspects of the object, as that which releases and preserves the erotics of individual subjectivity.

Provocatively, Bollas claims that the preservation of affective states – that is, their storage – is based on modalities of conservative or mnemic objects. This relates to the *storing* of affects within the object world of places, events and things.[25] This investment of affect in objects, both real and virtual, can remain 'stored' until such time as the individual is able to reclaim such self-defining experience in and through symbolic elaboration. In so doing, the individual might be said to be engaged in an act of 'emotional banking', depositing affects, moods and dispositions into the object world and storing such aspects of self-experience until they are withdrawn for future forms of symbolization and thinking. For example, the self-psychological analysts Atwood and Stolorow discuss the case of a man who regularly used a tape recorder to deposit and monitor his feelings outside therapy. 'This use of the tape recorder as a transitional object', they comment, 'both concretized the injured state of the self and reinvoked the empathic bond with the therapist, thereby enabling the patient to regain a sense of being substantial and real.'[26] This is suggestive of what we mean by *affect storage*.

Different objects, of course, have different levels of significance for individuals. For Bollas, individuals in the unconsciousness of day-to-day life invest various objects (both human and inhuman) to both contain and elaborate the complexity of the self. The investment of affect in objects is therefore something of an open-ended affair: such investment can either help to unlock or to imprison the creativity of the self. The imprisoning of the self within the object world – in which thoughts and feelings are not experienced as symbolic elaborations, but as things-in-themselves – is theorized by Bollas as a point of affective closure. Further, the mind is emptied of pain through the defensive use of omnipotent thinking and denial, and the self is fixed through an ideological framing (familial, religious, nationalistic and so forth) of what the world is actually like. The unlocking of the self through the storing of affects in the object world, however, permits a multiplication of experience and a transformation in pleasure, creativity and fulfilment. The use of an object as transformational, whether we speak of an immersion in music, literature or football, can help open the self to the multiplicity and discontinuity of experience. Likewise, in the context of mobile lives, the investment of affect in virtual objects, such as Facebook, Second Life or Skype, can function as a form of emotional containment, the storing of affect for subsequent retrieval, processing and thinking.

From this psychoanalytic standpoint, the creativity of self, which means the capacity to engage new experience as genuinely new, is closely tied to the openness of psychic life. Openness in this context involves a kind of processing – a thinking through – of emotions. A creative involvement with one's emotional life, as well as the emotional lives of others, stems from an openness to the complexity, and indeed multiplicity, of human experience. In this sense, both other people and surrounding objects can help facilitate experience that is transformational in impact. That is to say, containing environments supplied by other people and transitional objects assist in the processing of unthought emotion. Where individuals cannot live creatively, either because of dominant emotional imprints from past experience that are corrosive, or because their capacity for processing emotion is underdeveloped or impaired, chronic depressive and related pathologies are likely to emerge.

Although this psychoanalytic understanding of containment only refers to 'transitional objects' in a very general sense, there is no reason to suppose that the main lines of this argument do not apply with less force to the impact of digital technologies in day-to-day social life. While we are at the edge of where current psychoanalytic theory takes us, our claim is that digital technologies should be understood, at least in part, in relation to the containment of anxiety and emotional conflicts of the self. That is to say, mobile technologies are not only technical objects of adjustment through which people coordinate their activities with others. They are also constitutive of how people go about the production and transformation of their mobile lives. As anxiety, trust and technologies of mobile interaction are intricately interwoven, it is not surprising that miniaturized mobilities should function to some large extent as containing mechanisms. For miniaturized mobilities, we contend, are never free of the emotions, anxieties and conflicts of the individuals that use them.

The difficulties and complexities of containment are certainly evident from Sandra's story, a woman who has poured a good deal of her need for emotional contact into digital technologies. In a sense, there is much that is ordinary in Sandra's use of digital technologies as a mechanism of anxiety reduction. Like millions the world over, she uses mobile telephony, the internet and related electronic communications to keep in touch with significant others in her daily life. Although somewhat unremarkable from a lay standpoint (after all, this is arguably how people now live throughout advanced, network societies), it is worth underscoring the importance of such technologies to the emotional fabric of Sandra's life. Such technologies are deeply interwoven with all aspects of Sandra's professional and personal activities, from mobile conference meetings with colleagues (also 'on the move') to the scheduling and rescheduling of family get-togethers and outings. As we have seen, however, this mobile life extends well beyond the use of digital technologies to maintain relations of generalized contact or intimacy with others. Her technological activities also become the means by which she makes a connection with other, displaced (and sometimes only barely recognized or acknowledged) aspects of self-experience. Although an immersion in such technologies – in this instance, Picasa and iMovie – was gratifying in the early stages of her time living in London, with the sense that more and more of her evenings were taken up with such activities, it was as though Sandra was becoming disconnected from her own life. Perhaps this is why she expressed concern about the 'obsessional' aspects of such activity.

There is the sense here of digital technologies shifting in Sandra's experience from intoxicating to threatening. Listening to how she talks about her intensely mobile worlds of mediated interaction, it is as if she is describing a psychic power struggle between her personal and techno-logical lives, of which the latter comes to limit the former. What has limited Sandra's inner reality, it seems, is the isolation experienced as she goes about her entrenched ways of using, and her absorption in, these technolo-gies. It is as if this confrontation with mobile technology for Sandra has resulted in an engulfing of herself, an engulfment that has left the self drained and lifeless. Trapped in the isolation box of these new technologies, the emotional connections Sandra was seeking to re-establish with others – namely, her children and family – come to be eaten away from within. And this is even more the case when those relations-at-a-distance involve different countries or continents, and the families involved possess little network capital to enable relationship work and repair.

Sandra is not alone in finding that mobile technologies can switch from containment to engulfment. Research in psychology, for example, highlights the growing relations between problematic internet use and depression or psychic isolation.[27] Other recent research has focused on the psychological distress and connected pathological symptoms stemming from the maladaptive use of both mobile telephony and the internet.[28] A Japanese study of web-based communities found that excessive use of the internet increases depression and aggression, as well as the desire for further virtual communication, but (in contrast to findings in the above-mentioned research) does not impact on loneliness.[29] Much of the research concerning pathologies of the self arising in the context of mobile communications remains controversial, and there appears to be little overall consensus in the social sciences as to the emotional consequences of conducting much of one's life on small screens.[30]

As Norman H. Nie *et al.* have pointed out, however, social critique needs to shift away from general categorizations of whether mobile technologies are good or bad for sociability, and focus on how specific technological deployments affect the self and interpersonal relations.[31] In this connection, the psychoanalytic approach we have detailed to the generation of experience, mediated through digital technologies, is of considerable importance. It underscores the affective complexity of the self in its deployment of new communications technologies. This approach sees the benefits of new communications technologies, at the level of the self, as generating forms of experience that often involve creative dreaming or reverie. What accounts for disturbances in the self's engagement with digital technologies stems from closures in psychic life. When digital processes fail to function as emotional containers for experience, the individual can become overwhelmed by communications technologies, with disowned aspects of self-experience – ranging from paranoid anxiety to guilt, despair and depression. What gives rise to failures in emotional containment in conditions of complex mobile lives needs greater analytical attention than it has so far received in the social sciences. Similarly, how different forms of mobile connectivity – from SMS texting to video-conferencing to online fast communications – facilitate or constrain the autonomy of the self also demands further critical attention.

Conclusion

In this chapter, we have critically appraised the role of digital technologies in the constitution of mobile lives. Especially significant to living mobile lives are the multiple and intersecting software-operated, digital technologies that we term *miniaturized mobilities*. From Apple iPhones to Bluetooth wireless connectivity, miniaturized mobilities are corporeally interwoven with the body and serve to augment the mobile capacities of individual subjects in physical, communicative and virtual forms. We have outlined various ways in which new digital technologies enter into the patterning and restructuring of mobile lives, with particular concentration on the theme of emotional anxiety and its containment. Drawing from post-Freudian developments in psychoanalysis, we argued that digital life is increasingly organized as deposits, storage and retrieval of affect in and through miniaturized mobilities. From this perspective, we noted that virtual objects such as Facebook, Second Life or Skype are used, in part, for the 'holding' or containment of anxiety. We further noted that such containment can either facilitate thinking in relation to mobile lives, or can turn defensively back upon the self in various pathologies of mobile lives. Throughout, we have emphasized that the living of digital lives, realized increasingly through the augmentation of miniaturized mobilities, occurs in the broader context of complex networks of connection, and this provides the connection to the next chapter, on networks.

Figure 3.1 Internet lounge, Seoul Incheon International Airport, 2007

3   Networks and inequalities

Forthcoming destruction of houses and cities, to make way for great meeting places for cars and planes.

Filippo Tommaso Marinetti[1]

Networks and networking

A central argument of Chapter 2 was that the advent of digital technologies involves the creation of new kinds of mobile life, new kinds of sociality and new ways of relating to the self and others. In this chapter, we examine how mobile lives unfold through networks and specifically networked relations, facilitating the formation and re-formation of connections that people have with others. Although this book is concerned with mobile lives, this chapter will reveal how the movement itself is not as significant. Its importance stems from how it enables people to be connected with each other, to meet and to re-meet over time and across space. Movement makes *connections*. These connections form patterns or what are known as networks, which many commentators see as the critical feature of contemporary life. Much travel thus involves making new connections and extending one's network or sustaining one's existing networks.

This is especially evident in the lifestyles of global elites or 'globals', as we consider in Chapter 4, who roam the planet with multiple careers, overseeing vast capital investments, transnational operations and organizational downsizings and remodellings. Such networked patterns can have highly significant consequences for economies, societies and people's lives. Especially, in this chapter, we examine how such networks are a form of power or influence that can operate to benefit some social groups at the expense of others.

Networking is also to be viewed as a form of *working* that has consequences for people's lives. We will examine how travelling, communicating and networking are not cost free, as we have already noted and examined in the previous chapter. In Chapter 1, we encountered the idea of network capital: that networking is something that requires substantial resources: time, objects, access and emotion. In this chapter, we examine how this form of capital has come to develop through a mobility 'field', and we go on to examine its significant impacts upon social inequality in the contemporary world. We will see how those rich in network capital enjoy many benefits over and above their possession of economic or cultural capital. The chapter following this one explores the patterns of life of the 'globals' – a group where the temporal, object, access and emotional costs of 'networking' are made significantly lower through their high network capital. Overall, we establish in this current chapter, first, that networking is a resource-intensive form of work; and, second, that mobile lives involve the planning, holding and interpreting of meetings of very many different sorts. Movement is all to do with what we will call 'meetingness'.[2] We begin this chapter by analysing some features of networks before turning to the importance of meetings. We then examine the nature of network capital and of new kinds of mobility-generated inequality.

Manuel Castells, in *The rise of the network society,* argues that 'structures' with a clear centre, a concentration of power, vertical hierarchy and a constitution are now less significant in the contemporary world. Rather, he maintains, networks:

> constitute the new social morphology of our societies, and the diffusion of networking logic substantially modifies the operation and outcomes in processes of production, experience, power, and culture ... the network society, characterized by the pre-eminence of social morphology over social action.[3]

He argues that there are many such networked social phenomena, including network enterprises, networked states such as the European Union and many networks functioning within civil society. These all depend upon the work of interpersonal networking of the sort we encountered Simone engaging in, described in Chapter 1.

More generally, Luc Boltanski and Eve Chiapello describe the character of a 'connexionist' world. Such a world is to be found, they say, where 'the realization of profit occurs through organizing economic operations in networks'.[4] Such networks engender new forms of opportunism, which are different from those of market opportunism. They describe the networker or head of a networked project as: 'mobile, streamlined, possessed of the

art of establishing and maintaining numerous diverse, enriching connections, and of the ability to extend networks'.[4] Especially significant is
the person who can exploit what Burt terms 'structural holes' that others
have somehow missed or not taken advantage of.[5] Boltanski and Chiapello
then make a strangely characterized distinction between 'great men' and
the 'little people'. The former do not stand still, while the latter are rooted
to the spot. It is, they say, by moving around, by their mobility, especially
in exploiting structural holes, that great men create new links and extend
their networks. Indeed, in this 'connexionist' world, where high status
presupposes displacement, 'great men derive part of their strength from the
immobility of the little people'. This cumulative process means that, in this
network world, many live in a state of 'permanent anxiety' about whether
they are being disconnected, abandoned on the spot by those who are
moving around.[6] Finance capital has added to this fear of being rooted, of
being stuck in place and not being able to move and to network. There is
heightened anxiety about being too localist and not networked enough, not
able to exploit the structural holes. Such variations in the capacity to move
are structured by gender, ethnicity, age, (dis)ability and social class.

Other analysts of networks in economic life argue that such economies
generate more productive outcomes compared with economies that are hier-
archically organized. Yochai Benckler, in *The wealth of networks,* describes
the emerging nature of a 'networked information economy'. This involves
decentralization and peer production among very many people, as shown
in the enormously elaborate networks involved in developing open-source
software or large collaborations such as Wikipedia.[7] This 'we-think', as
Charlie Leadbetter expresses it, reflects the more general process by which
accumulation within networks, that is *who* you know, becomes more significant than *what* you know. This can, as he shows through many examples,
exemplify mass innovation rather than mass production.[8]

At its starkest then, to the extent that some knowledge is tacit, that is
informal and individually embodied through specific experiences, organizational success results from how people are able to access, develop and use
information. The more that there are formal and especially informal
networks, the more opportunity there is to create, to circulate and to share
tacit knowledge and develop and build new capital. In such contexts,
meetings and especially informal, face-to-face discussions become
especially significant. There are important ways in which social networks
can enable the exchange of tacit knowledge and can allocate resources. This
has been described as 'learning through interaction', and, hence, the
necessity for travel, co-presence and mobile lives in order that there is some
shared social context for developing and exchanging such tacit knowledge.[9]

However, such networking often socially discriminates against women especially and against others who are unable to enter or to sustain membership of such networks. We discuss this below through examining network capital.[10]

The most developed sociological programme of network research is that of Barry Wellman and colleagues. He argues that: 'We find community in networks, not groups . . . In networked societies: boundaries are permeable, interactions are with diverse others, connections switch between multiple networks, and hierarchies can be flatter and recursive.'[11] Such networked communities are not confined to a particular place but stretch out geographically and socially. Wellman suggests that these involve historic transformations in societies in the rich north from *door-to-door* to *place-to-place* to *person-to-person* communities.

First, people walking to visit each other typified door-to-door communities that were spatially compact and densely knit; there were 'little boxes' that were based upon geographical propinquity.[12] Significant others were encountered through walking or cycling to one another, and there was much overlap of family life, work and friendship. But such door-to-door communities became less significant with the increased speed of transport and longer-distance communications that especially took the male breadwinner out of the neighbourhood by car. Second, with 'place-to-place' communities, interactions moved inside the private home. It is the home in which entertaining, phone calls and emails take place: 'the household is what is visited, telephoned or emailed'.[13] Phone calls and, subsequently, email connect homes in disparate geographical locations and produce connections with those who are not living close by.

Third, since the 1990s, with person-to-person communities, the person 'has become the portal'.[14] The turn to person-to-person relations or what Wellman terms networked individualism stems from mobile telephony and related technologies. Each person becomes the engineer of their own ties and networks and is mostly connected, no matter where they are going or staying. Even while on the move, connections can be sustained. As Christian Licoppe reports: 'the mobile phone is portable, to the extent of seeming to be an extension of its owner, a personal object constantly there, at hand . . . individuals seem to carry their network of connections which could be activated telephonically at any moment.'[15] Networks are thus individualized, part of a wider individualization of 'reflexive modern societies', as discussed in Chapter 2. This networked individualism involves most people possessing many distant connections, or what are normally termed 'weak ties', connecting people to the outside world. Each person possesses a distinct, individualized pattern. According to Wellman *et al.*: 'This individualisation of connectivity means that acquiring resources depends substantially on personal skill, individual motivation and maintaining the right connections . . . With networked individualism, people must actively network to thrive.'[16] Obviously, there are huge variations in network capital and, hence, in the placing of people within a stratification order where 'networking' practices are so central.

This, in turn, connects to research on the so-called 'small worlds' thesis. Physicist turned sociologist Duncan Watts has sought to explain the empirical finding, noted in Chapter 1, that everybody on the planet, whatever their social location, is separated by only six degrees of separation. Whether or not this is literally correct, there seems little doubt that there are surprisingly few connections linking people around the world, even when they appear unconnected. It is common for people who believe that they are strangers to each other to find, after a relatively brief conversation, that they are in fact connected along a quite short chain of acquaintances. Their apparently distinct networks do in fact overlap. In John Guare's recently revived Broadway play, *Six degrees of separation*, it is stated that: 'Everybody on this planet is separated by only six other people. Six degrees of separation. Between us and everybody else on this planet.'[17]

The explanation of this is indicated by Mark Granovetter's analysis of the strength of 'weak ties'. His research showed that a striking 84 per cent of those seeking a new job were able to acquire such a job, not through someone they knew well, but through people they saw only occasionally and did not know well.[18] The extensive, *weak* ties of acquaintanceship and informational flow were central to successful job searches and, by implication, to many other social processes such as the spreading of rumour.[19] Such weak ties connect people to the outside world, providing a bridge other than that provided by the densely knit 'clump' of a person's close friends and family. Bridges between such clumps are formed from weak rather than strong ties. If people were only connected to the small group of close friends and family, then there would be a huge degree of separation of the world's population. However, if there are just a few, long-range, random links or weak ties connecting each of these 'clumps', then the degree of separation massively reduces. A limited number of long-range, random network links, if combined with densely knit lumps, produces a remarkably low degree of separation of each person from everyone else in the world. There is a normal distribution of individuals, with most people relatively weakly connected, and only a few moderately powerful nodes.

By contrast, however, websites are not normally distributed. A few nodes possess an enormous number of links that utterly dominate the networks and architecture of the internet. This pattern is sometimes described as an 'aristocratic system', where, through their networks, the rich get richer and have disproportionate influence, while the poor get poorer.[20] The global financial flows that move through the three main hubs of London, New York and Tokyo are a good example of an aristocratic pattern. This partly explains why financial values can violently fluctuate. What appears to be a safe investment is suddenly revealed to be quite the reverse, as rumours of financial collapse spread rapidly through a very few key financial nodes, as happened so dramatically in late 2008.

Finally, in this section, we might consider whether the developments in communications discussed in Chapter 2 are reordering the nature of 'knowing' people through the large expansion of very weak ties. Thus, people might be said to 'know' everyone in their email or mobile phone address book, or the members of an internet chat room, or all their 'friends' on a social networking site. There seems to be a huge increase in very weak ties through which others are known in one limited respect. Kay Axhausen argues that people in major European countries know an increasing number of other people, but that less effort is spent in 'keeping up' with most of those weak or very weak ties.[21] Barry Wellman maintains that the median number in people's 'personal community network' is 23, with between 200 and 1500 very weak ties.[22]

Simultaneously, much time has to be spent in sustaining one's far-flung contacts, as there is less likelihood of those quick, casual meetings that occurred when there was overlap between different, localized social networks. As we have seen, people thus spend much time planning and sustaining meetings with a fairly small proportion of those who are 'known', communicating especially to make arrangements and then travelling from a distance in order to 'keep in touch'. This is described elsewhere as the critical work of 'coordinating face-to-face meetings in mobile network societies'.[23]

This coordinating of meetings was particularly examined by Georg Simmel, who described how metropolitan life at the beginning of the twentieth century was dependent upon clocks, pocket watches and punctuality. He states that, if all the clocks and watches in Berlin were to suddenly go wrong in different ways, even if only by one hour, all economic life and communication of the city would be disrupted for a long time. Thus, the technique of metropolitan life is unimaginable without the most punctual integration of all activities and mutual relations into a stable and impersonal time schedule.[24] Clocks and watches made possible the mobilities and meetings of metropolitan life a century or so ago. Contemporary metropolitan life and its meetings are what we now examine.

Meetings

We have mainly discussed networks and networking without the key process in the small worlds literature that is co-present meetings.[25] Goffman noted decades ago that:

> The realm of activity that is generated by face-to-face interaction and organized by norms of co-mingling – a domain containing weddings, family meals, chaired meetings, forced marches, service encounters, queues, crowds, and couples – has never been sufficiently treated as a subject matter in its own right.[26]

We seek to remedy that neglect here, especially because such 'face-to-face interactions', such focused encounters, presuppose the *movement* of one, some or all of the participants, to attend such weddings, family meals, chaired meetings, forced marches, service encounters, queues, crowds, couples and so on. Each of these meetings is an element within a more complex social-and-material system of family or business networks, social movements, service industries, sports crowds, relationships and so on. The meetings are part of, and help to sustain, such networked relations. Networked individualism we might note is anything but individualistic!

The importance of such physical travel and organized meetings helps to interpret Watts' criticism of much network literature: 'Network ties . . . are treated as costless, so you can have as many of them as you are able to accumulate, without regard to the difficulty of making them or maintaining them'.[27] Watts uses this to query the empirical significance of the aristocratic model we discussed above. This model seems apposite in the case of the internet, because search machines do their costless 'travelling' across billions of pages (not costless in terms of energy requirement, as we are increasingly aware). But establishing and maintaining ties for many social groupings are not at all cost free, because of the importance and complexities of travel, a word originally from the French *travail,* or work. We have discussed this 'work' in Chapter 2. The more that networking relations are virtual, the more likely is an aristocratic network pattern. But, other things being equal, the more that there are 'meetings' within a given network, the fewer the inequalities in the network will tend to be, and the more normal the distribution.

The work of establishing and maintaining network ties is illuminated in David Lodge's sociologically informed novel, also called *Small world.*[28] It describes how networks of professionals have to spend time meeting up, with the network only reproducing itself through periodic meetings that cement its weak ties. The novel especially focuses upon 'conferences' where the most common refrain between delegates is, of course, 'it's a small world', as they discover various overlapping networks. Lodge describes the complex, multilayered and richly gossipy nature of conferences and other 'occasioned meetings'. *Small world* brings out that what get exchanged through intense and dynamic conversational interactions are rich social goods: of friendship, power, projects, markets, information, rumours, job deals, sexual favours, gossip and so on. Central to networks, then, are 'meetings' and, hence, travelling through time–space in order to 'cement' weak ties at least for another period until the next meeting, when much of the conversation will be about the previous meeting and who was or was not present!

Thus, although people may 'know' others in a short chain of acquaintances and, hence, generate the 'it's a small world' experience, this produces less affect than if people intermittently meet. Indeed, in some senses, people might be said only to 'know' each other if they do meet from time to time, assuming that they have what we refer to below as sufficient network capital. However, intense meetings at one period of time, say as students, can carry the relationship without as many frequent meetings, especially if distance, lack of income or young children prevent frequent travel. Overall, though, networks presuppose intermittent meetings. These are not cost free, and because of that people can only sustain networks with a limited number of other people (as discussed in Chapter 2).

We noted above that social networks appear now to be less coherent, with fewer overlapping, multiple affiliations. This is because people's residences and their activities, their families and their friends are significantly more geographically dispersed. Within the rich north, this dispersal has happened for various interdependent reasons:[29]

- the increase in the actual number of households worldwide and their reduced average size;
- the 'greying' of the world's population and people's tendency to retire to places different from where they have worked/lived;
- wider car ownership associated with the general spreading of lower-density suburban housing;
- airline deregulation and the growth of the budget airline model;
- high-speed rail networks, often stretched across continents;
- the internationalizing of much business and professional life;
- the growth of large, transnational communities and of leisure/family travel within such communities;

- the tendency for a significant proportion of a national population to live abroad;
- the general growth within tourism of the category of 'visiting friends and relatives' (VFR tourism);
- the internationalizing of higher education, partly because of the significance of the status of being 'internationally credentialled';
- the growing numbers of weak ties generated by new modes of communication and information storage.

And yet a network only functions as such if it is 'activated' through the intermittent co-presence of some or all of its members. What we can call 'network activation' occurs if there are periodic events, each week or month or year, when it is more or less obligatory for meetings to occur. Examples of this obligatory 'meetingness' include the daily meeting of a teenage group, weekly meeting of an extended family, monthly strategy meetings in a company, annual Thanksgiving celebrations within far-flung American families, or biannual conferences in an international professional organization. Very often, what is exchanged is tacit knowledge or understanding. And when people meet face-to-face for work, for family life or for friendship, this normally involves long-distance travel for some or all of the participants involved. The average distance people in the rich north have to travel in order to sustain their networks has significantly increased.[30] This in turn makes those who, for various reasons, are unable to travel regularly such long distances less effective at making and sustaining their networks (such as women with small children or other dependents).

We should, moreover, pause to reconsider 'tourism' in the contemporary world, and reflect on how it needs as a category to be 'de-exoticized'.[31] The geographical 'stretching out' of social networks makes what is tourist-type travel often desirable and necessary. Although speaking on the phone, text messaging and email are crucial, everyday practices of 'staying in touch' among distant friends and kin, they only afford socialities of a 'disembodied' and 'dematerialized' kind. One cannot buy a round of drinks or cuddle one's grandchild or kiss the bride over the telephone/ Skype or through an email or videoconference. Co-present talk is embodied and may involve food, drink, music and a shared physical place, places temporarily 'full of life'. Some places indeed are particularly ambient in affording the conditions for face-to-face sociality. Travel is thus about being co-present with significant *faces*, being their guests and receiving their hospitality and perhaps enjoying their knowledge of local culture. In Sweden, it is thought that about half of all travel stems from meeting up with friends and family.[32]

Sometimes, tourists are viewed as free-floating individuals seeking to maximize their hedonistic pleasures. But this view ignores the many obligations that choreograph tourism escapes, which can be more or less binding and more or less pleasurable, requiring intermittent face-to-face co-presence. In particular, obligations to family and friends involve very strong normative expectations of presence and attention. A significant 70 per cent of people surveyed in the UK agree that, 'people should keep in contact with close family members even if they don't have much in common'.[33] There are social customs, obligations and activities that substantial majorities of the UK population identify as among the top necessities of life. These events include: celebrations on special occasions such as Christmas (83 per cent), attending weddings and funerals (80 per cent) and visits to friends or family (84 per cent), especially those in hospital.[34] Warde and Martens say about family meals:

> It is important to be present, if it is possible, because the meal symbolizes a socially significant, temporally specific occasion. To have eaten the same meal the day before or the day after would not be a satisfactory substitute, even if many of the same people would be present.[35]

Thus, fulfilling social obligations often requires co-presence, rituals and sustained quality time, often at very particular moments and within specific kinds of ambient place.

So it is that, when distant friends or family members do meet up, each visit may now last longer. People may compensate for the intermittence of meetings and the cost of transport (time, money and weariness) by spending a whole day or weekend or week(s) together, often staying in each other's homes. Obligations of tourist travel, of visiting and showing hospitality, become central to tourist travel *and* indeed social life at-a-distance, as cheaper and faster tourist travel compresses 'stretched out' networks. Given that mobility is integral to social life, we can no longer equate closeness, ties and intensity of communion with geographical nearness and daily or weekly interactions. One respondent in research in 2005 described these obligations:

> [Travel] is essential. I don't think we could go on just by making emails and phone calls. It is very necessary for us to go and see friends and family . . . I think it would be emotionally bad for us if we didn't. We need to travel.
> (Male sales advisor in fitness and health club, late-twenties)[36]

Figure 3.2 Connect Zone, Seoul Incheon International Airport, 2007

Moreover, this research also showed how people are enmeshed in social dramas where travel depends upon negotiation, approval and guilt, and has social and emotional consequences. In many instances, 'guilt trips' set in motion physical trips. As another respondent noted:

> I don't like going [to the family in Italy] I must admit. I'm not a massive fan of going. But I did . . . my mum wanted me to go . . . Yeah, because I get the old guilt trip and then I feel like I have to go.
>
> (Male doorman, early twenties)

Indeed, if people are absent from a compulsory family get-together, it will be noted, and their social face is likely to be damaged:

> [My partner's] family are very rigid in the fact that there are certain days of the year like Easter, Boxing Day where it's a kind of compulsory family get together, so you have to make that effort to go down there. Your absence would be noted if you weren't there.
>
> (Male architect, early thirties)[37]

Tourist-type travel thus enters the lives of many, including otherwise 'immobile' people with friends and families living in distant places. Tourism becomes not the privilege of the rich few, but something involving and affecting many, as otherwise 'immobile' people might occasionally visit or host distant kin or be heartbroken when they remain at-a-distance. Tourists, we might say, are no longer only found in hotels, sightseeing coaches, museums and on beaches, but also in inner city flats, suburban homes, supermarkets and local bars.

We have so far been mainly examining meetings with specific others within a business, family or friendship network. But networks of weak ties often also depend upon there being meetings within particular places where people of a certain social category will be encountered. Certain places are known to be good for networking, although it may not be known precisely who will be there on specific occasions. This 'generalized co-presence' often involves 'showing one's face', and that face then gets reported to others. Travel and the weak ties within far-flung networks generate a kind of 'presentism' that, in turn, further extends weak ties. Certain parts of cities, campuses, cafés, bars, pubs, conferences, clubs, street corners and so on are highly appropriate for such generalized co-presence and presenting one's face.[38]

This networking pattern is to be found among relatively prosperous young professional people in city centres, such as new media workers in central London.[39] Research shows that 'network sociality' comes to be organized around ephemeral but intense, focused, fast and overloaded social ties. Clumps of persistent ties almost disappear, and most connections are long range, but with a strong importance of intermittent 'meetingness'. As these connections spread, so the networks of dominant weak ties get further extended. As one young media worker noted: 'so these meetings and these conferences for me are about being seen and seeing other people again, saying hello being sort of in the back of their mind and it's usually like a two-minute conversation.'[40] Sociality is less based upon a shared common history and narrative. Rather, information is key: the immediacy of the particular, what people can offer in the quick exchange. Moreover, work and play are increasingly assimilated, with workplaces designed to look like play places, and leisure places being places for work. Times of play and times of work are less tightly drawn as especially the 'party' and other 'networking events' are transformed into work. The categories of friend and workmate cross from one to the other. Networking practices for these media workers in the late 1990s involved: 'cars, trains, buses and the underground, of airplanes, taxis and hotels, and it is based on phones, faxes, answering machines, voicemail, videoconferencing, mobiles, email, chat rooms, discussion forums, mailing lists and web sites'.[41]

The field of network capital

Practices of networking can be re-posed in terms of twenty-first century mobile lives. Kay Axhausen notes the array of tools that are now necessary for successful 'networking' in the contemporary world of the rich north.[42] These include a car or the budget for taxis; budget and access for long-distance travel; location-free contact points (answering service, email, website); and sufficient time or assistance to manage these components, especially when one or another 'fails'. What we emphasize here is that mobilities themselves are not as important as are the social relations of networking. These are the 'real relations' that multiple mobilities contingently make possible.

As noted in Chapter 1, we treat network capital as a form of capital that is analogous to the other forms of capital famously analysed by Pierre Bourdieu.[43] There are various key features of his approach. First, the 'spaces of positions' in class structures are conceived of not as structures that produce unambiguous interests and outcomes but as 'fields'. Classes and other social forces are thus not to be understood as simply realizing pregiven 'interests', but rather as stemming from a field of struggles. Second, these struggles involve many different sites and terrains, including especially those around aspects of 'culture'. Tastes are never 'pure'; people struggle symbolically to distinguish themselves from others through distinctions of taste. Moreover, there are multiple forms of capital, with no necessary homology between them and especially not between economic and cultural capital. Finally, central to such struggles is the habitus of each social force. Habitus is: 'the capacity to produce classifiable practices and works, and the capacity to differentiate and appreciate these practices and products (taste), that the represented social world, i.e. the space of life styles, is constituted'.[44] Such habituses stem from, and generate, bodily expressions of taste. Class and other struggles are embodied, a point we have been making throughout this book (especially in Chapter 2).

In seeking to demonstrate that there is network capital, we have to characterize the 'field' of mobilities. And, of course, we are not suggesting that there were no travel and communications until, say, the second half of the twentieth century. However, over the course of that century, a number of transformations served to create a major field of mobilities, spun off from, and serving to generate, a major resource in the contemporary world, namely that of network capital.[45] These transformations include:

1   the sheer scale of domestic and international movement around the world;
2   the array of different mobility systems, feet, bike, car, lorry, canal, train, tram, shipping, helicopter, aircraft and so on;
3   the developing scale and impact of modes of international movement: asylum and refugee travel; business and professional travel; discovery travel; medical travel; military mobility; post-employment travel; 'trailing travel'; travel across diasporas; travel of service workers; tourist travel; the visiting of friends and relatives; work-related travel (see Chapter 1);
4   the significance of the automobility system, which is central to contemporary economy and culture and, through the search for cheap, plentiful oil, to international politics;
5   the entanglements of physical movement and communications, so that these have become highly bound up with each other, as contemporary twins;
6   the development of mobility domains that bypass national societies, such as shipping, air travel, high-speed train travel, the internet and mobile telephony;
7   the significance of various kinds of movement to the governance of contemporary societies, especially following September 11 and the heightened 'security-ization' of mobile populations;

8 the centrality of mobilities for people's social and emotional lives (as detailed in this book).

Thus mobilities develop into a distinct field with characteristic struggles, tastes and habituses. It is a site of multiple intersecting contestations. This field has spun off from economic, political and cultural processes and is self-expanding, giving rise to an emergent form of capital, network capital, that is a prerequisite to much life in the rich north of contemporary capitalism. And as people move around and have to develop these personalized life projects through setting the individual free from *these* structures, so they extend and elaborate their social networks, which are more personalized, more specific to them and less shared. As a consequence of networked individualism, so various distinctions of taste develop, between the modes of movement, the classes of traveller, the places that are moved to, the embodied experiences of movement, the character of those who are also moving along with one and so on.

We use the concept of 'network capital' to bring out that the underlying mobilities in themselves do nothing. What are key are the social consequences of such mobilities, namely, to be able to engender and sustain social relations with those people (and to visit specific places) who are mostly not physically proximate, that is, to form and sustain networks. So network capital points to the real and potential social relations that mobilities afford. This formulation is somewhat akin to that of Marx in *Capital,* where he focuses upon the *social* relations of capitalist production and not only upon the *forces* of production per se.[46] Our argument is that it is necessary to examine the social relations that the means of mobility afford and not only the changing form taken by the forces of mobility. Network capital is the capacity to engender and sustain social relations with those people who are not necessarily proximate, which generates emotional, financial and practical benefit (although this often entails various objects and technologies or the means of networking). As we saw in Chapter 1, it consists of the following eight elements: an array of appropriate documents, visas, money, qualifications that enable safe movement; others at-a-distance who offer hospitality; movement capacities; location-free information and contact points; communication devices; appropriate, safe and secure meeting places; access to multiple systems; and time and resources to manage when there is a system failure. Those social groups high in network capital enjoy significant advantages in making and remaking their social connections, the emotional, financial and practical benefits being over and above, and non-reducible to, the benefits people derived from economic and cultural capital.

We saw above how Wellman argues that there is a shift taking place towards person-to-person connectivity. Each individual, with their specific network, is key, while place, home and context are less significant in structuring networks. This shift to personalized networks is associated with leisure time being increasingly 'harried', and therefore 'meetingness' may be hard to bring about, except for those with high levels of network capital.[47] This is because of: increases in hours worked; the fragmentation of working hours, so that people's leisure times coincide less; increases in the variety and complexity of leisure activities; and the greater need for multitasking of leisure time to maintain friendships across distance. These processes result in an increasing 'society of the schedule', as people's daily time–space patterns are somewhat desynchronized from work, community and place and, hence, from each other.[48] Organizing meetings can become especially demanding with a decline in collective coordination. Those low in network capital often struggle to sustain a sufficient degree of 'meetingness' and, hence, can be powerfully 'socially excluded'.[49]

This is also because of the shift from 'clock time punctuality' (as described by Simmel) to 'flexible punctuality' effected through mobile communications.[50] As described in Chapter 2, mobile phones today are as ubiquitous as watches were a century ago. Ownership is not related to income or class. Ling describes how the mobile:

> challenges mechanical timekeeping as a way of coordinating everyday activities . . . Where the automobile allows flexible transportation, up until the rise of mobile telephony there has been no similar improvement in the real-time ability to coordinate movements. When you were en route, you were incommunicado. The mobile phone completes the circle.[51]

So, although meetings are crucial, their timing and spacing can be negotiable on the move. Mobiles free people from spatial fixity and are one of the most common items used on a journey. Trains, buses and cars are no longer characterized by 'isolation', as when Simmel wrote, but by connectivity and 'communicative travel'.[52] Calls and messages on the move are crucial practices for making, extending and reaffirming networks. Ling argues that:

> Micro coordination is the nuanced management of social interaction. Micro coordination can be seen in the redirection of trips that have already started, it can be seen in the iterative agreement as to when and where we can meet friends, and it can be seen . . . in the ability to call ahead when we are late to an appointment.[53]

The link between mobility and ongoing, flexible coordination is well captured in the concept of 'rendezvous'. According to Castells *et al.*: 'In the practice of rendezvous-ing, people walk or travel toward their destination, while deciding which destination is it is going to be on the basis of that instant communication in which they are engaged.'[54] There is a shift from the punctual mode to a more fluid and pervasive mode of coordination and 'rendezvous-ing' as times, spaces and participants are (re)negotiated on the move.

It stresses the need for such network capital: 'To not have a *keitai* [mobile phone] is to be walking blind, disconnected from just-in-time information on where and when you are in the social networks of time and space.'[55] Rettie summarizes the network capital aspects of mobile telephony: it enables the increasing and sustaining of social support; it extends communication time between people; it instigates face-to-face meetings and, hence, their anticipatory pleasures; it develops knowledge of the schedules of others, which is itself a form of intimacy; it enables phatic or social communication with no informational content; and it nurtures relationships more generally.[56]

Even so, in any network, the 'nodes' with the largest number of weak ties will be advantaged. Meetings for them will engender more weak ties and, hence, extend their future networking capabilities. This virtuous circle, dependent upon network capital, is sometimes known as the 'Matthew effect'.[57] There are positive feedback mechanisms whereby the network rich get richer and the network poor poorer, so producing further social inequalities.

Nothing could be more understandable. High network capital allows significant participation within meetings. Studies of 'global virtual teams' show the importance both of occasional meetings and of effective and reliable communications in-between such meetings. Maznevski and Chudoba's meta-analysis and their own longitudinal research bring out the necessity for network capital to ensure an appropriate temporal rhythm of both physical meetings *and* communications. This rhythm 'is structured by a defining beat of regular, intense face-to-face meetings, followed by less intensive, shorter interaction incidents using various media'.[58] They show that organizations unable to ensure such a pattern will be less effective, partly because of the failure to generate and mobilize tacit knowledge.

This networked dimension of social ties is especially ironic. The greater the scale of network capital, and, hence, the greater the networking that is made possible, the more that access to such capital is necessary in order to participate within such a 'networked society'. Feedback mechanisms extend the need for travel and communications as the scale of network capital expands and heightens the range, extent and heterogeneity of people's networks, even though trust and tacitness seem to remain so significant.

We now briefly consider some cases where significant inequalities in network capital have been of broad sociological significance. The importance of network capital and its unequal distribution was graphically revealed by Hurricane Katrina, which impacted so dramatically upon New Orleans, in the US, in August–September 2005.[59] This hurricane showed the extraordinary distributional consequences of uneven levels of network capital within disasters. Predominantly affluent whites were able to flee in advance because of their ownership of cars, contacts and communications. The network capital poor – blacks, women, children, the elderly – were left both to the impact of the hurricane and its enormous scale of flooding, and to the network capital-weak resources of the federal, state and city authorities. Only the TV pictures taken from low-flying helicopters demonstrated to the world that was watching just what happens to those living in large areas of a major city when network capital has more or less 'sunk' to zero.

Similar inequalities were starkly visible in the 1995 Chicago heatwave, a topic very relevant to future climate change issues, which we deal with in Chapter 7. In areas of Chicago that afforded opportunities for people to get out and about, to visit shops and local services, Eric Klinenberg showed that deaths from the heatwave were fewer.[60] The connectedness of houses with habitable streets, accessible parks, shops, cafés, neighbours and so on provided affordances for everyday walking, meeting and especially for *talking* with others. Where affordances were rich and diverse, then people would go out and about even in very high temperatures *and* they were more likely to survive. In areas where people were walking and talking, where, in other words, they had good network capital, they were less likely to die from heat, even though their standard of living was approximately the same as in areas where death rates were much higher.

Robert Putnam more generally deals with the social causes and consequences of co-present 'conversations' in everyday life.[61] He laments how there is a declining rate of face-to-face conversations within the US. For Putnam, the quantity of co-presence is not a given amount but has seemingly declined since the 1960s. Americans talk less frequently face-to-face. This is also borne out by similar research reported by Richard Layard into the causes of happiness and how the growth of TV seems to reduce overall happiness levels through the ways in which it reduces 'meetingness'.[62] According to Putnam, it is 'good to talk' face-to-face, as this minimizes privatization, expands social capital, makes people live longer and promotes economic activity, in mutually sustaining ways. Living a life 'on a screen' is not a satisfactory substitute for good conversation. If more relationships are conducted on-screen, then Putnam says this produces less conversation, poorer social interaction and a weakening of social capital. Miller describes, in *Conversation: a history of a declining art,* various 'conversation avoidance devices', which have a negative effect upon people's conversational skills.[63] He provides much supporting documentation of the negative effects of this long-term decline in face-to-face meetings and talk, as also noted in Chapter 2.

Another manifestation of network capital inequalities can be seen in how, around the world, 3000 people die *each day* from car crashes, and 30,000 are injured.[64] By 2020, car crashes will be third in the world ranking of disease and injury. However, most of the victims of car crashes do not own a car. There is, thus, weak network capital for those without access to a car. There are huge inequalities between car owners/users (normally men high in network capital) and cyclists, pedestrians and especially children (who are vastly lower in network capital). A car-based mobility system results in a massive scale of death and injury, largely effected upon the vulnerable bodies of pedestrians and cyclists. This slaughter results in annual deaths greater in number than those slain in warfare since the end of the Second World War.

Conclusion

This chapter has revealed the need for people to experience sufficient physical travel for the pleasures and productivity of meeting and talking to people to be sustained and developed. In a global world, trust and tacit knowledge both still seem to presuppose intermittent co-presence from those often highly distant.

This co-presence generates other effects that Sheller characterizes as 'civic freedom and mobility'.[65] Thus, if all else were equal, a 'good society' would not limit travel, good meetings and great conversations. Such a society would extend such co-presence to every social group and regard most infringements of this as undesirable. As the airline BA puts it: 'there's no substitute for face-to-face contact'. Network capital should be enlarged, and social exclusion would be lessened through spreading such capital as equally as possible. A socially inclusive society would elaborate and extend the capabilities of co-presence to all its members. It would minimize 'coerced immobility', both to improve psychic health and to heighten equality. Initiatives in transport, planning and communications should promote networking and 'meetingness' (and limit the degree of 'missingness') for all social groups. This dynamic notion of citizenship values the 'freedom to' meet, talk, interact, communicate, network and conduct relationships at-a-distance. This would entail a really radical transformation of network capital. For example, the many gender inequalities with regard to network capital revealed in *Gendered mobilities* would need to be rethought and reorganized on a massive scale.[66]

But there are three problems with this argument, which subsequent chapters explore. First, network capital is heavily skewed and typically induces resentment, as we examine in Chapters 4 and 6 when considering research on the life-chances and lifestyles of the 'globals' and the places of excessive consumption that they have come to generate and occupy. Second, work and personal relationships at-a-distance can be realized, but there are substantial personal and relationship costs, as we examine in Chapters 4 and 5. Third, such forms of mobile living presuppose huge and growing supplies of many resources, especially oil, and that their consumption does not turn out to have major external diseconomies, such as worldwide temperature increases. This in turn raises the question of whether various forms of mobile life today involve a megalomaniac overvaluation of extensive and intensive mobilities as such. The possibility that mobile living might significantly reduce in the possible near future is examined in Chapter 7, which examines what will happen as oil begins to run down and the effects of climate change begin to kick in. Will a psychically poorer life on the screen be forced upon us anyway by 2050?

4 The globals and their mobilities

The globals can afford the safety industry equivalents of haute couture. The rest, no less tormented by the gnawing sense of the world's unbearable volatility yet themselves not volatile enough to surf the waves, have as a rule fewer resources and must settle for inferior mass-production replicas of the high fashion art. The rest can do even less, in fact next to nothing, to mitigate the uncertainty and insecurity endemic in the world they inhabit.

Zygmunt Bauman[1]

Moving beyond: the globals

Is the mobile economy breeding a new global elite? In the past, the price of admission to the world's richest elite was vast holdings of land, ownership of industrial plants, ownership of massive factories and control over large workforces. Today, and by contrast, membership of the global elite is reconfigured in terms of both the 'new flexibility' of the weightless, information economy and (perhaps above all) the speed of mobilities.

The generation of great wealth among the ranks of the ultra-rich or global elite, whom we call, following Bauman, 'the globals',[2] has occurred in an economic context of the widespread financial deregulation of markets and the comprehensive privatization of 'social things'.[3] Seeking to capture the socio-economic contours of the new economy, analysts have spoken of an age of 'turbo-capitalism', 'late capitalism', 'neo-liberalism', 'disorganized capitalism' and 'liquid modernity'[4] (neo-liberalism will be further explored in Chapters 6 and 7). There have been many economic and financial developments that have shaped the emergence of our new mobile age of disorganized capitalism. These developments are complex, and here we simplify them by noting some events that have most directly affected these economic transformations: the collapse of Bretton Woods; President

Figure 4.1 Global time display, Kuala Lumpur International Airport, 2007

Nixon's repudiation of gold in the 1970s; the oil shocks of 1973; the Wall Street crash of 1987; the dot-com bubble and subsequent wreckage; the September 11 terror attacks; and the global economic and financial meltdown of 2008.

Against this socio-economic backcloth, several factors are worth noting at the outset with regard to today's globals, particularly if we are to distinguish them from previous global elites. First, today's globals, operating in an institutional context of fast-paced networking and mobile life, are, for the most part, relatively unconstrained by nations, national societies or communities. We will return to this point later in the chapter, but for now we merely note that the international, mobile realm of the twenty-first century is the first to generate a socio-economic elite that is *global*.

Second, not only are the assets and financial holdings of globals truly staggering, but the speed and dynamism with which globals generate, increase and multiply their total annual incomes have intensified on a dramatic scale.[5] From foreign-exchange dealing on Wall Street to software innovation in Silicon Valley, globals command vast personal agglomerations of wealth, travelling in transatlantic private jets to designer mansions dotted around the world. And, crucially, the private jets are an indication, not only of super-wealth, but also of the highly mobile nature of globals themselves and of their money, shifting as they do between various countries and regions, tax regimes and legal systems, while living extraordinary, sumptuous lifestyles well above even the highest standards of 'locals' living in territorially fixed societies (see Chapter 6 for further discussion of taxation and tax regimes in relation to mobile lives).

How should today's global elite be studied in relation to the new mobility systems unleashed by the global economy? What are the consequences for social inequality of a new super-elite? This chapter examines in detail the mobile lives of globals, situated in the broader context of sweeping changes to national economies, identities and cultures. In the following section, we review different kinds of evidence that support the claim that the globals have recently emerged as a new social class. We argue that, although there is evidence that indicates the rise of a new global elite as a superclass, what is absent from recent discussions is any sustained consideration of the 'experiential texture' of the *lives of globals*, as well as the richly networked individualism that such lives entail. In an attempt to overcome this limitation of much sociological research, the following section of the chapter outlines a case-study of one such global high in network capital. In the third section of the chapter, we draw out some more general lines of analysis from the case study, highlighting the central social forms in and through which the identities of globals are constituted, reproduced and transformed.

The globals: emergence of a new super-elite

Mega wealth has become a master signifier of the new global economy, generating in the process many new kinds of mobility, place and identity. Today's cultural fascination with mega wealth is increasingly in various displays of conspicuous, lavish consumption, from SUVs and diamond-encrusted mobile phones to personal jets and 500-foot yachts. The global electronic economy generates not only great wealth, but also forms of power and privilege for a new elite that transforms previous kinds of class antagonism and social inequality.

Winner-takes-all global capitalism generates new and extreme types of inequality. Contemporary sociologies of wealth and financial power and studies of the super-rich suggest various indicators of widening social inequality, especially in neo-liberal economies.[6] These indicators include the following:

- the United Nations World to Work Report 2008, which underscores that the gap between high- and low-wage earners increased dramatically since the early 1990s, with inequalities across seventy countries projected to remain excessive even with the global economic crisis of 2008;[7]
- the United States Congressional Budget Office 2008 Review, which reports that income for the bottom half of American households rose 6 per cent since 1979, while the income of the top 1 per cent skyrocketed 228 per cent;[8]
- across North America and Europe, the pay of chief executive officers grew exponentially – in Europe from 40 to 300 times that of the average employee; in the US, CEOs of the fifteen largest companies earned 520 times more than the average worker in 2007, up from 360 times more in 2003;
- the wealthiest 1 per cent of US households had a net worth that exceeded that of bottom 95 per cent of households in total;
- the Forbes 2008 Rich List identified 1,125 global billionaires (the first time the list had crossed into four figures); the total net worth of these individuals was $4.4 trillion, up $900 billion from 2007.[9]

Throughout the 2000s, up to the global financial crisis of 2008, hedge funds, securitizing and other kinds of speculative financing were core ingredients in how globals made their wealth. And the growth in the numbers of wealthy, not only the rich but also the ultra-rich, has been staggering. Robert Frank estimates, for example, that since 1980, in the

United States alone, the number of millionaires rose from half a million to 10 million, while the number of billionaires spiked from thirteen to over five hundred.[10]Although there was a marginal growth in wealth of those at the bottom of the employment ladder (especially immigrants), the incomes of the middle three-fifths of the American workforce went into decline in real terms. In this connection, Corey Dolgon's eye-opening study of the lavish lifestyles of the Long Island super-wealthy captures well how the lifestyle of globals is intricately interwoven with a low-wage working class and stagnating lower middle class.[11]

Analysing these various indicators of growing social inequality has involved social researchers and journalists considering different aspects of peoples' lives and occupations, encompassing material differences but also symbolic and cultural differences. Karen Ho's ethnological research on Wall Street, for example, uncovers how high-flying financiers project from their own daily experience of trading things and cutting deals onto the wider economy by seeking to make everything 'liquid' or tradable – including the jobs of middle- and low-income earners.[12] Gillian Tett has traced rising inequalities of wealth to the intensive, short-term deal-making of investors and bankers, specifically the role of credit derivatives in the lead up to the global financial crisis of 2008.[13] But perhaps nowhere is the proliferation of inequalities more discernable today than as a result of multiple mobilities. In *The super-rich: the unjust new world of global capitalism*, Stephen Haseler underscores the importance of mobility thus:

> Super-rich multimillionaires are the world's true global citizens – owing loyalty to themselves, their families and their money, rather than to communities and territorial boundaries . . . Their money is highly mobile, and so are they themselves, moving between their various homes around the world – in London, Paris and New York; large houses in the Hamptons in the United States, in the English and French countryside, and in gated communities in sun-belt America, particularly Florida, southern California and Arizona, and for the global super-rich the literal mobility of yachts in tropical paradises not scarred by local poverty.[14]

Access to new, complex and digitized mobility systems – from mobile phones and computer databases to yachts and private jets – is thus central to contemporary global experiences of great wealth, power and prestige. Yet the rapid increase in the wealth of globals during recent years has occurred at the cost of unprecedented levels of poverty. As Edward Luttwak notes: 'all countries that have undergone turbo-capitalist change, from the

United Kingdom to Argentina, from Finland to New Zealand, now have their new billionaires or at least centi-millionaires, as they all have their new poor.'[15] To which we might add that one central, defining feature of the new poverty to which Luttwak draws attention concerns its embedding in complex systems of immobility, such as the contracted cleaning staff who service the business and first-class airport lounges that globals routinely pass through.

In sociological terms, the emergence of a new super-elite should be cast against the backdrop of the institutional shift from organized, solid modernity to disorganized, liquid modernity.[16] The idea here is that the 'shake out' of nationally organized economies and societies by the dislocating processes of globalization has penetrated all the way down to the restructuring of work, the professions, social divisions and status processes. John Scott expresses this as follows: 'national capitalist classes themselves are being increasingly fragmented along the lines of the globalized circuits of capital and investment that they are involved in.'[17] Scott's assessment of the logic of wealth transformation occurs from the standpoint of methodological nationalism, with the 'global' represented as an external force rewriting the 'local'. But if we switch optics and consider the question from a more global perspective, we begin to see that these changes are even more far-reaching. Specifically, global finance, new technologies and multinational firms are creating highly mobile, detached forms of professional and executive experience that are transformational of the new economy.

Multi-millions and mobile manoeuvrings

'Has my secretary offered you a cappuccino?' exclaims Wim Eisner, as he glances at his gleaming Vacheron Constantin wristwatch, while sitting in a plush London office monitoring the FTSE.[18] The bank of screens displaying movements across world markets, as they happen, remains a constant presence throughout our interview. Eisner answers all questions thoughtfully and carefully, while all the time keeping an eye on the various ratings of the large banks, investment houses and insurance companies.

The discussions with Eisner, one of Europe's leading investment bankers, had been scheduled for months in advance. As a result of the 2008 global economic meltdown, however, the first scheduled interview was cancelled at short notice, owing to his need to travel to the US. An impromptu interview was subsequently arranged (again, at very short notice), as the day following the interview Eisner was leaving the UK for ten days' further travel in Asia, the Middle East and Australia. Such scheduling and rescheduling, most often last-minute, are clearly integral aspects of Eisner's daily working life. Trying to wrest some sense of continuity out of the interviews with Eisner is also taxing, primarily owing to the many intervening telephone calls from clients and frequent interruptions from colleagues. Like many globals, Eisner thrives on chaos and complexity.

Eisner got rich investing other people's money in short-term money markets, futures and hedge funds. He then got even richer through investments made in the rapid industrialization of China and India, as well as the buying up of cheap stocks in the leading Asian economies. Armed with an economics degree from the University of Chicago, he was one of the few who smelt trouble with the American sub-prime housing crisis of late 2007 and made the calculated move to sell up his own investments across world stock markets. He subsequently began putting his money to work elsewhere and decided that the time was right for a change of job along the way. As a reward for timing the market to near perfection, he took three months off work. During that time, he and his wife – a successful businesswoman in her own right – holidayed at various exclusive resorts that have recently expanded (see Chapter 6). The remainder of the time, they bounced between their four homes; they also commenced renovating a mansion recently purchased in Brittany.

At the time of interview, Eisner had been heading up a private investment bank in London for three months. He explains that the global crisis of 2008 represents an enormous professional challenge, but notes that his working schedule hasn't really changed from what he was doing previously:

> Usually I am up at around five in the morning and at the office by six thirty. I meet with clients throughout the day, which more often than not involves email and phone calls – unless I am meeting with a client for lunch. I go home at about seven, have dinner, and try to find some time to talk on the phone with my teenage daughter – who is at a private boarding school. Then it's back to the paperwork and late-night conference calls.

The late-night calls, it transpires, are routine. Eisner is part of his bank's Global Leadership Program, which involves dealing with the New York office several times a week. All this is presented as 'routine', although, tellingly, Eisner casually mentions that he is often abroad for work.

As it happens, he was working away from home on a staggering 268 nights in 2007 – a figure calculated by his secretary at the conclusion of our first interview.

Life in the fast lane of investment banking has changed enormously in recent years, mostly as a result of communications and travel revolutions. Investment bankers cultivate less the look of the dashing businessman than that of the prosperous tourist: expensive suits, open-neck designer shirts and lots of business/first-class travel. Eisner is able to travel the globe so regularly, partly because the individuals and firms that employ him demand this bodily presence, and partly because new information technologies make it easy to track and trace the movements and activities of his staff back in London. The elite network of globals in which Eisner moves operates largely with reference to short-term projects, business on the move and continual mobility. What support the flowing work worlds of such globals, however, are the largely immobile staff based at head offices. Implicated in all mobile lives, as we noted in previous chapters, are various immobility regimes.

That mobility is always intricately intertwined with immobility is a point that clearly applies to Eisner's professional and personal situation. For example, he and his wife employ a live-in housekeeper as well as a personal assistant. The personal assistant is charged with 'organizing' the professional and social lives of the Eisners, right down to 'scheduling' weekend get-togethers with their daughter, often in far-away cities where one of the parents is located for work. Regarding work itself, Eisner's extensive mobilities depend primarily on the management strategies he deploys for running the office at a distance. 'One thing I've learned over time in the management of staff', he comments, 'is that you get the best out of people by leaving them to get on and produce, but also keeping tabs on their productivity and performance just so that people know that they must deliver.' From such a calculated and detached perspective, Eisner is able to retain management control without being overly burdened by the daily detail of the office. As a result, he estimates that only around 15 per cent of his time is ever spent on management or administrative duties.

Attachment is the prevailing vice of those who have not managed to adapt to the new ethos of 'flexibility' promoted by the global electronic economy. Without explicitly saying so, Eisner makes it evident that there is little room in his professional life for attachment to colleagues or places. The new regime of short-term projects, episodic contacts and fast-assembled/disassembled teams means that the course of Eisner's daily life has little sense of continuity or routine. Or, perhaps more accurately, what structure there is to Eisner's working life is constantly being redefined and restructured. Eisner captures this nicely in his self-description of professional roles and responsibilities: whether performing as an investment banker, or a manager, an expert on hedge funds, a networker or a real-estate guru, it is part of Eisner's talent to make any contradictions between these roles appear untroubling. Indeed, one of the most noticeable aspects of Eisner's working life, as he recounts it, is the requirement to shift continually between different sectors of the broader economy; almost all aspects of the global marketplace and its dazzling digital technologies are used by Eisner to fashion and restructure his working life, involving continual mobility, detached cooperativeness, short-term connections and networked associations.

Overall, there is much that is attractive, indeed seductive, about Eisner's professional life of intensive mobilities and fast happenings – a vast income, luxury residences, global travel, high social connections and a 'designer' lifestyle. Eisner confides that he and his wife are the envy of their friends and acquaintances. Intriguingly, the relentless demands for travel and networking arising from Eisner's job are not experienced as constraining. Far from the stereotypical 'time-poor' senior executive, Eisner describes how he finds himself 'plunging' into ever-new projects, work tasks or networked possibilities. In fact, the global lifestyle that allows Eisner to 'get away from it all' (the office, colleagues, family) recasts him as someone always *getting ahead of himself*. He is, by his own reckoning, always planning and replanning the future. His professional networks appear to feed ongoing financial and work possibilities, which drift in his self-imposed manoeuvrings and compulsive reinventions of self. If Eisner's world of corporate entries and exits engenders increased personal freedom, this is partly because he is a self-described 'global' and certainly hugely rich in network capital. As he navigates the complex systems of the global economy (electronic money flows, financial databases and the spreadsheet culture of investment banking) with ease, Eisner's language is resolutely that of the corporate 'insider'.

But there are significant limits here as well. First, there is a familiar conflict between the global and the local, which raises seemingly insurmountable dilemmas with regard to Eisner's experience of the world. Eisner describes his usual sense of feeling overwhelmed – 'sometimes I become quite flat' – upon his return home from corporate travel. He talks about his family's demands on his time: his daughter has suffered from various illnesses (including eating disorders) in recent years, and he finds himself carrying out 'make-up' or 'repair' time in their relationship when making time to see her after periods away. Then there is his marriage: 'it's odd going from weeks of phone calls and texting to sitting opposite each other in the kitchen'. And, finally, the demands of his staff. He finds it irritating that his staff so often present issues as urgent the moment he arrives home – just when he is trying to 'catch up' with domestic demands.

Second, switching between the time of work-related travel and the time of routine practices is unnerving to Eisner. There is undoubtedly a somewhat cold, detached pleasure that he derives from the 'empty time' of global roaming – airport check-ins, first-class lounges, limousine transfers, hotel business suites. These are sites where obligations to others are minimal, and Eisner can engage his passion for decontextualized living to the hilt. The more fixed social relations he experiences in London, by comparison, are drab.

Mobilities in the global fast lane: on the arts of elite escape

The new institutional mobile realm, with its ever-changing, frenetic networking, promotes a novel relationship to the self, to other people, as well as to shared cultural life among present and aspiring members of the global elite. As we can glean from Wim Eisner's experiences, the new institutional regime puts a special emphasis on swiftness, speed, weightlessness, dexterity and flexibility.[19] These are ideological values coveted by advanced capitalism, but the point to note is that they press in deeply upon the self. Subjected to these institutional changes, the globals have been the fastest to embrace this ideology. And there are, we argue, six important forms in and through which the making and remaking of the lifestyles and life-strategies of global elites now occur. These social forms comprise *detached engagement*; *floating*; *speed*; *networked possibilities*; *distance from locality*; and *mapping of escape routes*. We now briefly consider the impact of these social forms in shaping the identities of globals.

First, what Wim's revaluation of values indicates is that life in the fast lane with other globals requires a sense of *detached engagement*. Such engagement through disengagement ranges from 'dropping in' to organizational discussions through email while working abroad to the monitoring of professional contacts in thick networks. It is also evident that the prospects for the detached engagement of individualized actors increases the higher they are within an organization or firm. At the top, crisis is normalized, and change is ever present, and so shifting from one network to another network with speed and agility becomes central to professional and personal success. Knowing how to move in the networked world, perhaps even more than the acquisition of specific technical skills themselves, is fundamental to what Luc Boltanski and Eve Chiapello call

Figure 4.2 Departure hall, Seoul Incheon International Airport, 2007

'the new spirit of capitalism'. As Boltanski and Chiapello summarize this ethos, the global business elite are:

> putting an accent on polyvalence, on flexibility of employment, on the ability to learn and to adapt to new functions rather than on the possession of skills and acquired qualification, on the capacity to gain trust, to communicate, to 'relate'.[20]

We should perhaps note that the inverted commas around 'relate' do not, in our view, indicate a lack of expenditure of emotional energy invested in work and professional networking. On the contrary, and as Eisner's story suggests, many globals feel themselves to be taxed to their limit in terms of their daily communications and relationships with colleagues. But the point is that less and less often in today's fast-paced mobile world does the growing speed of networked communications lead many globals to 'open themselves up' to others. From one angle, this is hardly surprising. Living in networked time means being continually on the move, both physically and emotionally.

Second, abetted by various economic forces including financial deregulation, globals turn towards *floating* both their organizational responsibilities and their control over subordinates within firms. By floating, we stress the collapse of managerially structured executive routines, as well as of the mentality of long-term 'careers'.[21] To say that mobile-driven organizations promote this floating orientation is to say that, like all obsolescent paradigms, the 'scientific' approach to management that dominated advanced societies during the late twentieth century – involving the continuous presence of executives and ongoing surveillance of employees – has become a formidable barrier to progress in the early twenty-first century. By contrast, and strikingly, the new approach to management involves a kind of non-management. The French economist Daniel Cohen says of today's global business elite: 'there are no more white collars who give orders to blue collars – there are only collars of mixed colours who confront the task they have to resolve'.[22] And the task to be resolved, we might add, is more often than not an episodic project – each episode of which creates further opportunities for networking, as well as the likely improvement in opportunities for employment elsewhere or further promotion. This is why floating is both network-driven (see Chapter 3 above) and self-interested. Eisner could afford to start job discussions with other companies so soon after commencing his new executive position because much of his working time is spent on short-term, fast-changing projects. Not only is there the opportunity to engage in these networking discussions with other senior professionals, but the networked identities promoted by mobile organizations seem to demand this of such people.

Third, globals define their identities increasingly through the intensity and extensity of their networking mobilities, especially their *speed*. For example, Eisner is arguably a new kind of global to the extent that he is a technician of speed, always on the move, ready to travel at a moment's notice, adept at navigating the corporate sensation of speed and global shift of movement. Multitasking across space and time is part of this, but another part is thinking and acting in *instant-response mode* – as the next corporate directive arrives by email, text or fax. It is as if, shifting through the fast lanes of the global electronic economy, part of Eisner's talent is to 'swoop down' on particular corporate institutions, possible mergers or financial deals and show companies how they have become trapped in set ways of doing things. Note again, though, that it is the speed of Eisner's command over mobility-systems that makes a difference to the financial world in which he moves. He is at the centre of global finance working in London; he is ever ready for 'virtual consultation' via his mobile or video conferencing; he arrives to 'lock in' the deal (in Singapore, Hong Kong or Dubai) and then, just as swiftly, has exited. 'Speed of movement', writes Zygmunt Bauman, 'has become today a major, perhaps the paramount factor in social stratification and the hierarchy of domination'.[23] Eisner's speed of movement is necessary to 'keep up' with the networking, deal-making and swirl of contemporary market forces. As Bauman explains, this

> capital travels light with no more than cabin luggage – a briefcase, laptop computer and cellular telephone. That new quality of volatility has made the engagement redundant and unwise at the same time: if entered it would cramp movement and thus become a constraint on competitiveness and limit the chances of increased productivity . . . [B]eing free of awkward bonds, cumbersome commitments and dependencies holding back movement was always an effective and favourite weapon of domination; but the supplies of that weapon and the capacities to use them are nowadays doled out less evenly than ever before in modern history.[24]

Fourth, globals organize much of their professional and personal lives in and through *networked possibilities* – the basis upon which those high in network capital achieve ever higher forms of connectivity with other globals via networks, connectors and hubs. Here, the 'networked' dimensions of the self, in contrast to the self as a generic phenomenon, presume a reflexive architecture of informational connections. How far certain individuals are able to exploit networked possibilities depends to a large extent on how rich they are in terms of informational connectivity, as discussed previously in Chapter 3.

Fifth, if globals are intricately interwoven with the culture of global capitalism, this is partly because they have learnt the language of cosmo-politanism. As a political doctrine, cosmopolitanism is concerned with, among other things, what we owe each other as persons as the result of a shared humanity.[25] As an element of the lived experience of the elite we are considering here, however, the cosmopolitanism of globals retains the more attractive qualities of the high culture propagated by political theorists and philosophers, but combines this with an understanding of 'humanity' fashioned in the image of the consumerist space of designer brands and opulent living. That is to say, this is a version of cosmopolitanism that fits hand in glove with the values of transnational corporations, or, as some have dubbed it, a kind of depoliticized, post-modern culture.[26] Elsewhere, this has been termed 'banal globalization'.[27] This worldview is pitched towards the post-national or transnational, certainly as far as business, economics, media, information and technology are concerned. As such, *distance from locality* expressed as distaste for traditional identities and communities is a key social form influencing the making of identities of such globals under conditions of a mobile life.

Finally, the mobile life of globals is almost exclusively about *elsewhere*. Much of Eisner's professional and personal life, for example, can be seen as a detailed *mapping of possible escape routes*. We are, essentially, talking about life experienced as a series of exits. From this angle, each exit is, in turn, followed by new entrances. And these entrances then entail further exits. This notion of escapism raises, of course, the thorny question of what it is, exactly, that globals are escaping from. For those preoccupied with escapism, the lure of what one is escaping to is often imagined as altogether different from what one is escaping from. But this is rarely the case. Adam Phillips, in a recent study of escapism, writes:

> A person who is running away from something, the Hungarian psycho-analyst Michael Balint once remarked, is also running towards something else. If we privilege (as psychoanalysts and others do) what we are escaping from as more real – or in one way or another, more valuable – than what we are escaping to, we are preferring what we fear to what we seem to desire. Fear of something (or someone), and the wish to escape from it, confer a spectacular reality on it. (If you want

to escape from someone, they have become very important to you.) Things are not frightening because they are real, they are real because they are frightening. Fear always confers power on its object.[28]

Fear, in this context, is the prospect of being overwhelmed by anxieties that concern entrapment, fixity, enclosure. Dread of immobility penetrates to the very roots of the psyche, partly because to be immobile in a society of intensively mobile processes is a kind of symbolic death. By contrast, to be 'on the move' provides a mode of orientation that, on the level of daily life, provides for a sense of independence as well as feelings of emotional security. The ultra-mobilities of globals might thus be seen as an attempt to 'master' an otherwise unsettling and dangerous world. The capacity to always be elsewhere is the capacity to thwart whatever debilitating circumstances arise within local contexts.

The self-stylization of globals

The life of the global can be thought of as a kind of aesthetic performance. That is to say, the power and prestige of global elites are less pre-existing social or structural categories than they are a type of identity that has to be enacted, performed and represented to others.[29] This is another way of saying that the constitution of global elites does not just happen through objective, depersonalized processes; to convey elitism means finding pathways or links between personal subjectivity and feelings on the one hand and the symbolic power or social capital relayed through globalism on the other. Just as Wim Eisner performs a global elitism for others through his relentless business travel, incessant virtual communications and lavish lifestyle, so other globals around the world undertake the ongoing daily work of an unconscious enactment and subjective representation of this new elitism.

Throughout the last ten to fifteen years, sociologists have sought to understand better the social practices that affirm a sense of exclusivity, superiority, status and wealth. These social practices of 'distinction', to invoke Pierre Bourdieu's term, turn increasingly on the symbolism of luxury, exclusiveness and expense in legitimating the growing separation between global elites and other groups. Many sociologists have emphasized in this connection the key significance of society's shift from industrial to post-industrial economies, bound up as this has been with a thorough-going transformation away from manufacturing production towards many different kinds of service, including, of course, 'financial services'.

In looking for clues as to what such large-scale shifts in the economy entail for today's inequalities of wealth and status, social theorists have concentrated on the social value derived from consumerism and consumer capitalism (further exploration is in Chapter 6). In a previous work, one of us developed the argument that disorganized capitalism differs from organized capitalism through, among other things, its increasing semioticization of economic life.[30] A focus on the growing semiotic dimensions of the new economy – finance, tourism and travel, information technology and many other services – has also been pivotal to much recent social science research.[31]

Movement – relentless, tireless, burdensome – has become the degree zero of contemporary societies, at once an index of social status (ranging from enforced migration to luxuriant global tourism) and the medium through which social relations are organized. It is not only that many people are travelling faster and further than in any previous historical era, although that is surely the case. It is rather that more and more people voluntarily travel without end – without ever arriving at a final destination – and that such travel in itself confers prestige, power and symbolic status. The mobile world, for its part, opens up to a new reckoning of economy and the political, and in the process confers an endlessly expanding multitude of new possibilities, pleasures and perils. In the society of networked lives, the frenetic pace of personal communications and professional connections functions as both a kind of imaginary self-enclosure and glamorous object of desire. The desirable life is not only about money and possessions; it is about movement, the capacity to escape, to be elsewhere, especially in certain kinds of distinct, ambient place. Mobility status today stands for an addiction to power and pleasure.

Today, through styling and stylization, 'the global' has become an increasingly well-identified social figure. As the spending and investment strategies of the wealthy reach such unprecedented levels as to generate an increasingly separate economy of the super-elite, globals undertake a series of stylizations aimed at the pursuit of luxury, good taste, exclusivity, authenticity, glamour and knowledge. From Bulgari luxury fashion goods to Bentley convertibles, from Louis Vuitton luggage to Prada designer clothes, the gap between wealth and extreme wealth is more defined through the acquisition, consumption and display of expensive goods, products and services.

When one of us began interviewing global elites in the mid 2000s, most interviewees had one key lifestyle thread in common: relentless travel. Whether illustrious investment bankers, new economy entrepreneurs or globetrotting architects, their lifestyles were linked through chauffeured limousines, airport business-class lounges and five-star hotels. Life 'on the move' was at once personally exhilarating and professionally taxing, but all agreed that they felt at the edge of a massive cultural shift. Few of the old social coordinates (career, family, social routine) held much weight any longer; life at the top had moved on, at least for these interviewees, and this seemed to produce lifestyles that seemed at least mobile, weightless, plural and freeing. It was as if, for these globals, someone had said, 'you don't have to live the way your parents did'. Quite a number of these interviewees were people born into considerable wealth, and so their childhoods had been filled with travel, journeys and adventures. However, these were still mobilities with a fixed reference point of 'home' at the back of their minds. By contrast, the mobilities lived by globals today seem more rootless. With homes dotted throughout the world, endless business travel and family life restructured around episodic get-togethers, the old social coordinates divided firmly between work and home appear to have somewhat evaporated.

Communication analysts Adam Jaworski and Crispin Thurlow have sought to probe the semiotic conditions and consequences of what they call 'super-elitism', specifically with reference to the stylization of elites in frequent-flyer programmes. Frequent-flyer programmes, they argue, at once generate social anxieties about status and confer symbolic prestige and power upon their members. According to this view, the normative production of luxury is intricately interwoven with a personalized framework by which 'rewards', 'awards', 'privileges' and 'entitlements' accrue to identities marked as 'elite'. This framework extends from material benefits such as wider cabin legroom or priority airport check-in to more semiotic indulgences such as luxury-brand champagne or the refined elegance of business and first-class lounges. As Thurlow and Jaworski note:

> frequent flyer programmes go to great lengths to promote design over substance, seducing passengers with the expressive utility of things and appealing to the indefinable nature of 'good taste'. Given the relative immateriality but semiotic potency of all these resources, frequent-flyer programmes are thereby able to fabricate an aspirational lifestyle by which to stylize their passengers as distinctive and superior.[32]

Adequately to generate all these new desires, affects, aspirations and addictions, as well as to inscribe them with broader symbolic markers of distinction, the intensive mobile fields of globalization must do more than rely on attitudes of distinctiveness and superiority. In the society of multiple and intensive mobilities, the gap between those keeping on the move and those less on the move – to say nothing of those not moving at all – is of fundamental significance to contemporary boundaries between self and others. 'To travel', as Robert Louis Stevenson famously put it, 'is a better thing than to arrive', which, in our own time of interdependent digitized systems of mobility, has been raised exponentially. We are dealing, then, with a symbolic register in which anxiety becomes expressed in and around the differentiated field of mobilities. 'Keeping on the move' appeals increasingly as a glamorously stylish life-strategy, linking as mobility does with new possibilities of desire, difference, otherness, exotica and plenitude. Concomitantly, and from the other angle, fears of 'getting stuck' become debilitating.

Globals, mobilities, space

What we have sought to explore in this chapter is the 'thick texture' of the lives, lifestyles and stylization of global elites. We have sought, in effect, to trace the lives of globals, particularly their enmeshment in complex networks as well as the lifestyles of networked individualism. As globals are largely de-anchored from traditional social coordinates of routine work, family commitments and community responsibilities, the experimental nature of their lives – the thrills and spills of globality, as it were – is particularly pronounced. To navigate these professional and personal complexities, globals employ a number of *mobile life-strategies* to create novel connections with their own identities, the lives of others and the wider network society. We have identified throughout this chapter various identity forms used by globals, consisting of detached engagement, speed, networked possibilities, distance from locality and the mapping of escape routes.

The social practices of globals suggest the new formulation of mobilities and mobile lifestyles. It must be acknowledged, of course, that the ultra-mobile way of living charted by globals remains a form of life conducted by only a miniscule elite (by percentage of the global population). Nevertheless, it is the mobile lifestyles of globals that are held up as a normative ideal in popular culture and the media, and in turn mimicked by many other people.

One remaining issue concerns the fascination of globals with space – with private, exclusive, luxurious space. From five-star hotel suites to private jets, from the playgrounds of private islands to the pampered amenities of penthouses or townhouses: globals consume an obscene excess of space.[33] Trying to make sense of this is an urgent issue for the analysis of mobile lives. One possibility might be that, in a world in which many spatial and temporal barriers have been eliminated, globals are seeking to reassert a sense of belonging in the act of consuming space. On this view, the production of luxurious and exclusive spaces occupied by globals appears as the other face of the dissolution of traditional social coordinates, secure places and established identities. It might be possible to see this 'globalization of privatized belonging' as a mobile life-strategy through which globals seek to feel 'at home' wherever they find themselves, as we discuss in more detail in Chapter 6.

Figure 5.1 Travelator, Dubai International Airport, 2007

5   Mobile relationships
Intimacy at-a-distance

Do we need distance to get close?

Sarah Jessica Parker

Negotiating mobile intimacies

Across rich societies, over the past few decades, there has been an explosion of interest in emerging intimate relationships dependent upon multiple mobilities. From 'commuter marriages' to 'distance relationships' to 'weekend couples', the shift to a personalized, detraditional world in which intimacy, sexuality and eroticism are negotiated and renegotiated across distance has emerged as a kind of normative model for intimate relationships in the twenty-first century.[1] Given the availability of mobile telephony, the internet, the car and cheap air travel, it is hardly surprising that more people have become fascinated with new ways of exploring their private lives and intimate relationships at-a-distance. At least one strand of contemporary social theory (reviewed later in this chapter) identifies cultural emphases on individualization, pure pleasure, desire and difference as core features of mobile intimacies. At the same time, however, the contemporary cult of 'intimacy at-a-distance' has a darker emotional undertone. How people experience intimacy at-a-distance is the theme of this chapter, a chapter that explores what we call 'mobile intimacy'.[2]

Consider the relationship of Robert and Gemma, a UK couple who married some 15 years ago and are now raising four children.[3] They are in various respects an exemplary instance of the contemporary 'distance relationship', negotiating as they do the rewards and perils of living life quite a long way apart from each other. An academic with a promising international career, Robert landed a 'plum research post' near Brighton a couple of years ago. Applying for the position, as he recounts it, was a kind of accident (as he wasn't really thinking of moving to another university), but when offered the job Robert realized it was too good to turn down. Yet the central difficulty for him was that Gemma did not want to move their family from south-west England, where they lived (and continue to live) in Exeter. Not only was Gemma professionally established as a doctor working at a practice in nearby Bristol three days a week, but she felt their children – the eldest two attending school – had all established solid friendships where they lived. There was also the matter of coping with the couple's eighteen-month-old baby, all of which led to the couple's decision that Robert would commute to Brighton and live away from the family home four nights a week. This was how, in Gemma's words, they came to 'do family life differently'.

The to-ing and fro-ing that comprise the weekly schedule of Robert and Gemma's relationship across distance is noteworthy. As a rule, Robert departs the Exeter family home on Sunday evenings, as it takes some four hours to travel to Brighton by train. From Monday through Thursday, Robert and Gemma negotiate the 'non-residential' aspect of their relationship. He concentrates on his university and research work, and she undertakes primary responsibility for looking after their children. Thursday morning sees Robert on a train back to Exeter, where he takes over parenting responsibilities from Gemma, so that she can undertake her professional commitments through to and including Saturday. This consequently leaves Sunday as the only full day for 'quality family time' – and even that is somewhat curtailed in the light of Robert's evening train departure, following the family meal, to the other side of England.

The personal and relational challenges that arise from maintaining this dual-career, dual-household (even if only for a portion of the week) are significant. Robert and Gemma are disarmingly frank in their assessment of the benefits and costs of juggling their relationship and family life across two careers and across distance. Both repeatedly stress the high degree of satisfaction they derive from their careers. Yet there are also very significant tensions and difficulties that their working lives carry for their intimate relations. Gemma acknowledges that the time spent away from each other involves all sorts of 'extra communicational crossed-wires', and that consequently much of the weekend quality time is spent attempting to recapture a sense of intimacy or 'romance', sometimes in other places. Gemma feels in particular that she works hardest at this emotional labour, seeking to excavate the couple's buried emotions from all their broader, rational planning and scheduling, which consume the bulk of their time. Robert, by contrast, is more upbeat, saying that the current work situation is not permanent, and that family life will one day return to 'normal'.

Such a narrative does not sit well in the context of other career possibilities that have arisen for Robert in recent months, including a job offer in Berlin. Certainly, for Gemma, the family home remains in Exeter, and any work Robert accepts on the continent will require an extension – and radicalization? – of their recently established distance relationship.

The centrality of communicating 'on the move' is especially important to the ways in which Robert and Gemma manage these relationship complexities. Robert spends many hours of his working week on public transport, but the time spent travelling is not one of emotional disconnection. Thanks to his iPhone, Robert is in regular email contact with both Gemma and his two older sons. Through email, he keeps abreast of his oldest son's schoolwork and sometimes 'helps out with homework whilst on the train'. Robert also uses the phone's iTunes when travelling to listen to music and, tellingly, finds himself listening over and again to songs that were favourites when he and Gemma first met. Through these music-induced reveries, Robert seeks to find a form of emotional contact with his partner while physically absent. Multiple technologies – from the internet to videoconferencing – provide ways for Robert to keep some daily, virtual contact with Gemma and the children, to do 'love online' with both his children and partner.[4]

Intimate relationships: from territorially fixed to individualized mobility

What distinguishes Robert and Gemma's contemporary 'distance relationship' from more traditional intimacies in the past? What, exactly, has changed to facilitate intimacy at-a-distance as a growing pattern? There have been three broad areas of rapid change, we suggest, which have transformed traditional relationship structures and forms of intimacy away from territorially fixed designations to more individualized and mobile patterns of relating. These areas concern globalization, transformations of intimacy and the reinvention of personal life. In what follows, we sketch some key features of this social change.

The first broad area involving massive changes to the very fabric of routine personal, social and economic life concerns globalization. Globalization, at least at the level of changes to human relationships, refers to a transformation in the dimensions of time and space between people and places, and among organizations, institutions, nations and cultures. This transformation has been interrogated with reference to the expanding scale, escalating speed, growing magnitude and deepening impact of transnational flows of people, objects, information, messages and images upon patterns of social interaction.[5] One significant consequence of these global transformations is the 'death of distance'.[6] While consisting of multiple processes, globalization generates increasing interconnectedness between peoples in different cultures, countries and regions and, importantly, 'unhooks' and 'dis-embeds' people from the constraints, but also the supports, of traditional structures of social interaction. In the fields of sexuality, gender and intimacy, this reorganization, reconstruction and compression of the distances between peoples and places has had dramatic implications – one result being the surge of distance relationships and commuting lifestyles, which in turn has served to intensify the dissolution of traditional structures of intimacy and family life.

The many controversies that surround globalization partly concern the extent to which an increasingly 'interconnected world' generates common global patterns. Some see the relationship between globalization and social order in terms of growing uniformity, or homogeneity. Others caution against such a view of social integration and argue that globalism does not generate a common set of experiences, values or worldviews. Yet there are emerging lines of consensus in the globalization debate, especially regarding the institutional processes facilitating compressions of time and space that underpin contemporary patterns of travel and communication across large distances.[7] As we have seen, these institutional processes include:

- the digital infrastructure of global communications linked to new information technologies;
- communications 'on the move', with mobile telephony now more common throughout the world than conventional landlines;
- the emergence of new global business models for the provision of discount travel and cheap airfares, which has led to an explosion in international journeys, now nearing one billion arrivals annually;
- the movement of peoples throughout the global economy for work and employment, family and friendship, linked to the growth of populations and major shifts in demography;
- the emergence of global networks, comprising broad cross-border interconnections and transnational processes relating to the multiple forms of mobile social practice we outlined in Chapter 1;
- the unfolding of a new type and form of 'life politics', involving personal autonomy and self-actualization.

There are clearly many ways of conceiving and categorizing these institutional processes in terms of the global age. There are even more ways in which people seek to adapt, adjust, cope with or react against such global transformations.

The second major contemporary social development is the *transformation of intimacy*. This has been traced to many roots and identified with various events – especially the sexual revolution of the late 1960s and early 1970s, as well as feminism and the women's movements – but its central focus has been the supposed 'crisis' of the nuclear family and of marriage. Among changes, sociologists argue that few are more profound than those transforming the texture of family life. Throughout contemporary, network-driven societies in the rich north, we are moving to a situation in which nearly half of first marriages end in divorce, and divorce and separation rates are higher for second and subsequent marriages.

Among conservatives, this decline is often cast as a sign of society's moral decay. The lament attributes it to several sources, from sexual permissiveness to feminism, from new parenting arrangements to the spread of gay rights. This new era, many conservatives argue, is one that spells the end of family ties that bind. Conservative critics have consequently sought to defend traditional familial values, from speaking up 'in defence of the bourgeois family' to sounding alarms about 'generations at risk'.[8]

The 'war over the family' that has broken out in recent decades is important for assessing changes to intimacy, relationships and sexualities. Certainly, a dramatic rise in both stepfamilies and one-parent families, as well as the sharp rise in births outside marriage, indicates that key changes are underway to the staging of everyday life in the contemporary era. And yet, although profound changes are undeniably occurring inside and outside the traditional family network, proclamations about the 'end of the family' are plainly out of step. Conservative critics do not readily acknowledge the fact that people very often remarry. The implications of this are far-reaching, and some sociologists are now suggesting that, rather than family breakdown, family life is undergoing a constructive renewal. The emergence of what has been called a 'post-familial family' is said to be taking shape, comprising a diversity of social forms and cutting across the apparent solid structures of the traditional family.[9] From non-marital cohabitation to gay and lesbian couples, from multi-adult households to open marriages, family life is becoming increasingly diversified, reconstituted and pluralized. Jeffrey Weeks captures this point:

> Within the broad limits of the term 'family' itself there are many internal differences arising from different class, religious, racial, ethnic and political beliefs and practices . . . It is wise today to refer not to the family, as if it were a fixed form, but to families, signifying diversity.[10]

Such transformations of family life are helping to create patterns of living best captured by the term mobile intimacy. Intimacy in conditions of intensive mobilities becomes flexible, transformable and negotiable. Mobile intimacy is fluid in both emotional and interpersonal terms. In *Liquid love*, Bauman underscores the 'looseness' and 'episodicity' of intimate relations in contemporary societies. He speaks, for example, of the rise of 'top-pocket relationships', those you can use when you need to and dispose of just as easily, as well as of the highly compartmentalized worlds of semi-detached couples (SDCs), those romantics who maintain separate pads and separate lives (a high-carbon liquid love, we might note!). Mobile intimacy involves relationships across distance and through space and is spreading to many social relations. These range from couples 'living apart together' (LATs) to 'business deals in brothels', from 'commuter marriages' to 'distance relationships', from 'love online' to 'weekend couples' and so on.

The third area in which the decline of tradition impacts upon the mobile complexity of intimate relationships is *reinventing personal life*. In contrast to industrial, solid or disciplinary forms of modernity, in which tradition or established habit inscribed self-identity within neighbourhoods based upon relatively slow forms of movement, the networked, liquid and mobile terrain of some lives today confronts people with a complex array of choices that are less clear-cut. On all standard measures, many people in parts of the world are more mobile *and* more changeable in their vocabularies of self and world. 'The great ideological certainties are giving way', writes Gilles Lipovetsky, 'before subjective singularities that may not be very original, creative, or reflective but that are more numerous and more flexible than before.'[11] This reinvention of personal life concerns various transformations of values, lifestyles and practices. The life of choice, the do-it-yourself life, involves a radical break with neighbourhood cultures, as well as ways of doing things, and is today reflected in a growing, widespread acceptance of 'relationship experimentation' in birth control, abortion, divorce, pre-marital sex, non-married partners and open marriages (not of course that all these are remotely available in all societies!).

These changes have significantly increased the possibilities for some experimentation in some societies in terms of personal life, sexuality and intimacy. Giddens has argued that such post-traditional lifestyle concerns open out 'the mobile nature of self-identity'.[12] By this, Giddens means to underscore the dramatic rise of choice within a plurality of possible options at the level of lifestyles and life plans. The explosion of discourses around choice is part of a new cultural tendency, and indeed compulsion, to develop life plans and relationship stories in ever more inventive ways, resulting in a heightened dramatization of what Foucault dubbed 'care of the self' in everything from psychotherapy and self-help literature to confessional television programmes and cosmetic surgery. Such lifestyle experimentation has particular application to the area of consumption in contemporary societies, as the multiplicity of choices presented within the ever-growing sectors of lifestyle consumption facilitates the adoption and enactment of novel social practices. This is somewhat akin perhaps to the idea of relationships as life choices made in a 'supermarket'. Aaron Ben-Ze'ev argues that we are witnessing the rise in 'flexible relationships'. Being able to 'love online' means that it becomes more possible to 'whet your appetite outside while eating at home'. It becomes easier, he says, to combine long-term commitment and short-term affairs through intermittent 'cyber-love'.[13]

The degree to which today's plurality of choices confronting people in terms of personal and professional life is either experimental or disempowering is much debated. The intensification of the 'mobile nature of self-identity' is not simply about a multiplicity of choices, however important that might be in a post-traditional social order. It is also, and crucially, about the opening of potential lifestyles in situations of work, leisure, friendship or family to novel options across distances, in different neighbourhoods at different times. Whether to go as a young person for 'overseas experience' in a country the other side of the world?[14] Whether to explore a job offer in a different country? Whether to undertake further education or training that would mean extra time away from partner or family? Whether to pursue an erotic connection with some distant other met in passing? Whether to retire to somewhere quite new and well away from established patterns of work, life and family?[15]

These are all aspects of the mobile intensification and reinvention of personal lives relatively de-synchronized from others and especially from those living within one's local neighbourhood.

Intimacy, space, mobility: a reassessment

Recent social theory has witnessed a number of major debates and claims regarding processes of social change affecting intimacy, intimate relationships and sexualities. Of particular relevance here, social theorists such as Giddens and Beck argue that identity in the global age involves the dissolving of 'traditional' forms of social life. They argue that the increased density of globalization fragments the power of traditional structures in peoples' lives, which in turn opens out identity to more experimental, individuated and reflexive ways of engaging with the self, others and the wider world. Other social theory, most especially feminism, sees accelerating mobilities much less favourably. Although we do not examine these social theories in detail, we address some of the specific social-theoretical claims concerning contemporary transformations of intimacy.

In *The consequences of modernity*, Giddens develops a powerful argument about the increasingly self-actualizing character of identity in contemporary societies. His argument centres on an increasing *reflexivity of personal and social life*. 'The reflexivity of modern social life', writes Giddens, 'consists in the fact that social practices are constantly examined and reformed in the light of incoming information about those very practices, thus constitutively altering their character.'[16] In current times, we see this acceleration in processes of reflexivity in various domains of life. This is evident, for example, in the ways that new information technologies impact upon the self and its relations with other people. As we have seen, recent changes in digital technology and, in particular, mobile telephony now mean that people can revise and reschedule their meetings, appointments and social events. This happens, not so much in advance of planned face-to-face interactions, but often as and when people are seeking to 'meet up' with each other. Through a mobile phone call, people can advise others (friends, family or colleagues) that they are running late and that their arranged meeting needs to be put back a short time. This is an example of the kind of reflexivity that Giddens thinks is at work in contemporary societies, the process of which he calls 'reflexive modernization', and it is, in his view, especially consequential for navigating personal life and intimate relationships today.

In *The transformation of intimacy*, Giddens explicitly connects the notion of reflexivity to sexuality, gender and intimate relationships. With reflexive modernization and the decline of 'tradition', identity for Giddens becomes a 'project' that has to be managed and defined against the backdrop of new opportunities and huge risks, such as artificial insemination, experiments in ectogenesis (the creation of human life without pregnancy), AIDS, sexual harassment and so on. As pre-existing traditions become undermined, so people become more drawn into dialogue and debate with themselves and others as to the choices that they make. In this connection, sexuality and intimacy become more open-ended, elaborated not through pre-given, neighbourhood-reinforced rules and roles, but through reflexively forged relationships. The self today, as the growth of therapy testifies, is faced with profound dilemmas in respect of sexuality. 'Who am I?', 'What do I desire?', 'What satisfactions do I want from sexual relations?' – these are core issues for the self, according to Giddens.

Consider his analysis of the changing social landscape of marriage and divorce. Throughout significant parts of the globe, there are now high levels of divorce and of remarriage. Giddens' thesis of accelerated reflexivity emphasizes that such statistics are not merely incidental to marriage today, but influence and reshape people's understandings of what marriage actually is. When a couple walks down the aisle in the early years of the 2000s, they do so 'knowing' (perhaps only half-consciously, otherwise in terms of a kind of practical consciousness) that the general chances for a lifetime marriage are on the decrease. The shift from marriage till-death-do-us-part to marriage until-further-notice is the result of people reflecting on the changing cultural practices governing identity, intimacy, marriage and divorce.

According to Giddens, people actively engage with novel opportunities and dangers that arise as a consequence of dramatic transformations affecting self-identity, sexuality and intimacy. For Giddens, divorce is undeniably a personal crisis, involving significant pain, loss and grief (and, we may add, for many a huge financial loss, especially for women and children in situations of dependence). Yet many, he argues, take positive steps to work through the emotional dilemmas generated by marriage breakdown. In addition to involving financial issues and matters affecting how children should be brought up, separation and divorce also call into play a reflexive emotional engagement with the self. Charting territory from the past (where things went wrong, missed opportunities and so on) and for the future (for example alternative possibilities, chances for self-actualization) involves experimenting with a new sense of self. This can lead to emotional growth, new understandings of self, and strengthened intimacies.

Against the conservative critique of marriage breakdown, Giddens thus sees the self opening out to constructive renewal. Remarriage and the changing nature of family life are crucial in this respect. He develops this point:

> Many people, adults and children, now live in stepfamilies – not usually, as in previous eras, as a consequence of the death of a spouse, but because of the re-forming of marriage ties after divorce. A child in a stepfamily may have two mothers and fathers, two sets of brothers and sisters, together with other complex kin connections resulting from the multiple marriages of parents. Even the terminology is difficult: should a stepmother be called 'mother' by the child, or called by her name? Negotiating such problems might be arduous and psychologically costly for all parties; yet opportunities for novel kinds of fulfilling social relations plainly also exist. One thing we can be sure

of is that the changes involved here are not just external to the individual. These new forms of extended family ties have to be established by the very persons who find themselves most directly caught up in them.[17]

Marital separation, as portrayed by Giddens, implicates the self in an open project: tracing over the past, imagining the future, dealing with complex family problems and experimenting with a new sense of identity. Further experimentation with marriage and intimate relationships will involve anxieties, risks and opportunities. But, as Giddens emphasizes, the relation between self and society is one of negotiation, change and development.

Like Giddens, Beck underscores the dissolution of the weight of traditional structures in the lives of contemporary women and men. His argument is that, with the corrosive impact of personal choice and public debate upon traditions and traditional ways of doing things, social life becomes peculiarly individuated; there is 'individualization'. Such a transformation in the status of tradition means that people are forced into making more active decisions about their lives, careers, families and relationships. An active engagement with the self, with the body, with relationships and marriage, with gender norms and sexualities, and with work and careers: these are the individualized parameters of 'reflexive modernization'. As Beck and Elisabeth Beck-Gernsheim explain:

> The normal biography thus becomes the 'elective biography', the 'reflexive biography', the 'do-it-yourself biography'. This does not necessarily happen by choice, neither does it necessarily succeed. The do-it-yourself biography is always a 'risk biography', indeed a 'tightrope biography', a state of permanent (partly overt, partly concealed) endangerment. The façade of prosperity, consumption, glitter can often mask the nearby precipice. The wrong choice of career or just the wrong field, compounded by the downward spiral of private misfortune, divorce, illness, the repossessed home, all this is merely called bad luck. Such cases bring into the open what was always secretly on the cards: the do-it-yourself biography can swiftly become the breakdown biography.[18]

Thus, they say that the demise of traditional worldviews ushered into existence with the advent of reflexive modernization brings in its wake individualization – a social process of which Beck says people are 'condemned'. New opportunities, but also new burdens, are the upshot of what we have termed 'networked individualism'.

There is much that is compelling in these accounts. Other analyses of current transformations of intimacy are not so affirmatively sweeping in their recasting of gender relations. Luce Irigaray argues that the phallocentric organization and management of space in contemporary societies harm the creation of an autonomous time and space for women. Like many French feminists, Irigaray contends that the ways in which space and time have been historically constituted have functioned either to contain or repress women and, by implication, men's relation to women as well. This sceptical reading of the state of gender relations is less to do with historically specific men or women, and instead concerns a social-historical tendency in the West to deny, displace and foreclose the facilitating, productive, maternal contributions of women and femininity. As she advances the argument in *An ethics of sexual difference*, representations of time and space are essential to identity itself and feminist ideals. 'The transition to a new age', writes Irigaray, 'requires a change in our perception and conception of space–time, the inhabiting of places and of containers, or envelopes of identity.'[19]

Irigaray's reflections on space–time, places and containers, as well as the notion of identities as envelopes, open questions about mobile lives, especially with regard to intimacy. She argues that masculine modes of thought are constitutive of a repression of the most primordial of spaces – the maternal body. In a quest for phallic mastery, says Irigaray, men foreclose their psychic relation to maternal space. In order to clarify what she means by this foreclosure or obliteration of the maternal, Irigaray explores how this space is repressed through the fantasy, paranoid projections of men specifically onto women's bodies and more generally onto femininity. She rather dramatically writes of the relation between the sexes: 'He enters into paternal power, to keep within him the life he drinks from the other. But enclosed within that form, she dies.'[20] This poisonous sexual relation is intricately interwoven in Irigaray's theory with conceptions of spatiality and temporality; hence its relevance to our analysis here. 'The production', writes Elizabeth Grosz of Irigaray's position, 'of a (male) world – the construction of an "artificial" or cultural environment, the production of an intelligible universe, religion, philosophy, the creation of true knowledges and valid practices of and in that universe – is implicated in the systematic and violent erasure of the contributions of women, femininity and the maternal'.[21]

The connections posited by Irigaray between masculine modes of inhabiting spaces (including movement between spaces) and the obliteration of femininity and the maternal raise crucial questions in relation to the general theme of what we have termed the network capital available to men and women in general and to specific groups in particular. It should also be noted that Irigaray equates the maternal with women, reducing the latter only to their reproductive (biological) role and ignoring the huge array of other social practices and relations within which women play major roles.[22]

Furthermore, neither Giddens and Beck on the one hand nor Irigaray on the other examine what we have been emphasizing here, namely the psychosocial impact of mobilities and especially the way that there are increasingly 'mobile' intimacies. What role, exactly, do mobilities and networks play in transformations of self and the organization of space and time? Can we adequately understand 'mobile lives' only in terms of broad categories such as 'modernity' and 'globalization', without interrogating how the radical escalation of mobilities (physical, communicative, virtual) transforms the constitution and reproduction of selves, relationships, intimacies and sexualities? It is, we argue, mobilities, networks and socialities that reorder the self in terms of an increasing propensity for the demands, differentiation and diversity of lives and emotions that are 'distanciated'.

It is movement that develops and enhances network capital, as we have argued above. Mobile worlds, we contend, construct novel configurations in processes of self-constitution, and especially so in relation to women's and men's relations to spatiality. Indeed, to the extent that mobile systems and lives add further complexity to experiences of space, place and time, one might wonder whether mobilities further drain the emotional energies of women and men, at least in parts of the contemporary world, in turn generating the commodification of sex, at least for many men? Does Robert's mobile life, for example, allow him to occupy other spaces, different sexualities, alternative intimacies? From one angle, a qualified 'yes' might seem appropriate. Robert's mobile life might appear more experimental and flexible than his previously 'fixed' family role suggests. And yet, from the optic of Irigaray's social theory, Robert's intensively mobile life might also be recast as highly masculinist, concerned primarily with the colonization of more and more space, as well as the denial of human frailty.

Certainly, if the particular theorists we have been discussing had appraised the role of mobilities more systematically, they might have seen how identities become, not only individualized, reflexive and gendered, but mobile in relationship to conceptions of the self, to others and to the social world.

Of course, twenty-first-century processes of globalization are not the first to witness multiple mobilities. As noted previously, the speeding up of the circulation of people, goods and information has been a core feature of the modern world certainly since the 1840s. However, today's complex mobility systems are developing novel characteristics, enabling the reorganization of personal and social life. These global transformations not only touch upon social institutions and organizational life, but press deeply in upon the self. That is to say, mobility transformations of the current age affect relations between home, work and social life and, indeed, the texture of lived experience and categorization of what is meant by personhood. The new kinds of mobilized identity are those involving the *stretching of self* in both psychological and social terms. This involves identities based upon plasticity, portability, contingency, communicational orderings, affect storage, as well as intimate, sexual and gender re-imaginings. Let us now turn to consider these points in detail, having considered these rather broad-brush theories of Giddens, Beck and Irigaray.

Mobile intimacy

Robert and Gemma's relationship, just like their family life, is complicated and individuated. Such is their desire to both live 'a life of one's own'[23] that the need for continual deliberation and renegotiation about when and how to coordinate relationship activities and family events gives rise to paradoxical and far-reaching challenges in their private lives. What appears paradoxical to Robert and Gemma is that their 'mobile relationship' contains more freedoms, but also more grey areas and insecurities, than before they started navigating intimacy at-a-distance. The opportunity for Robert to follow where his career takes him, and for Gemma to experience meaningful work and the challenges of higher education, brings a strong sense of autonomy, self-confidence and recognition by others. Yet the gulf between such professional independence, on the one hand, and the difficulties of 'living together separately', on the other, is often jarring and sometimes impossible.

The pressures as they navigate the uncharted waters of mobile intimacy are certainly about current and future risks, but also more. In this connection, their relationship at-a-distance raises some interesting questions. What kind of love affair are they having across distance? What kind of love experiment are they trying on, and out, through intensive mobilities? And what kind of relationship is 'mobile intimacy' for them? Is it, for example, something that needs to be actively negotiated or something that is self-propelling? If mobile intimacy requires continual planning to make relationships work, what risks arise from leaving events to chance? And is mobile intimacy all about 'choice', or does it have more to do with randomness, contingency and chance?

Mason's research in north-west Britain is helpful here. She argues *contra* Giddens and Beck that the 'individual, reflexive author' is the reality of only 'a highly privileged minority of white middle class men, apparently unencumbered by kinship or other interpersonal commitments'.[24] As we have seen when discussing Robert and Gemma, the 'individualization thesis' overlooks how commitments and obligations continue within families and keep them 'tied together', not least when children are involved. In her study of personal narratives about residential histories in north-west England, Mason shows that social identity and agency are relational rather than individualized:

> When the people in our study talked about where they had lived and why, they talked about relationships with other people, especially family and kin, but also friends, neighbours and sometimes colleagues and workmates. Indeed their discussions of context, contingency, constraint and opportunity were themselves highly relational in that they were grounded in and spoke of changing webs of relationship and connection rather than any kind of strategic individualism or motivation.[25]

Similar narratives about the need to maintain relationships at-a-distance were also seen in how the post-war generation of British working-class migrants to Canada and Australia constructed their immigration and family stories.[26] The stories told by these people were partly recollections of the pain and guilt of leaving people behind, of separating families. And, given that money was scarce, long-distance travelling high-priced, and communication slow and costly, these migrants thus tended to lose contact with family and friends back home. They had weak levels of network capital. Although many came to experience relative financial and professional success, their 'homesickness' almost ruined this success.

Migration now is different. Indeed, modern families around the world often comprise migrants and mixed-race families. The number of international migrants worldwide doubled between 1960 and 2000.[27] The migration literature shows that migration is rarely an isolated decision pursued by individual agents, but rather a collective action involving families, kinships and other communal contacts. King refers to this as indicating the importance of 'love migrations'.[28] Migrants travel to join established groups of settlers who provide transnational arrangements for them in receiving countries, while they are now able simultaneously to retain significant links with their country of origin and with chains of other migrants.

Figure 5.2 Sleep Inn, George Bush Intercontinental Airport Houston, 2007

So migration disperses family members and friends across vast areas, and thus the intimate networks of care, support and affection also stretch over large distances. Scholars of kinship and migration have long known that presence and absence do not necessarily conflict. Thus, 'geographical proximity or distance do not correlate straightforwardly with how emotionally close relatives feel to one another, nor indeed how far relatives will provide support or care for each other.'[29] Indeed, intimacy and caring take place at-a-distance, through letters, packets, photographs, emails, money transactions, telephone calls and intermittent visits. So caring, obligations and indeed presence do not necessarily imply physical travel and face-to-face proximity. People can be near, in touch and together, even when great distances tear them physically apart. These studies thus show that most people's biographies and mobilities are relational, connected and embedded, rather than individualized.

They are, however, individualized in the sense that each person's networks and relations are specific to them. People are enmeshed in social dramas wherein actions depend upon negotiation, approval and feelings, and have social and emotional consequences. Networks both enable and constrain possible 'individual' actions. This is the case, not only for people in relationships and families, but also for 'singles', who increasingly form tight-knit groups of friends where care and support flourish, according to Watters' account of *Urban tribes*. In general, we can see how friendship has become extremely significant in the rich north, especially for people who do not have children, and has come to structure and organize multiple mobilities.[30]

In what follows, we explore different components of mobile intimacy, focusing primarily on how new modalities of movement within and across national borders are reordering experiences of self, relationships and sexualities. There are at least six interdependent processes in the constitution and transformation of these intimate relationships at-a-distance, aspects also revealed by Katie Walsh's dissection of 'discourses of love amongst British migrants in Dubai', who are often maintaining complex relationships at-a-distance.[31]

First, mobile intimacy revolves around *diverse contingencies and coincidences*. That is to say, the shift from neighbourhoods to highly mobilized intimacy involves increasing levels of recognition of events, processes and happenings beyond one's power, as well as recognition of one's intimate relationships turning on a series of contingencies in time and beyond neighbourhood. In psychological terms, it was Freud who most powerfully underscored the impacts of the contingent, the accidental and the unintended – most notably in *The psychopathology of everyday life* (1904) – upon both self-identity and interpersonal relations. Examining in painstaking detail hundreds of minor accidents in daily social interaction to demonstrate that so-called 'accidents' are far from what they seem, Freud suggested that disowned parts of the self are given expression through accidents, mistakes, errors and failures. Using the subtitle 'Forgetting, slips of the tongue, bungled actions, superstitions and errors', Freud revealed how other selves and other desires within subjectivity are primarily gratified through traversing the very many chance events of daily life.

With multiple mobilities, the principal contours of new intimate relationships combine heightened awareness of the role of chance in shaping the future and ambient anxiety as to the potential risks and emotional losses this may entail. Viewed from this angle, Robert and Gemma's mobile relationship – arising as it has from various encounters with contingency, the continual negotiation of competing demands and their various compromises – appears in a new light: although the couple emphasize the various 'mistakes' made in negotiating the twin demands of their professional and intimate lives, another way of understanding their relationship might stress the exploration of alternative lives. From the 'accident' of shifting universities to the unintended benefits and losses of 'doing family life differently', the experience of mobile intimacy for Robert and Gemma has been one giving access to otherwise unknown selves, interests, pleasures, desires and potential lovers. 'Coincidences', writes Adam Phillips in Freudian vein, 'belong to those who can use them.'[32] Mobile intimacy, we might say, increasingly presumes contingency, coincidence and chance in relationships, both in the physical meetings with others and increasingly with others online.[33]

Second, mobile intimacy involves routine, ongoing, mundane and continual communicational orderings of relationships and family life. If physical mobilities (travel, transport and tourism) are a way out of 'traditional' family life, virtual mobilities offer people a way back to reconnect with their reconstituted families, whether they be joint-custody families, stepfamilies, distance relationships or non-cohabiting marriages. In this connection, digital technologies link couples at-a-distance and keep families 'plugged into' domestic events, plans and schedules (see Chapter 2 above). The lining of family residences with such technologies – computers, internet, email and phones – is fundamental to the ordering of 'family diaries', as we see in the case of Robert and Gemma. Bachen captures this point: 'No longer a sanctuary where the family was relatively shielded from intrusions from the outside world, the home is now a communication hub, infused with messages of diverse and increasingly global origins.'[34] The point, then, is that new communications technologies are not on the outside of human relationships. Such mobile machines are deeply inscribed within the tissue of mobile intimacies between parents, children, grandparents, grandchildren, aunts, uncles and so on. The internet and mobile telephony have enabled family relations to be more networked.

Third, mobile intimacy revolves around the use of mobile communications devices for experiences and explorations of the self and others. Communications technologies that people might plug into while 'on the move', as detailed in Chapter 2 and its discussion of miniaturized mobilities, typically include mobile phones, MP3 players, mini-DVDs and videos, as well as laptop computers. What is psychodynamically significant about the use of such technologies, from the vantage point of the self and its relationships, is that they provide a way out of the disparate pieces and fragmented connections occasioned by movement. That is to say, such technologies can facilitate the recovery, recapture and reconstruction of significant emotional elements of the 'remembered life' or 'self-told relationship', either because such technologies assist in sustaining many relationship connections at-a-distance or because they are productive of new kinds of construction of memory.

From this angle, communications technologies partly function as objects of *affect storage and retrieval* (see Chapter 3). For example, the fragmentary dimensions of Robert's working week, family connections and intimate life were oftentimes experienced as emotionally overwhelming or coercive. In his terms, it was often a 'drag' to be away from Gemma and the children so often. In so far as the demands of routine, relentless travel became limiting to Robert's internally recounted life-story and his usual ways of plotting his familial relationships, communications technologies offered various alternative possibilities for self-telling that he felt were beneficial. Listening to his favourite songs on iTunes while travelling, which in turn evoked very powerful memories of Gemma and of the vitality of their sexual relationship, was a means through which Robert could recapture the 'feel' of the intimacy he shared with his partner. Seen then less as a kind of emotional escapism and more as facilitative of new ways of self-telling and relationship plotting, Robert's use of affect storage through communicational technologies provides a glimpse into today's mobile forms for the telling of self, as well as the recounting of relationships.

Fourth, mobile intimacy depends on the regular moving back and forth between relationships, which in turn entails a sense of *portable personhood.*

The paradox of a mobile relationship is that it lends itself to tremendous fluidity and yet breeds a craving for lasting satisfactions. This paradox is one that can only be confronted, let alone negotiated, since the self exists in mature psychological form as temporally durable, constructed through self-narrative, involving fabrications of memory and embeddedness in social networks. If mobile relationships provide a whole new vocabulary for personal experimentation, this novel trajectory of intimacies, relationships and sexualities is therefore only possible to the extent that the self is portable, reflexive and individuated. In this connection, Robert and Gemma, like other dual-career and dual-household couples, live a life that is not only socially but spatially fragmented.[35] Maintaining their relationship and family life, while moving back and forth between jobs, residences and places of leisure, involves emotional work and complexity of affect. In any day, Robert and Gemma unwittingly rely on a sense of portable personhood to explore the challenges of work, friendship and family while still always returning to each other (even if only virtually or in fantasy) to reaffirm their relationship. The complexity of sustaining their relationship at-a-distance is, in turn, nurtured by attending to their possible future selves and states of mind. In this connection, portable personhood functions to bridge, not only spatial fragmentation, but also experiences of the present, past and future. To that extent, portable personhood reflects the imprint of what the late Cornelius Castoriadis termed 'radical imagination', involving the creation *ex nihilo* of representations, symbols and affects while on the move and without reference to any extra-subjective, foundational reference points.[36]

At the same time, this mobile self is also less likely to be fixed with one person for life. Annette Lawson argues that the culture of the individualized 'me' and an emphasis upon honesty, not honour, as the code of value are what have led to significant increases in rates of relationships outside the romantic 'couple'. Women, released from traditional constraints, feel freer to engage in conventionally masculinized forms of sex, while men, affected by the premium placed on open communication, now respond to the need for intimacy and affection in developing sexual relations. Annette Lawson thus describes the 'masculinization of sex' and the 'feminization of love', which have made adultery more frequent and more likely to be part of portable personhood in the context when multiple mobilities generate opportunities outside neighbourhood surveillance and regulation.[37]

Fifth, mobile relationships significantly reorder the domains of gender and sexual relationships. Studies of intimate relationships at-a-distance, particularly for couples without children but also for couples with parental responsibilities, reveal some greater autonomy for women than in conventional cohabitation relationships.[38] In large part, this is because of the relative freedom some women gain from pursuing careers in the manner traditionally associated with men, especially because, around the world, educational qualifications are on average now higher for women than those of men.[39] However, the extent to which women can hope to be treated equally to men in the current gender system is very highly contested, in part because of norms, practices and differences of power relating to how it is that women should prioritize their intimate relationships and family obligations over and above their working lives.[40] Holmes captures this imbalance of gender in distance relationships: 'Much of the responsibility for maintaining togetherness falls on women. Rationalised timetables make this role difficult at-a-distance because emotions, bodies, and caring cannot always be programmed to fit with organized visits and the problems of absence.'[41]

Sixth, the mobile intimacies of such couples with high income and network capital generate other jobs of domestic caring that can, in turn, spread around the world in a kind of chain. The term 'global care chain' was first used by Arlie Hochschild to refer to 'a series of personal links between people across the globe based on the paid or unpaid work of caring'.[42] Global care chains point to the massively growing global trade in domestic care services throughout wealthier countries of the world. Because of extreme poverty and growing inequality in many poor southern countries, as well as patriarchal relations, a huge supply of domestic workers is to be found, especially in South-East Asia, including particularly Thailand and the Philippines. These global care chains involve the transfer of emotional and physical care labour from those situated lower down the global care chain to those situated further up. Such a chain is normally generated by someone like Gemma who, in entering paid employment in a rich country, is unable to fulfil all her 'domestic duties' of childcare and house cleaning without working a 'double day'. This may well be because her partner is working significant periods elsewhere, as with Robert. In order to free herself from this double day, this woman buys another woman's labour, who will be poorer and is likely to be from abroad. Often the woman from elsewhere may be married with dependent children and has migrated to take up paid domestic labour. By doing this, she finds herself unable to discharge her own 'domestic duties', so creating a need for another 'woman' to substitute for her. This other woman is often drawn from an even poorer household in the sending country, or she may be a member of the migrant woman's own family. As one goes 'down' the chain, the value ascribed to the labour decreases and often becomes unpaid. Thus, at the end of the chain, an older daughter often substitutes for her mother in providing unpaid care for younger siblings.

Female labour is central to global care chains, with women supplying their own care labour while consuming other women's paid and unpaid care labour across the globe. Hochschild argues that such chains are a mechanism for extracting 'emotional surplus value'. The global scale of this is almost impossible to estimate because these workers live in and may only infrequently leave the house. Living in the house of their employer as 'part of the family', these migrant women are located in, and dependent upon, the host family. Many workers inside family households are unable to have their own friends or indeed lovers, at least in that same society. As Nayla Moukarbel expresses this, they are 'not allowed to love'.[43] Such women in the 'business of care' are also likely to be subject to abuse and exploitation, a topic dealt with in the following section.

Overall then, like so many other dual-career couples, Robert and Gemma appear to have reached various gender compromises in order to accommodate their working and intimate lives. Robert, for the most part, thinks the current arrangements work; Gemma, by contrast, notes that their caring duties rarely 'balance out'. Yet, whatever the precise imbalances of gender power here, Robert and Gemma do routinely manage to be 'somewhere else' (travelling, meetings, researching, studying, holiday-making) as a result of their ongoing agreement to support each other and to provide care to their children when the other is away. These 'gifts of support' are essential to their maintaining 'togetherness' while apart. And it is from this angle that some argue mobile relationships increasingly challenge stereotypical gender roles.[44] This may well be true, but, more than that, mobile relationships also underscore the inventiveness of intimacy when lived as an open-ended process. If traditional gender roles only permitted, at best, a complex replication of past ways of conducting relationships (based, for example, on parental cohabitation), mobile relationships by contrast are portrayed as freeing the potentially endless creativity of interpersonal dialogue and engagement. Mobile relationships are experiments concerned with the sharing of lives and the sharing of possible futures, but at-a-distance.

Mobilizing sex

It has become commonplace to claim that, in an age of extensive mobilities, gender identities and sexual intimacies are thus chosen, negotiated and constituted from various possibilities. Yet many sexual relations are not strategically chosen or mobile, as we saw above in the account of global care chains. Sex tourism, forced prostitution and the global sex industry demonstrate how forced mobilities *and* extensive immobilities are also central to contemporary gender relations. The transnational spread of commercialized sex is a significant component of neo-liberal globalization. This also shows how there can be no rapid increase in the mobile sexualities of some people without heightened immobility for others (in this case, largely illegal and organized in and through various male criminal networks).

From bar hostesses and lap 'dancers' to prostitution and domestic slavery, especially the forced trafficking in women by various crime networks, this is an extensive domain of patriarchal power. The activities of many trafficking gangs, including the Italian and Russian Mafia, the Chinese Triads and the Japanese yakuza, depend upon removing women from legal to illegal contexts and then replacing mobility with immobility. As Sietske Altink catalogues in *Stolen lives*, organized methods for trafficking women in the sex industry range from promises of a holiday or visa to more overt abduction and rape.[45] Many women who get trafficked will have been subject to regular sexual violence before their journey began, a journey often ending up in one of the places of consumption excess we examine in Chapter 6. From South-East Asia to Latin America to Europe, victims of trafficking are rendered immobile once they have arrived: they are transported from their country of origin, put under surveillance and housed by traffickers, and left without money, passports or permits. Thus are lives lived beyond neighbourhood, and the lack of neighbourhood regulation leaves women hugely vulnerable to organized male power.

The largely immobile lives of women trapped within the sex industry are instructive when contrasted with the lifestyles of those with 'high' network capital. This is especially so given how these forms may spatially overlap and impinge upon each other. Much of the 'business' undertaken by the globals we examined in Chapter 4 is conducted within locations where trafficked women are on display or part of the service that is provided to 'smooth' the deal. Major financial deals of the sort that Wim Eisner will engage in are often finished off in brothels, bars or lap-dancing clubs, where many of the available and displayed women will be trafficked or forced migrants from elsewhere.[46]

More generally, sex tourism is now part of the ambient culture of the sort of place that couples living apart together will travel to for their moments of quality time together. Jeremy Seabrook writes how:

It is a savage irony that sex tourism should be one symptom of global-ization, the 'integration' of the whole world into a single economy, when both the workers in the industry and the clients from abroad are themselves the product of disintegration – of local communities, the dissolution of rootedness and belonging, the breaking of old patterns of labour and traditional livelihoods; and the psychic disintegration of so many people caught up in great epic changes, of which they have little understanding and over which they have less control.[47]

Some feminist analyses portray women (and especially migrant women) who sell sex as passive victims and thus without agency. Other social analysts (some feminists, many post-feminists) argue that the label 'victim' ignores the complex experiences of many women who sell sex for a living and who work in low-prestige jobs in order to deal with specific life-issues, including the desire for travel similar to that of young men and other women. Certainly, the connections between marginalized women, migra-tion and the sex industry are complex and contradictory phenomena.

Our analytical focus here is with the recasting of human lives in terms of mobilities and immobilities through the global commercialization of sex. This also means recognizing how such mobilities and immobilities play out in varying social contexts and within different social strata. Laura Maria Agustin's *Sex at the margins* pays close attention to the mobilities – or, following Castells, 'space of flows' – of both sex workers travelling and travellers purchasing sexual services. For Agustin, the oppositions of work/leisure, worker/tourist, gazer/object, legal/illegal and home/abroad are not analytically fruitful, as such pure opposites are rarely found. As she reflects:

Everyone becomes an opportunist, women as well as men. Everyone looks for chinks to exploit for their personal benefit: places to live, jobs, husbands. Ownership of high-technology or expensive items such as laptop computers is not necessary, as migrants use cybercafes, phonecall shops and mobile phones like anyone else. Networked social relations are everywhere.[48]

What is striking about the growing commercialization of sex is its intricate entwinement with more extensive and cheaper movement and, specifically, the opening up of many societies to capitalist relations. It is also part of the neo-liberal period in which almost everything is seen as commodifiable, without boundaries. The global flows and mobilities of people connected to the growth of commercial sex involve both those rich in network capital and those poor in such capital. Agustin is correct to trace this commercialization of sex to mobility:

> Migrants selling sex are found travelling in every possible direction to, from and within Europe, and networks have arisen all over the world to facilitate finding jobs. Newcomers need to meet insiders with connections to the sex industry, whether they charge money for information and services or not.[49]

But such commercialization, in particular the reduction of all human inter-action to commodity status, has major ramifications for how people experience, and conceive of, sexual intimacy in their lives. Trips to work in the sex industry, as well as for those men travelling who purchase the sexual services of, mainly, women, have wider consequences for how people conceive of the connections between sexuality and intimacy.

Thus, it is during the neo-liberal period that there has been the strik-ing development of what Dennis Altman terms 'global sex', including prostitution and pornography.[50] As with other processes, it would be wrong to understand this commercialization of sex as a uniform process. It is a complex development. Such an increasing globalization of sexual 'services', especially through the relations of 'trafficking', enhances the mobilities of some, while contributing to the body-destroying immobilities of others. In the next chapter, we examine how one further aspect of this has been the proliferation of places such as Dubai, the Caribbean and Macao, where global sex has become routinized and part of the allure, part of that place. This then sours personal relations for all, and not just for those directly subject to its power. These tend to be places where gender relations are most likely to be patriarchal.

This 'industry' is also often highly interconnected with other 'industries' of excess and addiction, such as gambling and drugs. Within the context of those 'industries', it may be that, as Agustin argues, there is a certain amount of negotiation for some women some of the time, but the possibilities of this are hugely constrained by the power, wealth and force of this industry and the overwhelmingly male interests at work within it.

Conclusion: stretching or stretched?

Some 18 months after concluding the interviews with Robert and Gemma, a chance encounter occurred between the couple and a member of the interview team. Robert and Gemma are still on the mobile trajectory of a distance relationship. He still resides elsewhere for part of the working week, in order to research and develop his university career; she remains the sole carer to their children at the family home in Exeter during these periods, and also remains at work as a GP at other times. But their building and rebuilding of a coherent and rewarding sense of intimacy has in recent months been further challenged by Robert's relocation to Germany for his career. The monthly family schedule now revolves around Robert's working away every second week, when he flies out of the UK on a Sunday evening and returns on a Friday. As part of this new, even higher-carbon schedule, Gemma continues work at a medical practice every second week, but has now shifted to four days. What perhaps is most striking about these new arrangements is the provisional nature they are accorded by the couple. The current arrangement is described as 'temporary'. Robert must decide by the end of the coming academic year whether he will make the move to Germany a permanent one. Gemma acknowledges the current situation is increasingly untenable. There is a sense, then, in which they are currently living on borrowed time, and each seems aware of the wider dilemmas the other faces in this respect.

All relationships are mobile, but some are more mobile and 'distanciated' than others. In historical terms, mobility has surely been valued in diverse societies and across cultures. But we can begin to grasp how both the acceleration and intensification of mobile relationships become distinctive of the twenty-first century. Mobile relationships of the twenty-first century are, to some extent, those cut free from the traditional structures of territorially fixed intimacies and in which people wander through multiple mobilities and accumulate different meanings in different situations, which they in turn bring back to their relationship for further consideration or exploration. The future possibilities of a life shared are, in a sense, a core aspect of the structure of mobile relationships. As each partner negotiates the to-ings and fro-ings of multiple mobilities, so the relationship becomes increasingly dependent on the reconstructive endeavours of the couple itself. What may be made of current and past situations, demands, problems and dilemmas is fundamental for addressing and anticipating what the future may hold.

Feminists are correct to argue that the social pressures of combining work and intimate relationships are stretching contemporary forms of intimacy to breaking point, at least for many women. Mobile relationships, with their cult of flexible careers and fluid identities, might seem well placed to avoid such corporate pressures and social norms. Yet the mobile lover's accumulated bank of text messages is a stark reminder of the difficulties of maintaining mature emotional connections while living 'on the move'. Holmes is then perhaps right to see distance relationships as providing, among other things, a sense of respite from romantic narratives of everlasting togetherness in today's high divorce and remarriage society. 'Periods apart', writes Holmes, 'might be one way in which couples can realistically last the distance.'[51]

But there is an even deeper structural contradiction at work throughout mobile relationships in the contemporary age. From one angle, mobile relationships would appear to fit hand in glove a social order in which others are rarely proximate (or, if proximate, not for long), people are intermittently 'on the move', and the wider economic system generates high financial benefit to those with significant levels of movement capacity. Who says multiple mobilities, in other words, says mobile lives. From another angle, however, multiple mobilities can have a weakening effect on the depth or quality of relations within intimate ties at the level of a whole society. That is to say, there is a kind of in-built tension or contradiction between the global mobile economy, which privileges speed of movement and fast rational calculations, on the one hand, and the socio-cultural order of intimacy in which personal and familial relationships become increasingly ordered around short-termism, episodicity and communications at-a-distance, on the other. The tension or contradiction is that, although the latter sphere of mobile intimacy might appear to be a perfect fit for the global mobile economy, it is in fact rendered unfit for purpose as it is eaten away or hollowed out of emotional content by the former.

One consequence of this in-built contradiction is a backlash against intimacy, which in part is spawned by the speed of the global economy. This is shown in the drawing of sexuality into a globally huge industry, one of the largest in the world economy. This can be seen in the globalization of pornography and the widespread development of a global sex industry. The relationships between rich male visitors and sex workers in Dubai, the Caribbean, the Philippines, Thailand and countless other places are where mobilities and enforced immobilities meet head on, as we explore in Chapter 6.

The global connections that organize such mobilities and immobilities generally remain hidden or screened from daily life, and certainly appear at a rather removed distance from the privileged world of the case study charted throughout this chapter. Yet Robert and Gemma are, whether they know it or not, part of this complex contradiction, which penetrates to the heart of both contemporary mobile relationships and global mobility processes. At the time of writing, they continue to navigate an intimate relationship based on the stretching of their identities. Just at what point that stretching tips into a sense of the relationship becoming stretched – of buckling under its own pressure – is unknown, but it gets replayed in very many relationships around the world where there are many comings and goings, unions and reunions, quality time and lonely interludes, opportunities and anxieties.

Figure 6.1 Holland Casino, Amsterdam Airport Schiphol, 2007

6   Consuming to excess

On a planet where more than 2 billion people subsist on two dollars or less a day, these dreamworlds enflame desires – for infinite consumption, total social exclusion and physical security, and architectural monumentality – that are clearly incompatible with the ecological and moral survival of humanity.

Mike Davis and Daniel Bertrand Monk[1]

One of the most extraordinary places in the neo-liberal world order, and indeed a place that many globals will have visited, is the small, former British protectorate of Dubai. It became independent in 1971 as a component of the United Arab Emirates. Drilling for oil begain in Dubai in 1966, but, as the oil soon began to run out, instead a gigantic visitor and consumption economy replaced it. Instead of producing oil, Dubai is a huge consumer of oil. This oil is used to build islands, hotels and attractions in what is said to have been the world's largest building site; to transport in and out very large numbers of visitors, workers and women in the sex industry; and to provide spectacular cooled environments for visitors where average temperatures are over 40°C. Dubai became a place for holidays and leisure, of meetings and conferences, which are held in some of the most consumer-excessive forms of contemporary hotels, and shopping complexes and visitor attractions. It is a place of and for mobile lives.

On the Dubai skyline dozens of mega projects are on the go. These constructions include two palm island developments that extend the coastline by 120 kilometres; a string of new islands shaped like the world; vast shopping complexes; a domed ski resort in the desert and other major sports venues; what was the world's tallest building; the world's largest hotel, the Asia-Asia, with 6500 rooms, expected to open in 2010; and the world's first seven-star hotel, the Burj Al Arab, with hundred mile views.[2]

This is a place of almost literal monumental excess. Dubai's ambition is to be number one in the world. According to Mike Davis, to become such a luxury-consumer paradise, especially for Middle Eastern and South Asian visitors, 'it must ceaselessly strive for visual and environmental excess'.[3] And it achieves this through architectural gigantism and perfectibility. There are many massive simulacra for play, of dinosaurs, the Hanging Gardens of Babylon, the Taj Mahal, the Pyramids and a snow mountain, simulacra more perfect than the original.

Trying to be a gated enclave of playful excess is an arduous, complex business, but one that Dubai has achieved well, partly because state and private enterprises are virtually indistinguishable in their commitment to this goal. This is a place of over-consumption, of shopping, eating and drinking, but also of extensive prostitution and gambling. Guilt, in what is nominally an Islamic country, is *not* to consume beyond the 'limit'.[4] And Dubai is only made possible by migrant contract labourers travelling from Pakistan and India and then being bound to a single employer. Labour relations are excessively exploitative, with up to 90 per cent of labourers working in Dubai being imported, with their passports being removed upon entry.[5] This is accumulation through dispossession, as David Harvey says about neo-liberal economic development more generally.[6]

Dubai has been described by Mike Davis as 'an oasis of free enterprise without income taxes, trade unions, or opposition parties (there are no elections). As befits a paradise of consumption, its official national holiday . . . is the celebrated Shopping Festival, a month-long extravaganza.'[7] There is a YouTube video on Dubai entitled *Do buy*. It is a place, as locals boast, for 'supreme lifestyles' of the sort examined in Chapter 4. Dubai thus developed into the iconic place of excess. It moved from being a substantial producer of oil to become the exemplary site of excess consumption, including of oil, in order to get people there *and* to power the sites of consumption excess.

How did this place come about, or, as Davis and Monk ask much more generally, how did the world come to be full of 'evil paradises', of which Dubai is a leading exemplar? We have examined in this book how people do move around the world and established that they do so for many good reasons. People may be visiting partners, workmates, friends or family, and they do so by going to distinct places, such as Dubai. In this chapter, we examine how, over recent decades, some extraordinary new places have come into being, places to attract visitors, where they can make new friends. They can also re-meet partners, old friends, family and workmates within new kinds of designed, themed spectacle. We focus on those places developing in the neo-liberal era where, as Davis and Monk say: 'the winner-takes-all ethos is unfettered by any remnant of social contract and undisturbed by any ghost of the labor movement, where the rich can walk like gods in the nightmare gardens of their deepest and most secret desires.'[8]

'Evil paradises' of seductive attraction are designed, constructed and imagined as places of and for movement. Indeed, '[Dubai] has become a place where global flows of capital, people, culture, and information land and intersect'.[9] Contemporary capitalism has ushered in places especially where the *globals* examined in Chapter 4 can consume to the extreme. And, more generally, there are many places where the self is fashioned and refashioned through being able to consume an exceptional range of goods and services from around the world within designed, themed places. Such consumption presupposes large numbers of consuming visitors roaming the world and consuming places made for them and for their excessive and playful consumptions. Some consumption takes the form of powerful addictions, and so there have developed further distinct places where treatments for such addictions are also provided (especially for the super-rich).

Before considering such places in detail, we examine aspects of this generally devouring consumer culture.[10] It is common to say that a key feature of the contemporary world has been the pervasiveness of consumerism or of a 'consumer culture'. This is the idea that people depend upon and form their identities not only through work and being members of a given social class or gender or age. Rather, identities are formed through purchasing, using and making symbolic capital out of purchased consumer goods and services. What are especially important are people's purchases, and their material and symbolic uses of these goods and services, and especially how such consumed items are organized into various brands. There have been many studies of consumer culture and many critiques of the superficiality and distorting effect of lives experienced through consumer objects, services and brands. Some argue that people increasingly live 'branded lives', with people forming their identities through the purchase and display of consumer brands that are, in a way, more important to them than their memberships of social classes, genders or ethnicities.[11] Thus it seems that a further consequence of multiple mobilities are more mobile identities.

We examine two aspects of this consumer culture thesis that other writers have mostly ignored. The first is the idea that these consumer goods and services, what we will term 'consumer experiences', are put to work by people. And, as they are put to work, so they enable the self to be produced and reproduced. They make the self a matter, in part at least, of 'design', somewhat analogous to the designing of relationships discussed in the previous chapter. Erving Goffman famously described the multiple process involved in the 'presentation of self in everyday life'.[12] But what we are now seeing is more the 'design and re-design of self'.[13] This can involve many aspects, including those of the shape and style of the body. Many TV programmes are concerned with 'makeover'. The makeovers of goods, services, homes, cars, self, relationships and especially the body are forms of work carried out with, and through, consumer experiences. The extreme form of this remaking of self is in terms of upgrading the body through cosmetic surgery. One of us has elsewhere described the significance of 'global makeover industries' that enable instant self-reinvention through various kinds of plastic surgery.[14]

The second idea is that the key process now engendering this kind of consumer culture is that of people's movement to other peoples/places, this taking many different forms, as seen in early chapters of this book. Yet the significance of these different forms has been mostly ignored in the analysis of consumer culture. Therefore, in this chapter, we try to *mobilize* the study of consumer culture and show how mobile lives are entangled with the purchase, use, branding and signification of multiple goods and services. Indeed, mobile lives are lives based upon high and often excessive forms of consumerism that take place at a distance from neighbourhoods. Places are consumed and, hence, they are fantasized, travelled to, stayed in, experienced through purchases of goods and especially services, and then remembered, often in the company of others. The 'consuming' of place is a complex, multilayered set of practices stretched out in time and across space and involving the consumption of many objects and services.

This chapter, like the last, is organized around the crucial distinction between 'neighbourhood lives' and lives that are lived and experienced 'beyond neighbourhood'. Major consequences stem from this shift from 'neighbourhood' to 'beyond neighbourhood'. The former involves the dominance of slow modes of mobility, especially walking and cycling. The scale of most work and leisure activities is a few miles, and much consumption and many family and friendship patterns are 'localized'. The disciplining of especially young men (and women) takes place within neighbourhoods and is often informal and communal. Consumption tends to involve conformity with neighbourhood norms, acting in accordance with such norms and not stepping out of line. Many agricultural communities and early industrial-urban communities in the rich north were organized on the basis of such strong neighbourhood lives, slow modes of travel and relatively circumscribed forms of consumption.

Even when working-class holidays developed in Europe at the end of the nineteenth century, these were often neighbourhood-based, involving groups of employees or neighbours journeying away together with much mutual regulation.[15] Such places of working-class mass pleasure were based upon a number of strong and marked contrasts, between work and leisure, home and away, workspace and leisure space, ordinary time and holiday time. Pleasure is derived from these contrasts, from being away for a week from domestic and industrial routines and places. Contrasting places provide a chance to 'let your hair down' for a week in a place of carnival before returning to normal.[16] In contrast, at home excess is regulated through the co-presence of family and, to some degree, of one's neighbourhood, also travelling along at roughly the same time to that same place.

However, we have seen in this book how a 'mobility field' has come into play. In various ways, the development of such a field shifts the nature of consumption beyond these neighbourhood lives. It is however important to realize that the consumption of goods and services is still socially embedded and is not just a question of the relationship of people to abstracted objects or services.[17] In the following paragraphs we set out some of the important forms in which 'consumption' has moved beyond and outside neighbourhoods, forms often not sufficiently distinguished from each other.

First, consumer culture involves the movement of objects manufactured in workshops and, especially, factories. These goods are then transported to where consumers live, or at least where they go shopping, often with friends or family. Food itself is increasingly processed in factories and then transported to consumers using new techniques of canning, refrigeration and so on. These factories produce many of the new shiny products that define modern life. Neighbourhoods become less significant in structuring modern experiences, which are increasingly organized through buying and using these consumer objects that are produced elsewhere and possess associated sign values. To be manufactured elsewhere, especially in places such as Milan, New York, Paris, London, is often a marker of the status both of an object and of those able to consume it.

Second, specialized large-scale shops developed beyond people's neighbourhoods. Consumers journey with friends or family to these 'cathedrals of consumption' and then carry the objects purchased back to their homes. Their homes come to be filled with such objects, and many distinctions come to be made between owners of different kinds of goods. Such 'cathedrals' date from the 1840s, with department stores first developing in Paris. These elegant nineteenth-century stores and arcades provided models of taste and style to be copied by many other places of, and for, consumption that then developed around the world in the twentieth century. Many further developments in retail design generated lavish environments for display. There is a fetishism in objects being laid out, waiting to seduce the potential consumer through their shape, texture, materiality, quality, design, price, branding and sign value.[18]

Third, consumerism not only involves purchasing objects used or located in or around people's homes. The means of movement are also consumer goods, beginning with animals, especially horses, but with bicycles at the end of the nineteenth century and then with cars during the twentieth century, which has been described as the 'century of the car'.[19] The car became not just an object for expert drivers, but something driven by and to some extent tinkered with by 'consumers'. An exceptional array of goods, services and cultures of movement became organized around the car, generating powerful 'automotive emotions', especially divided by class and gender.[20] According to Roland Barthes, cars are 'the exact equivalent of the great Gothic cathedrals: I mean the supreme creation of an era . . . and consumed in image if not in usage by a whole population which appropriates them as a purely magical object'.[21] And, indeed, much consumption does not occur simply in fixed places but through movement around places. There have developed new cartographies of movement and consumption, especially in the contemporary world, involving automobility. The significance of this is well shown in the case of the cartographies of night-time consumption practices in Rio.[22]

Fourth, alongside the purchase of objects, increasingly diverse and specialized services develop. Some of these are neighbourhood-based, but increasingly they are organized beyond neighbourhoods. This is especially the case for those services organized in and through collective or state forms, especially health and education. Increasingly, services necessitate consumers travelling beyond their neighbourhoods, such as going by train to the seaside hotel, journeying by car to the out-of-town leisure centre, or going by air to a Caribbean beach. These services increasingly involve bodily makeovers. Consumer culture is increasingly 'embodied'. Bodies become subject to chemical, physical and body-part modification as elements of consumer culture. Especially significant is how bodily makeovers enable people to upgrade the self, something significant in an era in which face-to-face meetings and giving a good impression at first glance are of much importance in business and professional life, as we saw in Chapters 4 and 5.[23]

Fifth, many consumer services are located within specialized places which then come to be known for that particular service. The place and the service are synonymous. These places 'beyond neighbourhood' are based upon the consumption of specialized and distinct services. And, at the same time, the places themselves become branded through the services produced and consumed within that particular place. One early example of this involved the spa towns that developed across nineteenth-century Europe, including Wiesbaden, Vichy, Baden-Baden, Harrogate, Budapest, Bath and so on.[24] 'Taking the waters' in certain spa towns became a fashionable therapy in these few socially select towns known for their 'watering services'. There are many other cases where a place and its service are synonymous. Such places include health tourism in Havana; higher education in Cambridge; golf in St Andrews; beaches in Sydney; favelas and beaches in Rio; casinos in Monaco; bookshops in Hay-on-Wye; financial services on Wall Street, New York; surgical tourism in Malaysia; Holocaust 'tourism' in Auschwitz and so on.

Finally, places are not necessarily 'fixed' in terms of their sign value. Indeed, we can talk of places moving closer (as with favelas in Rio) or further away from the centres of cultural life; places themselves can be 'on the move'.[25] Such movement has been especially marked in the neo-liberal period through the increased importance of designing for consumption via branding and especially via the construction of themed spaces. Scott Lukas describes the increased importance of such theming as follows:

> A themed space, whether a casino, theme park, or restaurant, employs a theme to establish a unifying and often immutable idea throughout its space . . . Theming is a motivated form of geographical representation in which meaningful connections are made amongst unifying ideas, symbols, or discourses.[26]

Theming, he says, is present in all towns and cities across the world, with businesses having little alternative to being themed and indeed to undergoing a fairly regular process of re-theming. Much of that re-theming involves reconstruction in terms of a theme that arrives from elsewhere and especially from what can be described as the plethora of 'global centres' that populate the contemporary world. In recent years, certain cities have provided models or exemplars of development that themselves move around the world, the Barcelona model following the 1992 Olympic Games being perhaps the most iconic.[27]

In many different ways there are countless consumer cultures that have developed beyond what we have characterized as neighbourhood lives. Such shifts beyond neighbourhood can be further analysed in terms of the shift from societies of discipline, as understood by Michel Foucault, to societies of control, as outlined by Gilles Deleuze. In the former, the disciplining of populations occurs within specific sites, such as the family, local community, school, prison, asylum, factory, clinic and so on.[28] Each of these sites possesses its own regulations and procedures. Surveillance is based upon fairly direct co-presence within that specific locus of power, within each 'local' panopticon. Power is internalized, face-to-face and localized. And consumption is specific and regulated through each site, including the 'family' and neighbourhood, based upon, as noted, slow modes of travel. These disciplinary societies with their high levels of spatial and functional differentiation reached their peak in mid-twentieth-century Europe and North America.

However, over the twentieth century, another system of power emerged beyond that of discipline. This is what Deleuze terms societies of control, where power is fluid, decentred and less site specific.[29] The places of disciplinary confinement are not so physically marked. Critiques of the effects of 'institutionalization' develop, and this leads to the closure of some places of disciplinary confinement (although not prisons, which expand, especially in neo-liberal societies). Treatment and correction increasingly take place within the 'community', but a community involving more distant forms of control through fast modes of travel. Surveillance is less face-to-face and localized. Many sets of social relations are no longer internalized within specific sites. Gender relations are less confined to the family; work is both globalized and, in part, carried out in the home; schooling partly occurs within the media and so on. States increasingly employ complex control systems of recording, measuring and assessing populations that move, beginning with the passport and now involving a complex 'digital order' that is normally able to track and trace individuals as they move about, searching ever new places of pleasure, friendship and work. So those living mobile lives are subject to enhanced forms of surveillance at-a-distance, and this is especially so of those forced to move as refugees or asylum seekers or temporary workers.

To grasp that capitalist consumption in the rich north escapes from neighbourhoods is to see that such populations are mobile, moving in, across and beyond 'territories'. Many people's lives are less determined by those site-specific structures, of class, family, age, career and especially propinquitous communities. Indeed, the media and especially the internet also bring other worlds into people's lives. And, as people move around and develop personalized life projects through being freed from some structures, so they extend and elaborate their consumption patterns, their social networks and what we have termed in earlier chapters their network capital.[30] At least for the rich third of the world, partners, family and friends are more a matter of choice, increasingly spread around the world, as noted in Chapter 5. There is a 'supermarket' of partners, friends and acquaintances, and people depend upon an array of interdependent systems of movement with which to connect to this distributed array of networks, but often meeting up within distinct places, some of which are places of 'excess capitalism'.

Paralleling this are changes in how many people experience 'place'. It becomes less something that is belonged to and dwelt within and more something that is experienced through visiting. People, we might say, are increasingly connoisseurs and collectors of places. This connoisseurship and, hence, the further spreading of mobility come to apply to very many places. These places come to be known about, branded, themed and collected. These markers of place in the contemporary world order include beaches, clubs, views, walks, mountains, history, surf, music scene, icebergs, historic remains, sources of good jobs, food, landmark buildings, the gay scene, party atmosphere, universities and so on.[31] Examples of newly arrived places range from narco-capitalist favelas in Rio or Capetown to the Antarctic, from the Paris tunnel where Princess Diana died to nuclear power stations, from Ground Zero to holidaymaking in the danger zone.[32] As fast as places are so generated and marketed, so they get visited. Places are thus sets of abstract characteristics that are indexed in multiple 'guides', and less sites dwelt within.

This further means that travel practices can move on and leave behind places that are no longer of significance. In such a 'touring' world, places come and places go, some places speed up, and others slow down or die as the connoisseurs of such places leave them behind (and they 'need' re-theming). Many seaside resorts in Europe and North America have been left to decline since they no longer count as places to collect in such a world, and they struggle for finance to be re-themed.

Indeed, places in such a world of visitors are often full of disappointment and frustration. This is captured well in Alex Garland's book (and film) *The Beach*.[33] People's fantasies of a place compared with what performances are actually afforded are a constant trope in tourist tales. The objects of consumption may not be available; the place to-die-for is overrun with cheap souvenir stalls; the service quality is degraded compared with the

Figure 6.2 Travelex queue, Prague International Airport, 2007

destination's place-image; eco-tourists discover that the pristine coral reef has been destroyed by earlier mass tourism; or middle-aged business people find their city centre is overrun by promiscuous, drunk 'party-goers'.[34] But what this frustrated desire often does is to generate further consumption, going to a different place, or the same place but at a different time, or staying in more expensive accommodation or spending more. Frustrated consumption can lead to more consumption through an ongoing cycle of anticipation, experience, frustration, new anticipation and so on.[35]

Contemporary capitalism and its mobile lives thus presuppose and generate many mobile bodies relatively detached from propinquitous family and neighbourhoods and increasingly touring the world. Many are emotional, pleasure-seeking and novelty-acquiring. Such bodies are on the move, able to buy and indulge new experiences located in new places and with new people. This has helped to generate the market that comprises what is often known as the 'experience economy'.[36] So, as people escape the disciplinary confines of family and local community based on slow modes of travel, so they then buy goods and services from the many companies and brands that constitute the experience economy. Capitalist societies involve new forms of pleasure, with so many elements or aspects or parts of the body being commodified (for those able to afford to). Expressive capitalism develops into a mobile and mobilizing capitalism with transformed, and on occasions, overindulged bodies, while many other people are employed in 'servicing' such bodies, and, as we saw in the case of Dubai, they too are also often on the move from other places. Bodies are commodified in and through moving about and being moved about. There is what could be described as 'binge mobility', and indeed bingeing is widespread in a neo-liberal world (even bingeing on financial derivatives!).

Neo-liberalism

Spurious kinds of 'freedom' produce the destruction of human autonomy; in choosing its personal liberations, the self can eradicate freedom. We have noted how Giddens describes increased 'freedom' as many people from the rich north are forced away from site-specific forms of surveillance to more distant forms of control. And yet part of that apparent freedom is the freedom to become 'addicted', to be emotionally and/or physically dependent upon certain products of global capitalism, be they legal (sugar), illegal (heroin) or semi-legal (tobacco). One of us refers to the way in which there is 'addiction to the ethos of instant self-reinvention'.[37] So places of excess are often places where significant numbers of people come to be addicted. Places of excess are places of significant addiction. Giddens suggests that compulsive behaviour has become very common in modern societies. Such compulsion is:

> linked to lifestyle choice. We are freer now than 40 years ago to decide how to live our lives. Greater autonomy means the chance of more freedom. The other side of that freedom, however, is the risk of addiction. The rise of eating disorders coincided with the advent of supermarket development in the 1960s. Food became available without regard to season and in great variety, even to those with few resources.[38]

Such addictions derive from compulsive repetition – habits that are hard to break because of their emotional content. In the contemporary world, the following industries depend for their profitability upon these addictions: tobacco, 'illegal' drugs, alcohol, gambling, food processing and sugar, the last two being central to the developing catastrophe of global obesity.

These industries of addiction have become marked during the last quarter of a century, as neo-liberalism became the global orthodoxy spreading out from the University of Chicago's Economics Department. 'Neo-liberalism' involves 'accumulation by dispossession'. It presumes that the market is 'natural' and will move to equilibrium only if unnatural forces or elements do not get in the way. It elevates market exchanges over and above all other sets of connections between people. It asserts that the 'market' is the source of value and virtue. Thus, peasants can be thrown off their land; collective property rights are made private; indigenous rights are stolen; rents are extracted from patents; general or traditional knowledge is turned into intellectual 'property'; the state sells off its collective activities; trade unions are smashed; new financial instruments and flows redistribute income and rights away from the 'real economy'; and property development financed by indebted firms and indebted buyers is the form taken by the neo-liberal 'gold rush'. While obliging national states to create and pay for large infrastructure motorways, high-speed rail links and airports, so the private sector speculatively funds and builds highly leveraged new developments, leased or sold to those with escalating indebtedness. These developments include suburbs, apartments, second homes, hotels, leisure complexes, gated communities, sports stadia, shopping centres and casinos. Sometimes these are all found in one place, such as Dubai.

Such neo-liberalism is articulated and acted upon within most corporations, many universities, most state bodies and especially international organizations, such as the World Trade Organization, the World Bank and the International Monetary Fund.[39] According to an influential American adviser/consultant, the principal value promulgated through neo-liberalism was 'to inspire us all to consume, consume, consume. Every opportunity is taken to convince us that purchasing things is our civic duty, that pillaging the earth is good for the economy'.[40]

During this period, new or designed places of consumption excess developed, involving various 'dispossessions', of workers' rights, of peasant land-holdings, of the state's role in leisure, of neighbourhood organizations and of customary rights. David and Monk refer to these resulting 'evil paradises', and examples to consider include Arg-e Jadid, a Californian oasis in the Iranian desert; the buildings for the $40 billion 2008 Olympics in Beijing; Palm Springs gated community in Hong Kong; Sandton in Johannesburg; and Macao. The last of these involves a $25 billion investment oriented to providing leisured gambling for the re-invented China and the resurgent 1.3 billion Chinese. Simpson notes that, in the very same year that Macao was declared a UNESCO World Heritage site, the first steps were taken in constructing a vast 'Fisherman's Wharf' of themed reproductions, of a Roman coliseum, buildings from Amsterdam, Lisbon, Cape Town and Miami, and an erupting volcano.[41] Globally, the next massive paradise is the planned €17 billion entertainment city to be called Gran Scala, located in north-east Spain. There would be 32 casinos, 70 hotels, 232 restaurants, 500 stores, a golf course, a race track and a bullring, located, of all places, in the Los Monegros desert, where water and oil are overwhelming resource issues.[42]

Such places of 'consumption' excess share various characteristics. Their speculative development is often only made possible by large infrastructural projects, often with celebrity architects. The associated new transport systems are typically paid for with public money. Building such places typically involves the profligate consumption of water, power and building materials in order to build on what is often reclaimed land (as in Macao or Dubai) or in deserts (Gran Scala, Abu Dhabi). Such sites are highly commercialized, with many simulated environments, more 'real' than the original from which they are copied. Gates, often digitized, prevent the entry and exit of local people and those visitors who do not have signs of good credit. Norms of behaviour are unregulated by family/neighbourhood, with bodies being subject to many different forms of commodification. They are beyond neighbourhood, with liminal modes of consumption and only pleasure and no guilt, unless insufficient consumption occurs. Indeed, these places are sites of potential mass addiction, especially to gambling and related forms of criminality. Such consumption zones come to be globally known for their excess; it is excessive behaviour that marks that zone as distinct. Thus, to take one example: 'Ibiza is a post-Oedipal social space in which there is no law (and no misbehaviour).'[43]

Moreover, many such places lie on or near beaches (and/or deserts). Indeed, in Dubai, massive construction projects have enlarged the very scale of the 'beach' through developing many 'artificial' islands. The environmentalist Rachel Carson explained the allure of the beach: '[the] edge of the sea is a strange and wonderful place', partly because it is never the same from one moment to the next.[44] It is an in-between place, neither quite land nor sea. And, over the past two centuries, the beach has gone from being a place of repulsion and danger to one of attraction and desire, and increasingly one that is built and indeed designed. It became a place to be dwelt upon by visitors, a place of landscape, leisure rather than work, a place especially for mobile visitors rather than locals. Beaches became the classic place for visitors to place themselves temporarily, with unusual props and in a state of undress, and to reveal the close approximation of that body to a designed, tanned ideal. For the affluent classes of Europe and North America, the beach became a place of immense affect, of paradise and excess, signifying a symbolic 'other' to factories, work and domestic life. This initiates many other forms of bodily adornment and physical and chemical modification that de-stabilize the self and make bodies 'mobile' and subversive of conventional hierarchies of (clothed) wealth and power. This thin line between the sea and the land becomes a central stage for multiple, contested and, on occasions, marginalized performances of contemporary leisure and tourism. Overall, the beach is 'the emblematic space for a life of leisure'.[45]

The golden beaches of the Mediterranean and the Caribbean especially became thought of as paradises on earth. Sheller describes the working out of such processes within the Caribbean, one of the original places of paradise.[46] Here, 'all-inclusive resorts' have been common. They carve out spaces for liminal consumption largely cut off from the surrounding territory and from local people, apart from those providing these 'excess services'. Gated and often fortified, they secure temporary consumption of excess away from the prying eyes of both locals and of those who might disapprove 'back home'. Sheller describes: 'the neoliberal respatialization of the Caribbean for the benefit of the super-rich, yacht-owning, aeromobile global elite'.[47]

Indeed, on occasions, whole islands provide secure sites for such excess consumption by the globals. Islands do not have to be literally 'gated', as can be seen in the planned development of the island of Dellis Cay in the Caribbean. The island provides its 'natural' barrier to the outside world. This development is aimed at the 'private jet-set', those who accumulate planes, houses and servants as others accumulate cars. Sheller summarizes how: 'entire Caribbean islands are being curated into exclusive resorts for the super-rich, and removed from the control and governance of local communities and . . . their governments.'[48] Dellis Cay involves seven world-renowned architects developing the entire 560-acre island. The development is master-planned by Zaha Hadid, who is also designing some of the residences, villas, restaurants, boutiques and the marina. Residences will range in price from $2 million to $20 million, and the development is due for completion by the end of 2010.

Crucial also to much Caribbean tourism are huge cruise ships, which are in fact rather like islands. These floating gated communities are organized around consuming to excess. The largest cruise ship in the world's history has been recently launched by Royal Caribbean Cruise Lines. It includes 1815 guest staterooms, the first ever surf park at sea, cantilevered whirlpools extending twelve feet over the sides of the ship, a waterpark complete with interactive sculpture fountains, geysers and a waterfall, a rock climbing wall and the Royal Promenade with many shops and cafés, all moving around in the middle of the ocean.[49] This is again an example of such consumption zones being premised upon the strict separation between local people (except as employees) and over-consuming mobile visitors allowed onto special zones of Caribbean islands reserved solely for such cruise ship visitors.

More generally, islands often form part of the unregulated, tax-free, off-shore economy, the 'offshore world'. This comes to be constituted through the stitching together of physical space with cyberspace.[50] Such offshore worlds are paradigmatic of neo-liberalism, of gated resort development, select tourism for the super-rich, the splintering of public infrastructures and the enabling of often dubious wealth to go offshore and, hence, out of sight of tax-collecting authorities. In the neo-liberal period, systems of excess production, consumption and privatization have become dominant. Societies of discipline morph into societies of control, and specialized and differentiated neighbourhoods morph into mobile, de-differentiated consumption zones of excess. As Sheller writes, 'Atlantic City is not alone in spawning a virulent form of casino capitalism and real-estate speculation; it is just one example of a wider global trend in economies of excess, spectacle, and speculation', of the toxic combination of spectacle-making and speculation.[51]

However, some might argue that this kind of elite casino capitalism only pertains to a small sector of the world's consumers, to the super-rich globals we encountered in Chapter 4. Hence, it is not of wider economic, social and political significance. Thus, we are overstating their importance. But, for various reasons that we now outline, this is not, we think, true at all.

First, these kinds of place establish exemplars of development that developers elsewhere then seek to emulate and to produce mass-market versions of such places of excess, including themed restaurants, down-market resorts and suburban shopping malls. So what gets imagined and constructed at the select or elite end then moves elsewhere; or, indeed, the same development itself moves downmarket, as some suggest is currently happening in Dubai.

Second, these forms of conspicuous consumption generate places in which many people have to work, often for low wages and in sometimes degrading conditions. Many such workers are themselves mobile. For example, 40,000 workers enter 'offshore' Monaco each day. Moreover, most of the consumption excesses examined here are productive of much illegal or semi-legal work and, hence, of related forms of criminality that impact upon the lives of many others.

Third, some of these places attract the super-rich often 'offshore'. This has the effect of reducing the tax-take of states and lowering the level and scale of public provision, both in the island resort and in the country from which visitors travel. The scale of such tax havens, and hence of resulting tax losses, is immense, with the estimate for the US approaching $100 billion a year.[52]

Fourth, these places of consumption are part of a 'splintering urbanism', excluding many people and, hence, reducing the availability of public space more generally around the world.[53] This is shown in how many beaches throughout the world are closed or semi-closed to 'locals' or indeed to poorer visitors (often marked by race) travelling from elsewhere.

Fifth, the development of these places for visiting has the effect of further extending the mobility field and, hence, producing further inequalities between the economic and network capital rich and the economic and network capital poor (as discussed in Chapter 3). These places are components of, and help to reinforce, what we have termed a 'touring world'. People in the rich north are confronted by choices that, according to Schwartz, make many of them anxious and miserable, with reduced levels of well-being.[54] The proliferation of choice takes time, involves uncertainty and produces immense anxiety that the wrong choice with regard to one's visit has been made. Schwartz says that consumers of goods and services regularly experience regret about what they did not choose as well as frustration with what they have chosen – a double whammy of consumer culture![55]

Sixth, these dreamworlds for the super-rich provide models of lives that, through multiple media and global travel, enflame the desire for similar kinds of experience in much of the world's population. These dreamworlds enflame desires for consumption, exclusion and security.[56] When people mainly experienced neighbourhood lives, then they would tend to compare themselves with others locally. Schwartz points out the contrast between neighbourhood lives and those beyond neighbourhood, where comparisons and dissatisfaction would appear to be excessive:

> We looked around at our neighbours and family members. We did not have access to information about people outside our immediate social circle. But with the explosion of telecommunications [and long-distance travel] . . . almost everyone has access to information about almost everyone else . . . This essentially universal and unrealistically high standard of comparison decreases the satisfaction of those who are in the middle or below.[57]

Finally, these places are a yet further extension of the hyper-high-carbon societies of the twentieth century. This occurs through their gigantic building, their profligate use of energy and water, and the vast use of oil used to transport people in and out. Veblen famously analysed *wasteful* consumption.[58] The possession of wealth is shown by the conspicuous waste of time, effort and goods. In order for consumption to be conspic-uous, it must be wasteful. Veblen applies this notion to the consumption practices of individuals. But, in the neo-liberal phase of capitalism, whole cities', regions' or islands' economies/societies are transformed into centres of 'wasteful' production and consumption. Much capitalist production in the neo-liberal era takes place without regard for need or public good. So the scale and impact of 'waste' production has moved upwards, especially with much of this economy of waste focusing upon gambles on the future, whether on the casino table, or on global commodities, or on mortgages, or on speculative property developments. There is also, we might say, a casual production and consumption of place, especially through theming. Places come and go, being produced and then used up, as the touring consumer and related investment move elsewhere once a place is worn out and exhausted. So there are gambles on the futures of places as the level of conspicuous waste is ratcheted upwards, certainly until the Great Crash of October 2008!

Conclusion

In Chapter 4, we considered the super-rich, the globals. We noted how they seek to escape tax-paying and responsibility, often through having houses or apartments offshore, as they jet around the world from one place of offshore excess to another. We explored how the notion of excess captures a series of shifts in contemporary societies: from low-carbon to high-carbon economies/societies; from societies of discipline to societies of control; and from specialized and differentiated neighbourhoods to more mobile, de-differentiated zones of consumption, excess and waste.

But, in the following and final chapter, we examine whether the world as toured is a world that may well have a shorter shelf life than most of us would ever have imagined. The ultra-high-carbon hubris of the early twenty-first century was excessive and all consuming. We will see how, in various ways, such excessive consumption provoked both global climate change and the running down of the key resource of oil, which had literally made this mobile world go round. We will examine whether the era of 'mobile lives' for many was, in fact, merely a shortish period in human history.

Indeed many of the beach locations and resorts examined in this chapter may well be washed away by rising sea levels and floods, including possibly those newly created palm islands of Dubai.[59] Already, the hubris that is Dubai would seem to have flipped. Its astonishing growth has dramatically gone into reverse. Expats are fleeing and leaving their cars, bought on credits at the airport; thousands of construction workers have been laid off; there is a predicted 60 per cent fall in property values; half the construction projects are on hold or cancelled; and the population is now shrinking. Paul Lewis pronounces: 'Too high, too fast: the party's over for Dubai.'[60] Is this history of the present in Dubai a forerunner of the history of the global present, as mobile lives may come to a shuddering halt or even a reversal within the next few decades?

7 Contested futures

America's cars are one of the world's largest sources of global warming pollution.

John DeCicco and Freda Fung[1]

The twentieth century

In this final chapter, we place mobile lives (and mobility systems) into future contexts, examining in what ways and to what degree they can continue into the twenty-first century. We show that continuing such mobile lives can only be understood in the context of the legacy of the twentieth century, a legacy that problematizes its continuing high-carbon economy and society. That century's 'free lunch' has resulted, after a decade of global optimism in the 1990s, in some bleak dilemmas for the twenty-first century. There are, we might suggest, no good outcomes. The car, the plane and their high-carbon friends would seem to have done their best to leave little standing, even as they themselves may disappear from view.

Marx and Engels' nineteenth-century analysis of the contradictions of capitalism enables this legacy of the twentieth century to be examined. They famously wrote in the *Communist manifesto* that modern bourgeois society: 'is like the sorcerer, who is no longer able to control the powers of the nether world whom he has called up by his spells'.[2] The sorcerer of contemporary capitalism has generated major contradictions. But, unlike Marx, we argue that the contradiction is not so much that of class conflict resulting from the growth of the revolutionary proletariat, but from how twentieth-century capitalist relations of production have undermined the very forces of future capitalist production.

In this new century, capitalism may be unable to control those powers that it called up by its mesmeric spells, set in motion during the unprecedented, high-carbon twentieth century. Thus, as Leahy writes: 'capitalism could come to a sticky end . . . without the supposedly essential ingredient of a revolutionary proletariat. Capitalism as a growth economy is impossible to reconcile with a finite environment.'[3] In particular, the high-carbon economy/society of the last century is the emergent contradiction with multiple positive feedbacks that twentieth-century capitalism unleashed. It was the genie that got let out of the bottle, especially because of the emphasis upon the mobilizing of people's lives, and that cannot easily be put back into that bottle. Capitalism is no longer able to control the exceptional powers that it generated, especially through new forms of excessive mobility and consumption, which undermine long-term forces of production through changing climates, eliminating scarce resources and undermining some conditions of human life and its predictable improvement. In the twentieth century, powerful, high-carbon, path-dependent systems were set in place, locked in through various economic and social institutions. And as the century unfolded, those lock-ins meant that the world came to be left with a high and unsustainable carbon legacy.

We thus presume a clear distinction between twentieth-century high-carbon societies and the twenty-first century, increasingly characterized by oil shortages, huge population increases and, hence, unsustainable resource needs, and the developing impacts of global climate change. Future generations may consider the ultra-high-carbon hubris of the last century to have been excessive and all-consuming as they pick over the legacy now remaining in their century.

How then did we get to this state of affairs? There were, we would argue, an array of powerful high-carbon systems that were unleashed in the middle years of the last century. These systems, interdependent with each other, produced a powerful, locked-in legacy or a 'system of systems'.[4] These five interdependent systems were:

- the development of electric power and national grids, ensuring that more or less every home in the global north is lit, heated and populated with electric-based consumer goods;
- the spread of the steel-and-petroleum car (with now over 650 million cars worldwide) and associated roads and widely distributed, or sprawling, infrastructure;
- the development of suburban housing that is distant from places of work and that must be commuted to and then filled with household consumption goods powered by electricity;
- the emergence of various technologies such as stand-alone telephones, computers, laptops, networked computers, mobile phones,

BlackBerries and so on, that network geographically dispersed colleagues, friends and families;

- the proliferation of many specialized leisure sites, fast food, national parks, sports stadia, theme parks, most necessitating long-distance travel from home and neighbourhood, especially by car and plane.

Many of these systems were initially trialled and developed as mass forms within the US, before and after the Second World War. These interdependent, high-carbon systems were a product of the American Dream and involved public funding for each system and their growing, path-dependent interrelationships. The American Century, as the twentieth century should be termed, involved the developing of the conditions for these five interdependent systems and then their moving out around the world via the actions of American firms and the military and American cultural practices. These spread the American Dream and forged the rise of the American Empire. Through these systems and military power, 'the USA shapes the world'.[5]

However, there is a huge contradiction in this. The US seeks to spread the American Dream worldwide (sometimes referred to as empire via 'coca-colonization'). And yet it is impossible for the rest of the world to have anything like the same scale or share of the world's resources as the US. The US accounts for one-third of global wealth, 22 per cent of world energy consumption and one-quarter of total carbon emissions. Its population is only 5 per cent of the world's total.[6] Even the rich EU bloc consumes energy and resources at only half the American scale.

With regard to movement, the US drives almost a third of the world's cars and produces nearly half of the world's transport-generated carbon emissions.[7] It would be impossible for the rest of the world to share this American Dream. This Dream is only possible through monopoly of the world's resources. American mobile lives have got there first, we might say. Moreover, the world's resources are in some cases, such as oil, highly limited and likely to become more so. There could be no literal globalization of mobile lives.

Indeed, climate change and increasing resource constraints are the outcome of powerful systems that are like a 'juggernaut' careering at full speed to the edge of the cliff.[8] To slow down, let alone reverse, increasing carbon emissions and temperatures and reducing resources for a mobile life requires the wholesale reorganization of social life and, in particular, the setting of these five systems into 'reverse' gear.

However, this is a massively challenging task, as such systems and the more general development of a 'borderless world' were enhanced in the last quarter of the last century through neo-liberalism.[9] This predominant form of economic, political and social restructuring transformed one economy and society after another.[10] As we saw in Chapter 6, neo-liberalism asserts the power and importance of private entrepreneurship, private property rights, the deregulation of markets and the freeing of trade. It elevates market exchanges over and above all other sets of connections between people, and asserts that the 'market' is the source of value and virtue. Deficiencies in the market are thought to be the result of its contingent imperfections and not its structural form.

States are often central to the elimination of 'unnatural' forces, to the destruction of many pre-existing sets of rules, regulations and forms of life seen as slowing down markets and economic growth. And sometimes that destruction is exercised through violence and attacks upon democratic procedures, as in Pinochet's first neo-liberal experiment in Chile in 1973. The state is often used to wipe the slate clean and to impose sweeping free-market solutions, as, from 1973 onwards, in Latin America, Reagan's US, Thatcher's Britain, post communist-Russia and eastern Europe, 'communist' China, post-apartheid South Africa and indeed much of the world.[11] We saw in Chapter 6 just how neo-liberalism has been central to developing those twentieth-century mobile lives we examine in this book. We will now consider some of the processes that are undermining uninterrupted growth and the spreading of mobile 'forces of production' in this twenty-first century.

Climates, energy and people

First, and most dramatically, twentieth-century capitalism seems to have resulted in changing global temperatures. They have risen over the past century by at least 0.74°C, and this appears to result from higher levels of greenhouse gases in the earth's atmosphere.[12] Greenhouse gases trap the sun's rays. As a result of this 'greenhouse' effect, the earth warms. More-over, such greenhouse-gas levels and world temperatures will further increase significantly over the next few decades. With 'business as usual' and no significant reductions in high-carbon systems, the stock of green-house gases could treble by the end of the century. The Stern Review states that average temperatures may rise within a few decades by between 3°C and a staggering 10°C (rather than the 6°C most analysts suggest). There could be a 5–20 per cent reduction in world consumption levels.[13] Even a worldwide temperature increase of 3°C overall is completely beyond known experience and would change temperature patterns, rainfall, crops, animals and life worldwide.

The scientific evidence for climate change is less uncertain than when the first Intergovernmental Panel on Climate Change (IPCC) report appeared in 1990. By the 2007 report, the IPCC declared that the warming of the world's climate is now 'unequivocal', based upon extensive observations of increases in global average air and ocean temperatures, widespread melting of snow and ice and rising global average sea levels. The report further shows that carbon dioxide is the most important of the human-produced, or anthropogenic, greenhouse gases. Its concentration levels exceed by far the natural range identified over the past 650,000 years. Carbon dioxide's high and rising levels thus stem from 'non-natural' causes. There are many elements of global warming: increase in Arctic temperatures, reduced size of icebergs, melting of icecaps and glaciers, reduced permafrost, changes in rainfall, reduced biodiversity, new wind patterns, droughts, heatwaves, tropical cyclones and other extreme weather events.[14]

Through the IPCC, the organized actions of thousands of scientists around the globe have come to transform public debate, and this is also reflected in various movies, including *The Day after Tomorrow* (2004), *An Inconvenient Truth* (2006) and *The Age of Stupid* (2009).[15] This organized 'power of science' is probably unique in its mobilizing of actions and events around the perceived crisis of global climate change. This emerging climate change orthodoxy has mostly marginalized 'climate change deniers', with around 2005 marking the year when the climate change debate seems to have tipped.[16] The Pentagon announced that climate change will result in a global catastrophe, costing millions of lives in wars and natural disasters, and is a much greater threat to global stability than that of terrorism. Sir David King, the UK government's chief scientific adviser in 2004, claimed that climate change is a far greater threat to world security than that of international terrorism.

However, there is still significant uncertainty as to the scale, impact and speed of future climate change over the next century. The global climate models used to predict rates of greenhouse gases and temperature increases contain very many 'unknowns', what Beck terms the 'inability-to-know'.[17] The IPCC reports are based on reaching a complex scientific and political consensus and thus do not factor in all the potential and more uncertain feedback effects. As world temperatures increase over the next few decades, these increases will almost certainly trigger *further* temperature rises as the earth's environmental systems are unable to absorb the original increases.[18] The most dramatic of these positive feedbacks would involve the whole or partial melting of Greenland's ice cap. This would change sea and land temperatures worldwide, including the possible turning off or modification of the Gulf Stream. Another potentially significant feedback involves how climate change has led to the first recorded melting of the Siberian permafrost, with the potential subsequent release of billions of tons of the most powerful greenhouse gas, namely methane.[19] Climate change produces climate change as, according to Lovelock, 'there is no large negative feedback that would countervail temperature rise'.[20]

Moreover, recent ice core research shows that, in previous glacial and inter-glacial periods, abrupt and rapid changes occurred in the earth's temperature. Earth does not engage in gradual change.[21] Rapid changes have been the norm not the exception. Moreover, temperatures at the time of the last Ice Age were only 5°C colder than they are now. And, in the Arctic, recent increases in temperature have been really marked, with feedbacks creating local warming of 3–5°C over the past thirty years.

Thus, various diverse yet interconnected changes within the earth's environmental systems could create a vicious circle of accumulative disruption occurring, as Pearce expresses it, 'with speed and violence'. The World Health Organization calculated as early as 2000 that over 150,000 deaths are caused each year by climate change, such changes being global, cross-generational and highly unequally distributed around the world.[22] The planet will endure, but many forms of human habitation, especially those that involve being 'on the move', may not. Moreover, climate change is increasingly intersecting with a global energy crisis, and this may further undermine those mobile lives examined in this book.

There are many ways in which today's global economy and society are deeply dependent upon, and embedded into, abundant cheap oil. Most industrial, agricultural, commercial, domestic and mobility systems are built around the plentiful supply of 'black gold'. Homer-Dixon notes: 'Oil powers virtually all movement of people, materials, foodstuffs, and manufactured goods – inside our countries and around the world.'[23] It provides at least 95 per cent of transport energy. Oil is remarkably versatile, convenient and, during the twentieth century, was relatively cheap. Hence, 'the Great Addiction' (to oil) remained, as it became vital to virtually everything done and especially to everything that *moves* on the planet. This oil-based infrastructure was a twentieth-century phenomenon, with the US as *the* disproportionately high energy-producing and -consuming society.[24]

But the peaking of oil supplies occurred in the US as far back as 1970, famously predicted by Hubbert in 1956.[25] The US now imports 60 per cent of its oil, and this may rise to 75 per cent by 2030.[26] Worldwide, the largest oilfields were discovered over half a century ago, with the peak of oil discovery being in the mid 1960s. There have been no huge new discoveries since the 1970s. All but two of the world's hundred largest oilfields date from before 1970. Strahan refers to the 'imminent extinction of petroleum man' as, for every barrel of oil now being discovered, three to four are consumed.[27] Oil production may now have peaked, although this is hugely contested. There is a very pronounced rate of decline in production once an oilfield is over its peak, and most oilfields now are. Many commentators think that it will be difficult to raise the current production of oil much above the current output of 86 million barrels per day.[28]

Former Shell executive Jeremy Leggett describes the 'Empire of Oil' as being 'without doubt the most powerful interest group on the planet', more powerful than are most nation states.[29] And these private corporations and state enterprises have exaggerated the size of their reserves through various legal and illegal means, suggesting that the peaking of global oil is further away than other commentators tend to posit. Indeed, more and more energy is now required in order to extract the oil remaining in most fields.

Moreover, the power of the empire of oil has resulted in the foreign policies of many high-consuming states being significantly driven by global oil interests. According to some, the US's desire to increase oil access beyond its shores – as a result of the decline in domestic oil production – has resulted in its attempted subjugation of Middle Eastern oil interests in the name of the 'freedom' of citizens of the 'West' to drive and to heat/air-condition their homes.[30]

Energy will almost certainly become increasingly expensive, even with a long-term global depression, and there will be increasingly frequent shortages.[31] This is especially so with the world's population continuing to increase in size; its profligate consumption of oil to move almost everything, including water; its use of oil in almost all manufacturing and agricultural processes; and the exceptional rate of current and future urbanization. There is not enough oil to fuel such worldwide systems, with experts estimating that, with 'business as usual', global production would need to double by 2050.[32] Geo-political instabilities in many oil-producing countries are simultaneously producing increased fluctuations and destabilizations in oil supply and doubts about future energy security. Even relatively minor fluctuations result in oil-price spikes and protests both for and against cheap oil.[33]

The Age of Easy Oil occurred between the first discovery of oil in 1859 and its probable demise in the early decades of this century.[34] Overall, James Kunstler considers the system effects of such peaking of oil:

At peak and just beyond, there is massive potential for system failures of all kinds, social, economic, and political. Peak is quite literally a tipping point. Beyond peak, things unravel and the center does not hold. Beyond peak, all bets are off about civilization's future.[35]

The crucial issue is how societies around the world manage what some term the 'energy descent' at a time of potentially huge changes involving climate change and large increases especially in urban populations. The world went urban on 23 May 2007, this being 'transition day', when the world's urban population exceeded the rural.[36] And where once cities were viewed as the cradle of civilization, they now produce huge social inequalities, environmental decline and 'global slums' for at least one billion people.[37] These cities are places of death, with poor levels of public transportation and high use of cars. The result is 'sheer carnage', with 1 million people, many of whom never own a car, killed in road accidents each year in Third World cities.[38] And such city-based populations use much more oil and other expensive energy than rural populations. Helping to generate these urban slums is the growth in the world's population by about 900 million people per decade, the largest absolute increases ever recorded.[39] The world population is expected to reach 9.1 billion by 2050, that is if global warming, the peaking of oil, wars or global epidemics do not intervene by dramatically increasing death rates and reducing the scale of globalization.

There are some hugely significant consequences of these multiple, interdependent developments, such consequences being far worse in the global south and for women and children because of the 'climate of injustice':[40]

- Increases in the number and scale of 'failed states' and of 'failed city states' (such as late 2005, New Orleans): states are often unable to cope with oil shortages, droughts, heatwaves, extreme weather events, flooding, desertification, highly mobile diseases and the forced movement of up to 200 million environmental refugees.[41] States also have to deal with such issues, although their tax revenues have been recently reducing through the proliferation of tax havens designed to avoid or evade tax payments.
- Rising sea levels and storm surges: these will result in the flooding of roads, railways, transit systems and airport runways, especially in the coastal areas that are central to global transportation and shipping. This will also make problematic the continued movement of visitors in from the rich north. An early example could be the washing away of the

Maldives, something already being prepared for with the search for a 'new homeland'.[42]

- Growing insecurities in the supply of clean, usable water: there are huge demands from growing populations, especially those now moved to mega cities that have to both buy and transport their food and water from outside, using carbon-based systems. A global temperature increase of 2.1°C would expose up to 3 billion people to water shortages.[43] Some commentators now refer to 'peak ecological water', only 0.007 per cent of water on earth being available for human use.[44]

- Increasingly significant problems of food security: much food production depends upon hydrocarbon fuels to seed and maintain crops, to harvest and process them and to transport them to market, partly because of the exceptional food miles involved.[45] As oil shortages develop, 'food could be priced out of the reach of the majority of our population. Hunger could become commonplace in every corner of the world, including your own neighborhood'.[46] There will be many food protests with flooding, desertification and generally rising costs, as well as the tendency for 'rich' societies to buy up land in 'poor' societies to ensure food security (as is now happening in Qatar).

- Significant reductions in the standard of living around the world: rising energy consumption and efficiency have been major sources of expanding income and wealth around the world. Oil came to be embedded within the development of the high-carbon American economy and society. Oil made the world go round. But with reduced energy and the effects of climate change, world consumption levels and income will probably fall, as has happened every time oil price increases occurred over the past half-century. There could be a profound 'de-globalization'. When oil production goes past peak, so too may the size and effectiveness of the world economy and society.[47] After reviewing potential energy sources available in the twenty-first century, Leahy maintains that there 'is no way forward without a drastic reduction in consumption and production. As far as energy is concerned, the reduction has to be maintained indefinitely'[48] (whether developments in solar or new energy might produce a different outcome is, however, considered below).

These processes undermine the continuation of the high-carbon societies of the twentieth century. Such high-carbon forms of life cannot continue; there will be an ending to the carbon hubris that has been the overwhelming legacy of the last century. It is likely that components of that ending will occur sooner rather than later and in poorer places first, but with many effects elsewhere. Because these are 'global' risks to high-carbon economies and societies, their consequences will not be reducible to specific places but will seep out across much of the globe. Such global risks, according to Beck, involve: delocalization, spatially, temporally and socially; incalculability; and non-compensatability.[49]

Futures

We have thus seen how twentieth-century capitalism generated the most striking of contradictions. Its pervasive, mobile and promiscuous commodification involved utterly unprecedented levels of energy production and consumption, a high-carbon society whose dark legacy we are beginning to reap. This contradiction could result in a widespread reversal of many of the systems that constitute capitalism as it turns into its own gravedigger. A 'carbon shift' is inevitable. In the twenty-first century, capitalism seems to be unable to control those powers that it called up by the spells set in motion during the unprecedented high-carbon twentieth century, which reached its peak of global wastefulness within the neo-liberal period. So what does the future hold? If there is a major carbon shift, what kind of world can we anticipate by the middle of this century? Will it involve the reversal of the high-carbon movement that was the legacy of the twentieth century? How should we anticipate the future? How will future historians refer to the next few decades? Will they be known as the climate change years, or maybe even the end of (mobile) civilization years?

We now consider various scenarios of future societies that could feasibly exist by around 2050. We distinguish between futures that are possible, those that are probable and those that are preferable. And the last of these, the preferable futures, are often neither probable nor even possible. Moreover, even preferable futures will involve many winners and losers around the world. And achieving one set of goals means not achieving other goals. So there are very complex choices here, even if it were possible to establish which future is preferable at a general level and even how it could be best realized.

The four scenarios developed in this chapter are drawn from (but somewhat differ from) a Foresight Programme prepared for the UK government using scenario-building specialists. Various other scenarios for the middle of this century have also been consulted.[50] We set them out in a fairly general way, but it is clear that future patterns will unfold very unevenly within and especially across societies. Each scenario has very distinct implications for the future of the mobile lives described in previous chapters. But also it must be acknowledged that many visions of the future have previously not unfolded as had been predicted. As there are many 'failed technology futures', we at least set out some alternative future scenarios.[51]

Perpetual motion

The first scenario is that of hypermobility, that the patterns of mobile lives based on new communication and transportation practices develop on an extreme scale. Resource shortages and the effects of climate change turn out to be much less significant, with movement getting more extensive, frequent and part of people's very 'persona'. New sources of transportation energy (solar, hydrogen, nuclear or another) effect a move to a post-carbon, ultra-high-mobility future.

This is a 'hyper' world; people are 'always on', with messages and individual media continuously streamed to miniature intelligent devices, especially when 'on the move', which people would be much of the day and night. Average citizens are travelling four to five hours a day, and so overcoming the notion of a constant travel time. New kinds of fuel and vehicle overcome limits of space and time. Personalized air travel, São Paulo writ large, would be common through the use of second- (or third-) generation biofuels. Cars would be unfashionably stuck on the ground as a Corbusier-inspired future beckoned all to the skies, including regular flights into space with Virgin Galactica. Regular trips into at least inner space would be common.[52] The final frontier would indeed be overcome with the privatization of space travel, and the long decline of the idea of space travel would be reversed with the realization of multiple 'rocket dreams'.[53]

Devices will connect consumers directly with global wireless networks. The lifestyle and retail advantages of an 'always on' connection are clear. Such devices manage personal finances, using 'agent-based' technologies to switch funds automatically between different assets to maximize returns. They also make arrangements, and even friendships and appointments with others chosen for their presumed compatibility. More generally, people are forced into a life of 'distant connections' through others moving; hence, the even more extensive development of miniaturized communication devices, some implanted and constituting the sources of smart connections, friendships and practical arrangements.

There is also extensive telepresencing, involving both video-conferencing and virtual reality to create three-dimensional, high-speed, fluid interactions across different geographical locations. The software automatically stitches together feeds from several cameras by integrating the visual data from each camera's location and the direction in which it is pointing.

Moreover, travelling and having distant connections with those in other societies are the predominant forms of status, except for forced migrants and exiles. Electronic communications do not *substitute* for physical travel but enhance it. This is a global phenomenon, and so it is difficult to somehow stop those living in one society from engaging in such perpetual motion with significant others, and such reductions would anyway reduce economic and social well-being. Living a life 'on the screen' is still not as attractive as being with others in one's networks face-to-face from time to time.

In this highly connected world, social life and work are intense, and the boundaries between them increasingly blurred. Some thrive on the buzz of activity that results, but early burn-out is common, and stress is a way of life for most. Even low-paid service workers are so used to being 'always available' that holidays are no longer seen as a break. Stress is undoubtedly the major new health issue, with estimates suggesting that this costs a major proportion of national income.

This scenario is certainly not probable, given what we have argued above. However, it could just be that an unexpected 'technological fix' occurs that dramatically changes energy costs and availability, which somehow makes mass movement, especially above the ground, and multiple communications more or less cost-free. This has been described elsewhere as the 'Star Trek' vision of the future, and it could support a global population of 9 billion.[54] But many would consider that this scenario is less preferable to certain others because societies based on such high levels of movement will be even more unequal, with access to network capital being the major source of social inequality.

Local sustainability

The second scenario is what many environmentalists argue for, namely a worldwide reconfiguration of economy and society around 'local sustainability'. This Schumacher model would involve a network of self-reliant (and probably also semi-isolated) communities, in which people live, work and mostly recreate. This eco-communalism:

> could emerge from a New Sustainability Paradigm world if a powerful consensus arose for localism, diversity, and autonomy ... Eco-communalism might emerge in the recovery from 'breakdown'. Under conditions of reduced population and a rupture in modern institutions,

a network of societies, guided by a 'small-is-beautiful' philosophy conceivably could arise.[55]

This would involve some dramatic global shift towards lifestyles that are much more intensely local and smaller in scale. Friends would have to be chosen from neighbouring streets; families would not move away at times of new household composition; work would be found nearby; education would be sought only in local schools and colleges; the seasons would determine which foodstuffs were consumed and when; and most goods and services would be simpler and produced nearby. Indeed, it will be unfashionable to live and bring up children in anything apart from such 'compact cities' (a little like the way that suburban living became fashionable in the middle years of the twentieth century). Status attributions would have to be re-localized. This scenario depends upon new kinds of 'friendship', on choosing to know mostly those who live close by and can be walked to, and being unperturbed by a lack of long-distance travel and connections. Long-distance travel would be uncommon, and lives would again become organized around 'neighbourhood'.

There would have to be extensive building of such new local 'communes' to facilitate such localism. Planners, politicians and citizens would collaborate in the redesign of urban and rural centres, neighbourhoods and mobility systems focused upon local access and high-level facilities.[56] There would need to be some distinct new materials and techniques to enable the building of such compact cities. Indeed, the development of such compact places will probably require new kinds of legal entity, or private–public–community partnerships, simultaneously able to invest in and to develop various post-car means of individualized movement.

This may be in part a response to dramatically decreased availability of cheap energy and increased global contestation for what is available. For example, the intense economic meltdown triggered by the collapse of the US economy may be the harbinger of a global push to such local sustainability.[57] Alternatively, such a shift could result from climate change or environmental disruptions and resulting social conflict. If these geo-social disruptions are critical, this could produce increasing social disenchantment against privileged consumerist and especially mobile lifestyles. Values of community and eco-responsibility could, through a global crisis, come to be viewed as more valued than those of consumerism, competition and unrestrained mobility.

Such a 'contraction' in human affairs would open up opportunities for more revitalized and cooperative community-based social relations. James Kunstler predicts that 'the twenty-first century will be much more about staying put than about going to other places'.[58] In an extreme post-peak-oil scenario, the use of a car may be seen as a luxury. Resentment among those unable to drive because of oil shortages could lead to cars being vandalized or drivers being abused. Kunstler mainstains that the future will involve comprehensive downscaling, downsizing and re-localizing and the radical reorganization of lifestyles in the rich north. He states that:

> Any way one might imagine it, the transportation picture in the mid-twenty-first century will be very different from the fiesta of mobility we have enjoyed for the past fifty years. It will be characterized by austerity and a return to smaller scales of operation in virtually every respect of travel and transport. It will compel us to make the most of our immediate environments.[59]

Thus, there would be the partial replacement of the car system with a wide range of local forms of transport and movement. Long-distance movement is uncommon because of oil and resource shortages. Many forms of life are locally centred and concentrated. Because much movement is local, so feet, the bicycle and many new low-carbon forms of transport are found alongside motorized forms, with much recycling of vehicles and parts.

However, this scenario of local sustainability is 'possible' but not probable. It requires huge reversals of almost all the systems of the twentieth century, as well as a much smaller global population. There would have to be a massive restructuring of economic activities and the de-globalization of economy, finance and social life. There would be the large-scale reduction in the conventionally measured 'standard of living' and its replacement with the 'Happy Planet Index', where, in 2009, Costa Rica came out on top.[60]

It is hard to see all the events occurring that would seem necessary for its emergence. If climate change and peak oil effects are so overwhelmingly significant, creating a new 'disaster', then the next scenario is more probable than local sustainability, but much less preferable.

Regional warlordism

One scenario envisaged is 'tribal trading' or what we call 'regional warlordism'. This scenario is similar to what another report characterizes as 'barbarization'; here, the 'socio-ecological system veers toward worlds of sharply declining physical amenities and erosion of the social and moral underpinnings of civilization'.[61]

In this 'barbaric' climate change future, oil, gas and water shortages and intermittent wars lead to the substantial breakdown of many of the mobility, energy and communication connections that straddle the world and were the ambivalent legacy of the twentieth century. There would be a plummeting standard of living; a re-localization of mobility patterns; an increasing emphasis upon local 'warlords' controlling recycled forms of mobility and weaponry; and relatively weak national or global forms of governance. There would be no monopoly of physical coercion in the hands of national states.

Infrastructural systems would collapse, and there would be increasing separation between different regions, or 'tribes'. Systems of repair would dissolve, with increasingly localized recycling of bikes, cars, trucks and phone systems. Much of the time they would not be working. Cars and trucks would rust away in the deserts or would be washed away in floods. Certain consequences of climate change may partially rectify themselves, as oil and other resource use declines, and the overall world population may plummet. There is a post-oil localism.[62]

Systems of secured long-range mobility would disappear except for the super-rich. Rather like in mediaeval times, long-distance travel would be extremely risky and probably not engaged in unless people were armed. The rich would travel mainly in the air in armed helicopters or light aircraft. Each warlord-dominated region would potentially be at war with its neighbours, especially for control of water, oil and gas. With extensive flooding, extreme weather events and the break-up of long-distance oil and gas pipelines, these resources would be contested and defended by armed gangs. Those who could live in gated and armed encampments would do so, with the further neo-liberal privatizing of many collective functions.

This scenario could also be described as 'Fortress World'. One reaction to a global contraction of resources would be for richer nations to break away from poorer nations into protected enclaves. Outside such fortified enclaves there would be increasing 'wild zones', from which the rich and powerful would exit as fast as possible, if and when the oil, food and water no longer flow. Such wild zones would be left to ethnic, tribal or religious warlordism, to the multitudes that from time to time re-enter safe zones as migrants or as slaves or as terrorists. In Fortress World:

> the elite retreat to protected enclaves, mostly in historically rich nations, but in favoured enclaves in poor nations, as well . . . Technology is maintained in the fortresses . . . Local pollution within the fortress is reduced through increased efficiency and recycling.

Pollution is also exported outside the enclaves, contributing to the extreme environmental deterioration induced by the unsustainable practices of the desperately poor and by the extraction of resources for the wealthy.[63]

This scenario involves 'walled cities', similar in some ways to those in the mediaeval period and providing protection against raiders, invaders and diseases.

More generally, in September 2005, New Orleans captures what this scenario might be like for a major city in the rich but highly unequal 'north'.[64] TV pictures taken from low-flying helicopters demonstrated to the world what happens to those in a major city when an extreme weather event washes away much of the economic and network capital of the poor, including their capacity to move. These pictures showed how whole populations are 'disposable', as bloated corpses of the floating black poor were displayed on the hundreds of millions of TV screens around the world. Katrina also showed the vulnerability of the oil supply to the localized flooding that took place in the Mississippi delta. The world's refineries were already working to maximum capacity and could not raise production when the refineries in the Mississippi shut down, and so shortages were common, and oil prices soared.[65]

Even more starkly, parts of the global 'south' already show signs of transformation through global climate change. Bangladesh, on the low-lying Ganges, is the country worst affected by global climate change and yet produces tiny levels of carbon emissions. These emerging global relationships have been termed 'climatic genocide', with millions being forced to migrate away from global climate change risks, so far mainly experienced in the poor 'south'.[66] Life under this scenario would be nasty, brutish and 'shorter', both in the rich north and in the poor south, with the probable huge extension of global slums.

Some cars and trucks will remain, but they will mainly be rusting versions from previous decades. Enormous efforts and skills need to be deployed to keep these wrecks moving and to stop them being commandeered. Few new methods of movement are found. This is a post-mobility pattern. In some ways, the use and re-use of cars in current developing societies indicate the kind of improvisational, tinkering car culture likely to develop.[67] Many video games present versions of this *Mad Max 2* scenario, such as Supreme Ruler 2020. *Mad Max 2* famously depicts the future through a bleak, dystopian, impoverished society facing the breakdown of civil order because of oil shortages. Power comes to rest with those able to improvise new mobilities, including especially that of short-term flight.[68] Oil is indeed black gold in *Mad Max 2* scenarios. This might be a probable but not preferable future.

Digital networks

Adherents to the neo-liberal shock doctrine hold that crises can be productive of new forms of life in generating vast, clean canvases.[69] And remaking can often be undertaken through dispossessing people of their democratic and other rights. So global forces may find energy insecurity and climate change attractive, as this context could provide the clean slate to force through the fourth scenario here, the digital networks future that involves many new products and services to be developed and delivered by 'low-carbon' corporations.

Here, new software 'intelligently' works out the best means of doing tasks, whether this involves meeting up or getting to some place or event. If people did need to travel, then there would be small, ultra-light, smart, probably battery-based 'vehicles' that would be hired, a bit like the bikes that can be hired now in Paris or Barcelona. Streets would be full of often speed-controlled micro-cars, demand-responsive minibuses, bikes, hybrid vehicles and pedestrians, seamlessly integrated together with larger-scale public transport. Smart 'cards' control access and ensure payment for all forms of movement.

We may thus be close to a tipping point when personal vehicles come to be combined with a 'smart' infrastructure so as to develop an integrated network system rather than a series of separate vehicles. This would represent a major shift as personal vehicles are reconstituted as a system rather than as separate 'iron cages', which they were during the century of the car. Electronic regulators embedded in lampposts and in vehicles would regulate access, organize price and control the vehicle speed. Some such vehicles would be driverless. The movement of vehicles would be electronically and physically integrated with other forms of mobility. One future scenario describes the 'personal multimodal pod in which passengers can stay in comfort throughout a journey leaving all the hassle of switching between different transport modes and network levels to the pod'.[70] There is a mixed flow of those slow-moving micro-cars, as well as bikes, hybrid vehicles, pedestrians and mass transport. These are integrated into networks of physical *and* virtual access. There would be electronic coordination between motorized and non-motorized transport and between those 'on the move' in many different ways. This scenario would not involve a return to the *dominance* of publicly owned, managed and timetabled buses, trains, coaches and ships. That public mobility model has been lost because of the car system, which necessitates and generates individual flexibility, comfort and security of personal vehicles. This scenario involves the integration, through information, payment systems and physical access, between personal vehicles and collective forms of transport.

And, at the same time, neighbourhoods will be redesigned so as to foster 'access by proximity' through denser living patterns and integrated land use. People will live in denser, much more integrated urban areas that maximize co-presence. Such redesign would 'force' people to bump into each other, as their networks will overlap, and there will be many 'meeting places' for different groups of citizens.

This scenario would involve some notion of carbon allowances as the currency to be allocated, monitored and individually measured, so dramatically constraining much physical movement and other consumption forms. Where movement does occur, then this would be subject to rationing through price, or need or some kind of quota. It is clear that air and space travel would need to be the most heavily rationed of the forms of transport so far found.[71]

Much of the time, such physical travel would be replaced by virtual travel. These forms of virtual access will have developed so that they effectively simulate many features of physical co-presence with other people. An early version of this is the Halo system of video-conferencing, which simulates the illusion of a boardroom. As the website promises: 'life-size, real-time, eye-to-eye conferencing with outstanding audio and no delay. Halo gives the sense of being in the same room together. And best of all, it's right down the hall'.[72] Tele-immersion environments may be able to simulate the pleasures and especially the complexities of face-to-face interactions. They will enable users in different locations to collaborate in a shared, simulated environment as if they were in the same physical room. Computers will recognize the presence and movements of individuals and objects, track those images and then permit them to be projected in realistic, multiple, geographically distributed immersive environments, where individuals can interact with each other.[73]

Apart from such virtual environments, this scenario presupposes various digital technologies: data mining software; biometric security; integrated digital databases; the embedding of digital processing within the environment and moving vehicles; CCTV cameras; radio-frequency identity (RFID) implants to track objects and people; automated software systems for allocating road space; smart-code space to determine the route, price, access and speed of vehicles; and sensors and processors to enable vehicles to self-navigate.[74]

This scenario would seriously constrain the opportunities for physical movement. Components of this system are in place, and this is a distinctly possible future scenario. However, if we backcast from 2050 and consider what are the events necessary to make it come into being, there are some major complexities.

First, the tipping point in this scenario should not be read off from linear changes in existing firms, industries, practices and economies. Just as the internet and the mobile phone came from 'nowhere', so, if there is a tipping point here, it will emerge unpredictably. It will probably develop from a set of technologies or firms or governments that are not currently at the centre of the transport industry.[75] It is most likely that the post-car system will first emerge in a small society or city-state where there is very dense informational traffic, and with innovating market relations and a culture that fosters unexpected and disruptive innovation.

Second, such an infrastructure would be very costly to implement, although some of the 'hard technology' will be found in cities in the rich north over the next few years. But, at a time of increasing resource constraints because of climate change and financial crises, the costs may make it impractical to implement on a global scale, even if some prototype cities were able to develop such a model (city states such as Singapore). It is a 'first world' solution, although even here the difficulties of getting it to work are huge. And it would require utterly massive sums to develop such a system in the emerging mega cities of the poor south. Huge investment by private companies and large amounts of 'aid' from the rich north to the poor south would be necessary. But even then, there is the Jevons paradox: the more efficient the machines that are developed, such as low-carbon cars, then the more they will get used, and, hence, the less the energy that comes to be saved. To offset this Jevons paradox, it is almost certain that significant rationing will be needed.

Third, aspects of these digital developments threaten civil liberties.[76] They transform the nature of the individual person. Already, many states are seeking to integrate different databases that contain 'private' information on each person. This further extension would link that information with data on each person's movement by personal vehicle and public transport (as now with London's Oyster card). This would seriously limit the 'freedom' to walk, drive or move without record and without connections being made with other information held about that person. People and their movements become recorded and classified. However, 'smart solutions' will be contested in the name of 'freedom', especially within 'democratic' societies and where there is little 'trust' in the state. This contestation, at a time of many other conflicts around security and population management, will make such a scenario bitterly fought over. In this scenario, the future of *human* life may well depend upon moving across a tipping point to the 'digitization' of each self and the integration of multiple databases (what China calls the 'Golden Shield'). Such a system of tracking and tracing will involve noticeable changes to the very fabric of social life, freedom of movement and lifestyles.

This bargain involves what we might call a digital 'Orwellian-ization' of self and society, with more or less no movement without digital tracing and tracking and with few legally beyond or outside the control of digital networks. This may tame the car system (and other energy systems) if many developments take place simultaneously, including the tracking of each person's carbon allowance, which would function as the public measure of each person's worth and status.

Achieving that shift would require exceptional political leadership worldwide to ensure that personal rights are significantly protected. So far, there is no sign that states recognize the sheer economic, social and political complexities of implementing a future that would dramatically slow down the rate of carbon emissions, without huge reductions in personal freedom. And with large private-sector corporations devising new 'security products', there are many reasons why an illiberal securitized future is more likely.

Threats from climate change and limited energy supplies may become so palpable that there seems to be no alternative other than implementing systems of this sort. The shock of climate change may tip societies into these kinds of digital network and a post-car future. In any case, such freedoms have already been seriously curtailed with the worldwide 'securitization' of people's lives in the early years of this century. Under the sway of a post-September 11 atmosphere, and amid an orchestrated 'war on terror', many intrusive technologies are being introduced, so much so that the UK government's Information Commissioner says that people in Britain already live in a surveillance society.[77] But, if this is so, maybe people will conclude that such surveillance should be used for the purposes of 'defeating' climate change and will not necessarily contest the introduction of such a digital mobility future.

Multiple futures

So, there are four scenarios for the middle years of the twenty-first century. These could be described as the Corbusier, Schumacher, Hobbesian and Orwellian scenarios. None of these scenarios is without massive costs for human lives, democracy and social life. None is simply preferable, and none is obviously the most likely to develop. So whether, and to what degree, mobile lives continue is highly contestable. The reason for this constrained set of alternatives is the twentieth century. That century of unprecedented energy production and consumption paid little attention to future generations. The message with regard to mobility was 'drive and fly now', and the future will look after itself! We now know that the future will not look after itself, and indeed that the frequent drivers and flyers may soon be grounded if certain of these scenarios get to be realized.

Determinants of which scenario is more probable are the character and nature of the world economy and of economic discourse over the next few decades. We have already noted how neo-liberalism promotes the notion that only markets and the private sector should develop solutions to what economists term the external diseconomies of economic growth. Some neo-liberals simply expect the market to develop solutions without needing extra measures or state encouragement of any sort. The recent growth in biofuels is a good example of the kind of market solution favoured by neo-liberals to the peaking of oil and its dramatically rising price, and the growing scale of greenhouse emissions. It is probable that, for a further period, neo-liberalism will continue to set economic and political agendas, making widespread, concerted state actions to deal with climate change unlikely. This is also because states in an era of neo-liberalism are hugely beholden to the oil and other corporate interests that were routinely favoured in twentieth-century struggles.

But this is not certain, only probable. It could turn out that climate change and peak oil turn out to be issues of such significance that, through catastrophic events, they lead to the dramatic modification or rejection of neo-liberalism. After all, as economist Nicholas Stern writes, 'Climate change . . . is the greatest and widest-ranging market failure.'[78] Climate change shows that the private pursuit of individual gain around the world, especially since around 1990, has resulted in a collective outcome at the global level that threatens the future of capitalism. The private market seems to be destroying the very conditions of the market economy. There is an emergent contradiction at the heart of contemporary capitalism, and unfolding catastrophes might just tip economic and political discourse *and* practice away from neo-liberal orthodoxy.

Part of the strength of neo-liberalism had been its enabling the 'American empire' to remake much of the world in a neo-liberal vision. Neo-liberalism enabled American companies to dominate world markets. So-called freedom turned out to be the freedom of American companies to dispossess and then to take over industries, regions and whole countries. The US remade the world in its image through scores of bases worldwide, overt military power, think tanks, advisers, consultants and US-dominated international organizations such as the IMF and World Bank.

But this 'American empire' is now in relative decline, by comparison with the European Union, China and, in different ways, Islam.[79] The US is not the overwhelming global force, and it has to find its way within a world of contending powerful entities and a set of global processes that seem 'out of control'. This is, first, because the rest of the world no longer needs the US's 'protection' in relationship to the USSR, as during the long Cold War. More generally, there is a decline in the degree to which populations around the world 'admire' and look to the US as the obvious model of the 'good society', given its high rates of murder, crime, obesity, financial incompetence and fraud. Second, various sources of evidence on citations, patents and copyrights suggest that the US has not maintained the degree of scientific and technological leadership over the rest of the world, and especially over Europe, Japan and China, that it most possessed during the second half of the last century. Third, during the early years of the new century, the US has been isolated because of its refusal to implement the Kyoto Protocol dealing with climate change. Relatedly, its declining supplies of oil and gas noted above mean that it is reliant upon unstable, alternative and often distant and costly sources. Further, the US continues to generate huge budget, balance and payments deficits and extraordinary levels of indebtedness and financial insecurity. At the same time, the EU has so grown that its economy and society are now significantly larger than those of the US and it possesses in the euro the world's strongest currency (in early 2009) and one increasingly used for worldwide commodity transactions. Similarly, the rapidity of China's growth means that it will overtake the US in the sheer size of its market, in its very high level of savings and in its display of an alternative, if flawed, model of successful development to that of fundamentalist, deregulated market-capitalism.[80] Finally, the Great Crash of October 2008 commenced with the financial meltdown in American property markets, which has then spread worldwide. Instead of exporting the free-market American Dream, the US is exporting the American nightmare on Main Street. The highly mobile, consuming US is by no means still the undisputed world leader. The new century will be characterized by multiple and contending powerful forces.

Thus there is coming into play a set of perceptions, practices and policies that could tip contemporary societies into a post neo-liberal era of resource-capitalism, a capitalism in which there are massive limits surrounding the form, scale and character of economic and social practices and especially in the degree to which financialization is to be found. In September 2008, the value of the world's financial assets was $160 trillion, 3.5 times the value of world GDP.[81]

Climate change, like global financial crises and the peaking of oil, shows that the private pursuit of individual gain around the world has resulted in a collective outcome at the global level that undermines the very future of capitalism, hence the need for a resource-capitalism that delivers security, stability and sustainability. The long-term forces of production have to be regarded as the basis of all economies/societies. Resource-capitalism involves ensuring the long-term viability of the earth's resources, which capitalist economies/societies deploy and depend upon.

The need for such a resource-capitalism is now being articulated by various leading commentators. Stern's *The economics of climate change* is an attempt to bring about a new, post neo-liberal consensus. It concludes with the rallying cry that: 'reducing the risk of climate change requires collective action ... It requires a partnership between public and private sectors, working with civil society and with individuals.'[82] Likewise, Stiglitz's *Making globalization work* presents a similar, post neo-liberal line of argument, with chapters on making trade fair, lifting the resource curse, saving the planet and democratizing globalization. The book is organized around the claim that 'another world is possible'.[83] A further Nobel Prize-winner, Paul Krugman, critiques *The return of depression economics* and argues the need to develop a different economic model, especially from that of endlessly bursting bubbles.[84] Anthony Giddens, one of the West's leading 'public social scientists', has recently called for a positive model of a low-carbon future that will involve national and regional states thinking ahead, making interventions, countering businesses that block climate change initiatives, developing appropriate fiscal stimuli and planning overall for low-carbon futures.[85]

Future projections of the global economy and politics are exceptionally hard to figure out. But, if neo-liberalism was to be on a slippery slope because of the collapse of the American empire and the demise of the market fundamentalism post October 2008, and if climate change did become a matter of democratic politics and not just the opportunity for new corporate investment, then it might just be possible to avoid the scenarios of both perpetual motion and regional warlordism.

Catastrophe

But these are stiff conditions, and many writers by contrast are now arguing for a 'new catastrophism' in social thinking. Various academics, journalists, filmmakers and authors are claiming that, unless a huge array of changes rapidly occur, then the mobile, consuming society we have been describing in this book may go into reverse or indeed 'collapse'. A dooms-day scenario, an 'apocalypse now', is almost becoming commonplace.

Most notably, Jared Diamond maintains how environmental problems have, in the past, produced the 'collapse' of societies.[86] Populations grew and stretched natural resources, especially energy resources, to breaking point, particularly when such societies seemed to be at the very height of their powers. He suggests that human-caused climate change, the build-up of toxic chemicals in the environment and energy shortages will, in the twenty-first century, produce abrupt, potentially catastrophic decline. Such an apocalypse would consist of: increases in global temperatures that make much plant, animal and human life impossible; the running out of oil and gas; the increased lack of resilience of many societies; a global failure of economy and finance; population collapse; increasing resource wars; and huge food shortages; in short, a perfect storm that will make the Great Crash of 2008 seem a birthday party by comparison. Such processes will hugely constrain the possibilities of re-engineering future mobilities and energy uses so as to avoid a 'societal collapse', of the sort that happened to the apparently unchallengeable Roman Empire or the Mayan civilization, through internal contradictions.[87]

Other commentators are increasingly examining the nature of the current period of human history as that of the anthropocene. This developed from around 1800 and resulted in soaring carbon dioxide levels, a quantum step upward in erosion, widespread species extinction, ecosystem disturbance and ocean acidification. The earth moved in a fundamentally new direction, the anthropocene.

Within this period, mobile lives for millions could turn out to be only a short moment. For a century or so, the rich world went mad, before its contradictions so kicked in that twenty-first-century humans and machines will have to deal with a probably much slower legacy as societies go into reverse. The period of mobile lives may thus be a short interlude during the anthropocene period. Indeed, Joseph Tainter presciently wrote, over twenty years ago: 'however much we like to think of ourselves as something special in world history, in fact industrial societies [and their mobilities] are subject to the same principles that caused earlier societies to collapse.'[88]

Afterword

In recounting the stories of Simone, Sandra, Eisner, Robert and Gemma, we sought to describe mobile lives from the 'inside out', shifting from the terrain of ordinary, everyday mobilities to more extensive, global processes of mobility. We have shown that both of these orders – the everyday and the institutional – are highly structured and systematic. We have also shown, throughout the book, how mobile lives unfold on many different levels.

Mobile lives, first and foremost, are lived, experienced and reflected upon in the course of day-to-day life – with all of its pleasure and pressures. Everyday mobilization is intricately interwoven with what people feel, desire and think about their lives. Yet mobilities – physical, communicative, virtual – are also at the centre of broader institutional processes. Complex, powerful, interdependent knowledge-based systems constitute the mobilization of production, consumption, communications, networks and travel around the world. Understanding how mobile lives and mobility systems interweave and dislocate is crucial to grasping, as well as confronting, the politics of movement – of people, goods, information and ideas – in the contemporary age. Such interweaving and dislocation of mobile lives and mobility systems, we have argued, operate as assemblages that move both subjects and objects around. Mobile lives are organized into various assemblages – from miniaturized mobilities to portable personhood – in the constitution of contemporary mobility processes. We have written this book as a contribution to the analysis and critique of societies, systems, places and lives on the move.

Much of this book has concentrated on the current dominant mobility systems that developed during the 'mobility century', based especially on oil. However, as a consequence of the peaking of world oil and gas supplies, and when set in the context of the cataclysmic dangers posed by global warming, we also discussed alternative mobility futures and the lives or lifestyles that they may promote. It is clear from the mobile lives of Simone, Sandra, Robert and Gemma that many people are only at the beginning of confronting the threats, risks and dangers to which a world of extensive and intensive mobilities has given rise. There are also those – such as globals like Eisner – who refuse to face up to such collective dangers. But still, this leaves the troubling question of futures open. What then of future generations? What possible futures for the children and grandchildren of those whose stories we have told throughout this book? What might be the future contours of their mobile lives?

From one angle, such questions are plainly more or less unanswerable. There are simply too many variables, unknowns, contingencies and counter-factuals involved. But we should not underestimate the collective risks faced when assessing possible future trajectories of mobile lives. As Giddens warns:

> Our civilization could self-destruct – no doubt about it – and with awe-some consequences, given its global reach. Doomsday is no longer a religious concept, a day of spiritual reckoning, but a possibility imminent in our society and economy. If unchecked, climate change alone could produce enormous human suffering. So also could the drying up of the energy resources upon which so many of our capacities are built. There remains the possibility of large-scale conflicts, perhaps involving the use of weapons of mass destruction. Each could intersect with the others.[1]

It is against this disturbing backdrop that the future scenarios outlined in the last chapter – the Corbusier, Schumacher, Hobbesian and Orwellian scenarios – take on an even more tragic dimension. Whatever hopes there may be for future mobile lives, they are restricted by potentially catastrophic global processes – the very destructive reach of which might bring the world's existing mobile ways of life to a shuddering end.

Nevertheless, if social theory is to engage with the question of mobile futures, it must develop emancipatory and utopian resources. It must confront the imaginative capabilities of people to create fresh opportunities from even the most unpromising global situations. Glimmerings of Utopia, as Herbert Marcuse famously argued, are always discernible in current social practices – no matter how repressed or distorted.[2] How then to press for new mobile futures from the present? What kind of fresh thinking do today's mobile lives demand for the world's possible mobile lives of tomorrow? The great global crash of 2008 and the wider social consequences of worldwide economic stagnation generated various responses. In spite of the massive costs arising from high-carbon economy and society, it is still possible that today's mobile lives could function as a springboard for creating more sustainable lives in the future.

One striking development is the Transition Towns movement, which seeks to move the world from 'oil dependency to local resilience'. This movement was founded in Kinsale, Ireland, and then spread to Totnes, England, during 2005 and 2006. It has now spread around the world, especially recently. It seeks to develop policies to deal with the global significance of the ending of the 'petroleum interval' that we discussed in the last chapter. It starts off when a small collection of motivated individuals within a set of neighbourhoods come together with a shared concern of how they can respond to the challenges, and opportunities, of peak oil and climate change.[3] A Transition Initiative involves a locality working together to address the question: for all those aspects of life that this community needs in order to sustain itself and thrive, how does it significantly increase resilience to mitigate the peaking of oil (and drastically reduce carbon emissions to mitigate the effects of climate change)?

The downside of this movement is that it is localist in orientation and, hence, ignores many of the ongoing processes that structure and restructure the world, especially those involving a complex global division of economic and social labour. Indeed, there are so many mobile relations that make developing and implementing local solutions difficult or impossible, except as exemplars of future development.

A second development has been the dramatic rise in virtual meetings and videoconferencing as one outcome of the 2008 collapse. Companies and organizations turned to new digital technologies when facing the dilemma of reconciling the need for business travel with depressed profitability and increased costs of air travel as airlines went out of business and reduced flight frequencies.[4] Virtual communicative innovation allows organizations to save funds on flights, hotels and the leasing of office facilities while keeping employees geared towards global business engagement and market opportunities. Companies such as Cisco Systems have poured billions of dollars into developing specialized software for developing and marketing video-conferencing systems, recognizing that the future of business networking substantially depends upon communicative/virtual travel outstripping physical travel in the relatively near future.[5]

But there is no free lunch. It may be that, whatever virtual futures there are, living 'lives on the screen' is less satisfying than frequent meetings. Meetingness is a crucial human property and value, the stuff of social life. Indeed, we saw in Chapter 2 how Sandra finds that digital technologies can switch from containment to engulfment. By contrast, co-present talk is embodied and may involve food, drink, music and a shared physical place, places temporarily 'full of life'. Thus, what would need development is a virtual meetingness that effectively substitutes all, or at least most, of these emotional pleasures of being present with others face-to-face, emotion-to-emotion, body-to-body. So far, there is no digital technology that begins to achieve this. Also, we should note that virtual mobility is also much more carbon energy-intensive than previously realized, and this will be even more the case if very large bandwidth is used to simulate meetingness in the ways that we have just proposed.[6]

Third, consider that emblem of a post-global warming future, renewable energy. It is now widely agreed that the search for renewable power is fundamental to the struggle to limit catastrophic climate change. What is interesting, though, is the current exploitation of mobilities in the search for large flows of renewable energy – as companies, organizations and states work together across borders, undertaking many activities focused on alternative energy sources. European government and industry, for example, are developing a range of programmes for massive solar thermal plants spread across the Middle East and Sahara. The programmes aim, not only to provide renewable power to their host nations, but also to generate 15 per cent of Europe's electricity needs by 2050.[7] These solar thermal plans are projected to cost hundreds of billions of euros. Many administrators from European countries, as well as representatives from companies including Siemens, Deutsche Bank and Swiss Re, are involved in actively mobilizing throughout the world, seeking to establish frameworks and regulations for the realization of such a vast programme.

Yet again, the situation is far from clear-cut. Such alternative energy projects generate as many dilemmas as they claim to solve. One concern is that proposed solutions to the world's energy problems, from biofuel refineries to certain types of solar farm, result in the consumption of billions of gallons of water every year. The Solar Millennium project – financed by a German developer and comprising two large solar farms generating electricity in the Nevada desert – is estimated to consume 1.3 billion gallons of water each year to cool its power plants.[8] In this case, the attempt to create renewable energy security is actually bound up with potential destructive impacts upon the environment and thus functions as another threat to the future of mobile lives! Free lunches there are not, and this will also relate to these massive solar projects.

There are thus immense complexities involved in building sustainable mobile lives for the future. The fostering of new opportunities, it seems, is always deeply interwoven with fresh risks. But the current diversity of mobile lives should not stand in the way of preparing for the future, or indeed of planning for alternative mobile futures. As a new politics emerges around issues of movement and mobilities, many people seek to break from the orthodoxies of the present and consider new mobile paths of living. This book has been a contribution to further opening up the politics and practices of people's lives and their intermittent and deeply problematic mobilities.

References and notes

Preface

1 Andreas Schafer and David Victor, 'The future mobility of the world population', *Transportation Research A*, 2000, 34: pp. 171–205, 171.
2 Much of the empirical research for this project arises from funding secured from the Australian Research Council in the form of a Discovery Project Grant (DP877817). Some interview material is drawn from a Large Research Grant awarded by the British Academy and from a New Horizons project funded by the UK Department for Transport. Regarding the sociological method of semi-fictionalized case studies, see Anthony Elliott and Charles Lemert, *The new individualism: the emotional costs of globalization* (London and New York: Routledge, 2nd edition, 2009), pp. 196–7; and see, also, Susie Orbach, *The impossibility of sex* (Harmondsworth: Penguin, 1999).

1 Mobile lives: a step too far?

1 Leo Tolstoy, *A confession and other writings* (Harmondsworth: Penguin, 1987), p. 165.
2 This figure of Simone is a composite of various cases examined for this project and drawn from research funded by the Australian Research Council Discovery Grant.
3 Mark Buchanan, *Nexus: small worlds and the groundbreaking science of networks* (London: W.W. Norton, 2002), p. 121. More generally, see Aharon Kellerman, *Personal mobilities* (London: Routledge, 2006); Tim Cresswell, *On the move* (London: Routledge, 2006); and John Urry, *Mobilities* (Cambridge: Polity Press, 2007).
4 See Jonas Larsen, John Urry and Kay Axhausen, *Mobilities, networks, geographies* (Aldershot: Ashgate, 2006), on 'friendship' miles.
5 Nicholas Stern, *The economics of climate change. The Stern Review* (Cambridge: Cambridge University Press, 2007), p. 197.
6 See Staffan Linder, *The harried leisure class* (New York: Columbia University Press, 1970).
7 This is explored in Jonas Larsen, John Urry and Kay Axhausen, *Mobilities, networks, geographies* (Aldershot: Ashgate, 2006).

8   See Mark Buchanan, *Nexus: small worlds and the groundbreaking science of networks* (London: W.W. Norton, 2002); Duncan Watts, *Six degrees* (London: William Heinemann, 2003); and Jonas Larsen, John Urry and Kay Axhausen, *Mobilities, networks, geographies* (Aldershot: Ashgate, 2006), chapter 11.

9   On the concept of 'detraditionalization', see Anthony Giddens, *Modernity and self-identity* (Cambridge: Polity Press, 1991); and Ulrich Beck, Anthony Giddens and Scott Lash, *Reflexive modernization: politics, tradition and aesthetics in the modern social order* (Cambridge: Polity Press, 1994).

10 This patterning is explored in the case of media workers in London in Andreas Wittel, 'Towards a network sociality', *Theory, Culture and Society*, 2001, 18: pp. 31–50.

11 Dale Southerton, 'Squeezing time: allocating practices, co-ordinating networks and scheduling society', *Time and Society*, 2001, 12: pp. 5–25.

12 Martin Heidegger, *Being and Time*, trans. John Macquarie and Edward Robinson (New York: Harper & Row, 1962).

13 Scott Lash and John Urry, *Economies of signs and space* (London: Sage, 1994), chapter 9; Hartmut Rosa and William Scheuerman (eds.), *High-speed society* (Pennsylvania: Pennsylvania State University Press, 2009).

14 See, for early formulations, Scott Lash and John Urry, *The end of organized capitalism* (Cambridge: Polity Press, 1987); and David Harvey, *The condition of postmodernity* (Oxford: Blackwells, 1989).

15 Homi Bhabha, *The location of culture* (London: Routledge, 1994), p. 88. See Bülent Diken and Carsten Bagge Laustsen, *The culture of exception. Sociology facing the camp* (London: Routledge, 2005), pp. 86–8.

16 Christopher Bollas, *Being a character: psychoanalysis and self experience* (New York: Hill and Wang, 1992).

17 See Kingsley Dennis and John Urry, *After the car* (Cambridge: Polity, 2009), chapter 1.

18 Barry Wellman, 'Physical place and cyber place: the rise of networked individualism', *International Journal of Urban and Regional Research*, 2001, 25: pp. 227–52.

19 Zygmunt Bauman, *Globalization: the human consequences* (Cambridge: Polity Press, 1988), p. 2.

20 John Urry, *Mobilities* (Cambridge: Polity, 2007).

21 On the concept of cultural and economic capital, see Pierre Bourdieu, *Distinction: a social critique of the judgement of taste*, trans. Richard Nice (Cambridge: Harvard University Press, 1984); and *The logic of practice*, trans. Richard Nice (Cambridge: Polity Press, 1990). On symbolic power, see Pierre Bourdieu in his *Language and symbolic power*, ed. J.B. Thompson (Cambridge: Polity Press, 1991).

22 John Urry, *Mobilities* (Cambridge: Polity, 2007), pp. 197–8.

23 See Barry Wellman, Bernie Hogan, Kristen Berg, Jeffrey Boase, Juan-Antonio Carrasco, Rochelle Côté, Jennifer Kayahara, Tracy L.M. Kennedy and Phuoc Tran, 'Connected lives: the project', in Patrick Purcell (ed.), *Networked neighbourhoods* (Berlin: Springer, 2005); Albert-László Barabási, *Linked: the new science of networks* (Cambridge, MA: Perseus, 2002); and Kay Axhausen,

'Social networks and travel: some hypotheses', *Arbeitsbericht Verkehrs- und Raumplanung 197*, (Zürich: ETH, 2003).

24 Ulrich Beck and Elizabeth Beck-Gernsheim, *Individualization* (London: Sage, 2000). On the complexities of making and remaking arrangements for such a life, see Jonas Larsen, John Urry and Kay Axhausen, 'Coordinating face-to-face meetings in mobile network societies', *Information, Communication and Society*, 2008, 11: pp. 640–58.

25 James R. Lawler (ed.), *Paul Valéry: an anthology* (Princeton, NJ: Princeton University Press, 1977).

26 Tim Ingold, 'Culture on the ground', *Journal of Material Culture*, 2004, 9: pp. 315–40.

27 Manuel DeLanda, *A new philosophy of society: assemblage theory and social complexity* (London: Continuum, 2006).

28 Patricia Clough, Sam Han and Rachel Schiff, 'Review – *A new philosophy of society*', *Theory, Culture and Society*, 2007, 24: pp. 387–93.

29 This is a shortened and revised version of John Urry, *Mobilities* (Cambridge: Polity, 2007), chapter 3; see Mimi Sheller and John Urry, 'The new mobilities paradigm', *Environment and Planning A, 2006, 38: pp. 207–26.

30 Mary Chayko, *Connecting: how we form social bonds and communities in the internet age* (New York: State University of New York Press, 2002), pp. 69–70; see Émile Durkheim, *The elementary forms of the religious life* (London: George Allen and Unwin, 1915).

31 James Gibson, *The ecological approach to visual perception* (Boston: Houghton Mifflin, 1986), chapter 8.

32 See, on aeromobility and globalization, Saolo Cwerner, Sven Kesselring and John Urry (eds.), *Aeromobilities* (London: Routledge, 2009).

33 See Daniel Miller (ed.), *Car cultures* (Oxford: Berg, 2000).

2 New technologies, new mobilities

1 Christopher Bollas, *Being a character: psychoanalysis and self experience* (New York: Hill and Wang, 1992), p. 59.

2 The figure of Sandra is a composite of two case studies for research funded by an Australian Research Council Discovery Grant (DP877817).

3 See Eric Laurier, 'Doing office work on the motorway', *Theory, Culture & Society*, 2004, 21: pp. 261–77.

4 See Michael Bull, 'Automobility and the power of sound', *Theory, Culture & Society*, 2004, 21: pp. 243–59.

5 See www.pbs.org/transistor/background1/events/transfuture.html. Our thanks to Dan Mendelson for pointing out these developments and the research on them.

6 Paul du Gay, Stuart Hall, Linda Janes, Hugh Mackay and Keith Negus, *Doing cultural studies: the story of the Sony Walkman* (London: Sage, 1997), p. 17. The reference in the following paragraph is also to p. 17.

7 Manuel Castells, 'Informationalism, networks and the network society: a theoretical blueprint', in Manuel Castells (ed.), *The network society* (Cheltenham: Edward Elgar, 2004), p. 7.

8   Nigel Thrift, 'Movement-space: the changing domain of thinking resulting from the development of new kinds of spatial awareness', *Economy and Society*, 2004, 33: p. 583.

9   Barry Wellman, 'Physical space and cyberplace: the rise of personalized networking', *International Journal of Urban and Regional Research*, 2001, 25: p. 238.

10   See John Urry, *Mobilities* (Cambridge: Polity, 2007), Chapter 5.

11   Karin Knorr Cetina, 'How are global markets global? The architecture of a flow world', *Economics at Large Conference*, 14–15 November 2003.

12   Rich Ling, *The mobile connection* (Amsterdam: Elsevier, 2004).

13   See Jonas Larsen, Kay Axhausen and John Urry, 'Geographies of social networks: meetings, travel and communications', *Mobilities*, 2006, 1: pp. 261–83. Also see www.nytimes.com/2008/04/13/magazine/13anthropology-t.html for further elaboration on 'just-in-time' moments.

14   Glenn Lyons and John Urry, 'Travel time use in the information age', *Transport Research A*, 2005, 39: 257–76.

15   Glenn Lyons, Juliet Jain, David Holley, 'The use of travel time by rail passengers in Great Britain', *Transportation Research Part A: Policy and Practice*, 2007, 41(1): 107–20.

16   See Anthony Elliott, *Social theory and psychoanalysis in transition* (London: Free Association Books, 2nd edition, 1999).

17   See Patricia Clough, *Auto-affection: unconscious thought in the age of technology* (Minneapolis, MN: University of Minnesota Press, 2000).

18   For an overview of psychoanalytic contributions to the analysis of technological containment, see Anthony Elliott, *Subject to ourselves: social theory, psychoanalysis and postmodernity* (Boulder, CO: Paradigm Press, 2004). Also see Mark Poster, *The second media age* (Cambridge: Polity Press, 1995).

19   See Vincent Kaufmann, *Re-thinking mobility: contemporary sociology* (Aldershot: Ashgate, 2002).

20   See Paul Ricoeur, *Freud and philosophy* (New Haven, CT: Yale University Press, 1970). See also Anthony Elliott, *Psychoanalytic theory: an introduction* (Durham, NC: Duke University Press, 2002).

21   See Anthony Elliott, *Social theory since Freud* (London and New York: Routledge, 2004).

22   Wilfred Bion, *Learning from experience* (London: Heinemann, 1962).

23   Anthony Elliott, *Subject to ourselves: social theory, psychoanalysis and postmodernity* (Boulder, CO: Paradigm Press, 2004), chapters 4 and 5. See also Stephen Frosh, *Identity crisis* (London: Macmillan, 1991).

24   Christopher Bollas, *Being a character: psychoanalysis and self experience* (New York: Hill and Wang, 1992), p. 60 and, for following quotation, p. 59.

25   See Christopher Bollas, *The Shadow of the Object: Psychoanalysis and the unknown thought* (New York: Columbia University Press, 1987).

26   George Atwood and Robert Stolorow, *Structures of subjectivity: explorations in psychoanalytic phenomenology* (Hillsdale, NJ: The Analytic Press, 1984), pp. 88–9.

27   See Kimberly Young and Robert Rodgers, 'The relationship between depression and Internet addiction', *CyberPsychology and Behavior*, 1998, 1(1): pp. 25–8.

28 See M. Bernanuy, Ursula Oberst, Xavier Carbonell and Chammaro, 'Problematic Internet and mobile phone use and clinical symptoms in college students', *Computers in Human Behavior*, 2009, 25(5): pp. 1182–7.

29 Mielzo Takahira, Reiko Ando and Akira Sakamoto 'Effect of internet use on depression, loneliness, aggression and preference for internet communication', *International Journal of Web Based Communities*, 2008, 4(3): pp. 302–18.

30 Sherry Turkle, *Life on the screen* (London: Weidenfeld and Nicolson, 1996).

31 Norman H. Nie, D. Sunshine Hillygus and Lutz Erbing, 'Internet use, interpersonal relations and sociability', in Barry Wellman and Caroline Haythornthwaite (eds.) *The Internet in everyday life* (Oxford: Blackwell, 2002), pp. 215–43.

3 Networks and inequalities

1 Filippo Tommaso Marinetti, 'The new religion-morality of speed', in Hartmut Rosa and William Scheuerman (eds.), *High-speed society* (Pennsylvania: Pennsylvania State University Press, 2009), p. 59.

2 See, for earlier formulations, Jonas Larsen, John Urry and Kay Axhausen, *Mobilities, networks, geographies* (Aldershot: Ashgate, 2006); and John Urry, *Mobilities* (Cambridge: Polity, 2007).

3 Manuel Castells, *The rise of the network society* (Oxford: Blackwell, 1996), p. 469.

4 Luc Boltanski and Eve Chiapello, *The new spirit of capitalism* (London: Verso, 2007), p. 355.

5 Ronald Burt, *Structural holes* (Cambridge, MA: Harvard University Press, 1992).

6 Luc Boltanski and Eve Chiapello, *The new spirit of capitalism* (London: Verso, 2007), pp. 363–4.

7 Yochai Benckler, *The wealth of networks: how social production transforms markets and freedom* (New Haven, CT: Yale University Press, 2006).

8 Charlie Leadbetter, *We-think* (London: Profile Books, 2008).

9 See Meric Gertler, 'Tacit knowledge and the economic geography of context, or the undefinable tacitness of being (there)', *Journal of Economic Geography*, 2003, 3: pp. 75–99.

10 Sue Durbin, 'Who gets to be a knowledge worker? The case of the UK call centres', in Sylvia Walby, Heidi Gottfried, Karin Gottschall and Mari Osawa (eds.), *Gendering the knowledge economy* (Basingstoke: Palgrave, 2007). On mobility gendering, see Tanu Uteng and Tim Cresswell (eds.), *Gendered mobilities* (Aldershot: Ashgate, 2008).

11 Barry Wellman, 'Physical place and cyber place: the rise of networked individualism', *International Journal of Urban and Regional Research*, 2001, 25: pp. 227–52, 227.

12 Barry Wellman, 'Little boxes, glocalization, and networked individualism', in Makoto Tanabe, Peter Van den Besselaar and Toru Ishida (eds.), *Digital cities II: computational and sociological approaches* (Berlin: Springer, 2002). The famous UK studies of Bethnal Green in East London in the 1950s particularly show this: Michael Young and Peter Willmott, *Family and kinship in East London* (Harmondsworth: Penguin, 1962).

13   Barry Wellman, 'Physical place and cyber place: the rise of networked individualism', *International Journal of Urban and Regional Research*, 25, 2001: pp. 227–52, 234.

14   Barry Wellman, 'Physical place and cyber place: the rise of networked individualism', *International Journal of Urban and Regional Research*, 2001, 25: pp. 227–52, 238.

15   Christian Licoppe, '"Connected" presence: the emergence of a new repertoire for managing social relationships in a changing communication technoscape', *Environment and Planning D: Society and Space*, 2004, 22: pp. 135–56, 139.

16   Barry Wellman, Bernie Hogan, Kristen Berg, Jeffrey Boase, Juan-Antonio Carrasco, Rochelle Côté, Jennifer Kayahara, Tracy L.M. Kennedy and Phuoc Tran, 'Connected lives: the project', in Patrick Purcell (ed.), *Networked neighbourhoods* (Berlin: Springer, 2005), p. 4.

17   Duncan Watts, *Small worlds* (Princeton, NJ: Princeton University Press, 1999), p. 11; Duncan Watts, *Six degrees: the science of a connected age* (London: Heinemann, 2003), chapter 5.

18   Mark Granovetter, 'The strength of weak ties: a network theory revisited', *Sociological Theory*, 1983, 1: pp. 203–33.

19   Mark Granovetter, 'The strength of weak ties: a network theory revisited', *Sociological Theory*, 1983, 1: 203–33; Raymond Burt, *Structural holes* (Cambridge, MA: Harvard University Press, 1992), pp. 24–7; Albert-László Barabási, *Linked: the new science of networks* (Cambridge, MA: Perseus, 2002), p. 43.

20   Mark Buchanan, *Small world: uncovering nature's hidden networks* (London: Weidenfeld and Nicholson, 2002), chapter 7; Duncan Watts, *Small worlds* (Princeton: Princeton University Press, 1999); Duncan Watts, *Six degrees: the science of a connected age* (London: Heinemann, 2003), chapter 4. Technically this is a scale-free or power law distribution, rather than a normal distribution.

21   Kay Axhausen, 'Social networks and travel: some hypotheses', in Kieran Donaghy, Stefan Poppelreuter and Georg Rudinger (eds.), *Social aspects of sustainable transport: transatlantic perspectives* (Aldershot: Ashgate, 2005).

22   Barry Wellman, Bernie Hogan, Kristen Berg, Jeffrey Boase, Juan-Antonio Carrasco, Rochelle Côté, Jennifer Kayahara, Tracy L.M. Kennedy and Phuoc Tran, 'Connected lives: the project', in Patrick Purcell (ed.), *Networked neighbourhoods* (Berlin: Springer, 2005), p. 20.

23   Jonas Larsen, John Urry and Kay Axhausen, 'Coordinating face-to-face meetings in mobile network societies', *Information, Communication and Society*, 2008, 11: 640–58.

24   Georg Simmel, *Simmel on culture*, eds. David Frisby and Mike Featherstone (London: Sage, 1997), p. 177.

25   See John Urry, *Mobilities* (Cambridge: Polity, 2007), chapter 11.

26   Erving Goffman, *Relations in public* (Harmondsworth: Penguin, 1971), p. 13.

27   Duncan Watts, *Six degrees: the science of a connected age* (London: Heinemann, 2003), p. 113.

28   Duncan Watts, *Small worlds* (Princeton: Princeton University Press, 1999).

29   See John Urry, *Mobilities* (Cambridge: Polity, 2007), for details.

30 This is explored in Jonas Larsen, John Urry and Kay Axhausen, *Mobilities, networks, geographies* (Aldershot: Ashgate, 2006).

31 See Jonas Larsen, John Urry and Kay Axhausen, 'Networks and tourism, mobile social life', *Annals of Tourism Research*, 2007, 34: pp. 244–62, on the following. Lancaster's *Tourist* Information Centre has just been relocated within a cultural industries complex and is now known as a *Visitor* Information Centre.

32 Tom O'Dell, *Cultural kinaesthesis: the energies and tensions of mobility* (Lund, Sweden: Lund University, 2004), p. 15.

33 Francis McGlone, Alison Park and Ceridwen Roberts, 'Kinship and friendship: attitudes and behaviour in Britain 1986–95', in Susan McRae (ed.), *Changing Britain: families and households in the 1990s* (Oxford: Oxford University Press, 1999).

34 David Gordon, Laura Adelman, Karl Ashworth, Jonathon Bradshaw, Ruth Levitas, Sue Middleton, Christina Pantazis, Demi Patsios, Sarah Payne, Peter Townsend and Julie Williams, *Poverty and social exclusion in Britain* (York: Joseph Rowntree Foundation, York Publishing Services, 2000).

35 Alan Warde and Lydia Martens, *Eating out* (Cambridge: Cambridge University Press, 2000), p. 217.

36 Jonas Larsen, John Urry and Kay Axhausen, 'Networks and tourism, mobile social life', *Annals of Tourism Research*, 2007, 34: pp. 244–62, 259.

37 Jonas Larsen, John Urry and Kay Axhausen, *Mobilities, networks, geographies* (Aldershot: Ashgate, 2006), p. 105.

38 See, on the university campus as a place of meetingness, Ash Amin and Patrick Cohendet, *Architectures of knowledge* (Oxford: Oxford University Press, 2004).

39 Andreas Wittel, 'Towards a network sociality', *Theory, Culture and Society*, 2001, 18: pp. 31–50.

40 Andreas Wittel, 'Towards a network sociality', *Theory, Culture and Society*, 2001, 18: pp. 31–50, 67.

41 Andreas Wittel, 'Towards a network sociality', *Theory, Culture and Society*, 2001, 18: pp. 31–50, 69; he also notes the importance of old-fashioned business cards among cool media workers!

42 Kay Axhausen, 'Social networks and travel: some hypotheses', in Kieran Donaghy, Stefan Poppelreuter and Georg Rudinger (eds.), *Social aspects of sustainable transport: transatlantic perspectives* (Aldershot: Ashgate, 2005).

43 See Pierre Bourdieu, *Distinction: a social critique of the judgment of taste* (London: Routledge, 1984); Fiona Devine, Mike Savage, John Scott and Rosemary Crompton, *Rethinking class: identities, cultures and lifestyles* (London: Palgrave, 2005).

44 Pierre Bourdieu, *Distinction: a social critique of the judgment of taste* (London: Routledge, 1984), p. 170.

45 See data and arguments in Tim Cresswell, *On the move* (London: Routledge, 2006).

46 Karl Marx, *Capital,* vol. 1 (London: Lawrence and Wishart, (1867) 1965).

47 Stephan Linder, *The harried leisure class* (New York: Columbia University Press, 1970).

48   Dale Southerton, Elizabeth Shove and Alan Warde, *Harried and hurried: time shortage and coordination of everyday life* (Manchester: CRIC Discussion Paper 47, University of Manchester, 2001).

49   See Noel Cass, Elizabeth Shove and John Urry, 'Social exclusion, mobility and access', *The Sociological Review*, 2005, 53: pp. 539–55.

50   Overall, see Jonas Larsen, John Urry and Kay Axhausen, 'Coordinating face-to-face meetings in mobile network societies, *Information, Communication and Society*, 2008, 11: pp. 640–58.

51   Rich Ling, *The mobile connection: the cell phone's impact on society* (New York: Morgan Kaufmann, 2004), p. 69.

52   Glenn Lyons and John Urry, 'Travel time use in the information age', *Transport Research A*, 2005, 39: pp. 257–76.

53   Rich Ling, *The mobile connection: the cell phone's impact on society* (New York: Morgan Kaufmann, 2004), p. 70.

54   Manuel Castells, Mireia Fernández-Ardévol, Jack Linchuan Qui and Araba Sey, *Mobile communication and society: a global perspective* (Massachusetts: MIT, 2007), p. 172.

55   Cited in Manuel Castells, Mireia Fernández-Ardévol, Jack Linchuan Qui and Araba Sey, *Mobile communication and society: a global perspective* (Massachusetts: MIT, 2007), pp. 172–3.

56   Ruth Rettie, 'Mobile phones as network capital', *Mobilities*, 2008, 3: pp. 291–311.

57   'For unto everyone that hath shall be given . . . but from him that hath not shall be taken away even that which he hath'; see Duncan Watts, *Six degrees: the science of a connected age* (London: Heinemann, 2003), p. 108.

58   Martha Maznevski and Katherine Chudoba, 'Bridging space over time: global virtual team dynamics and effectiveness', *Organisation Science*, 2000, 11: pp. 473–92, 489.

59   Kevin Hannam, Mimi Sheller and John Urry, 'Editorial: mobilities, immobilities and moorings', *Mobilities*, 2006, 1: pp. 1–22, 7–9.

60   Eric Klinenberg, *Heatwave: a social autopsy of disaster in Chicago* (Chicago: Chicago University Press, 2002).

61   Robert Putnam, *Bowling alone* (New York: Simon and Schuster, 2000).

62   Richard Layard, *Happiness. Lessons from a new science* (London: Allen Lane, 2005), p. 78.

63   Stephen Miller, *Conversation: a history of a declining art* (New Haven: Yale University Press, 2006).

64   Death rates per 100,000 population vary from six per year to forty per year, with China reckoned to have one of the highest rates of car deaths. See Mike Featherstone, 'Automobilities: an introduction', *Theory, Culture and Society*, 2004, 21: pp. 1–24, 4–5; and WHO, *World report on road traffic injury prevention* (Geneva: World Health Organization Publications, 2004).

65   Mimi Sheller, 'Mobility, freedom and public space', *Mobilities in Transit Symposium*, Trondheim, June 2006; and see John Urry, *Mobilities* (Cambridge: Polity, 2007), Chapter 9.

66   Tim Cresswell and Tanu Uteng (eds.), *Gendered mobilities* (Aldershot: Ashgate, 2008).

4 The globals and their mobilities

1 Zygmunt Bauman, *Community: seeking safety in an insecure world* (Cambridge: Polity, 2001), p. 113.

2 See Zygmunt Bauman, *Globalization: the human consequences* (Cambridge: Polity, 1998), p. 99.

3 See Charles Lemert, *Social things* (Boulder, CO: Rowman and Littlefield, 4th edition, 2008).

4 See, among others, Edward Luttwak, *Turbo-capitalism: winners and losers in the global economy* (London: HarperPerennial, 1999); Fredric Jameson, *Postmodernism, or the cultural logic of late capitalism* (Durham, NC: Duke University Press, 1999); Scott Lash and John Urry, *The end of organized capitalism* (Cambridge: Polity Press, 1987); and Zygmunt Bauman, *Liquid modernity* (Cambridge: Polity Press, 2000).

5 See Stephen Haseler, *The super-rich: the unjust new world of global capitalism* (London: Macmillan, 2000), pp. 4–7.

6 See Sylvia Walby, *Globalization and inequalities* (London: Sage, 2009).

7 See www.un.org/apps/news/story.asp?NewsID=28590&Cr=INCOME&Cr1 =ILO.

8 See www.cbsnews.com/stories/2008/05/03/earlyshow/living/money/main 4068795.shtml.

9 See http://finance.yahoo.com/banking-budgeting/article/104557/The-World'sBillionaires;_ylt = AqbOGjBvWGzzXezTVP26NB4y0tIF.

10 Robert Frank, *Richistan: a journey through the American wealth boom and the lives of the new rich* (New York: Three Rivers Press, 2008).

11 Corey Dolgon, *The end of the Hamptons: scenes from the class struggle in America's paradise* (New York: New York University Press, 2005).

12 Karen Ho, *Liquidated: an ethnography of Wall Street* (Durham, NC: Duke University Press, 2009).

13 Gillian Tett, *Fool's gold: how the bold dream of a small tribe at J.P. Morgan was corrupted by Wall Street greed and unleashed a catastrophe* (New York: Free Press, 2009).

14 Stephen Haseler, *The super-rich: the unjust new world of global capitalism*, (Houndmills, Basingstoke: Macmillan, 2000), p. 3.

15 Edward Luttwak, *Turbo-capitalism: winners and losers in the global economy* (London: HarperCollins, 1998), p. 5.

16 See Zygmunt Bauman, *Liquid modernity* (Cambridge: Polity Press, 2000); and Scott Lash and John Urry, *The end of organized capitalism* (Cambridge: Polity Press, 1987).

17 John Scott, *Corporate business and capitalist classes* (Oxford: Oxford University Press, 1997), p. 312.

18 The case study of Wim Eisner derives from research funded by the Australian Research Council. Eisner is a composite figure deployed to disguise individual identities.

19 See Anthony Elliott and Charles Lemert, *The new individualism: the emotional costs of globalization* (London: Routledge, 2009).

20   Luc Boltanski and Eve Chiapello, *The new spirit of capitalism* (London: Verso, 2007).
21   See Richard Sennett, *The corrosion of character* (New York: Norton, 2000).
22   Daniel Cohen, *Richesse du monde: pauvretés des nations* (Paris: Flammarion, 1998).
23   Zygmunt Bauman, *The individualized society* (Cambridge: Polity, 2002), p. 27.
24   Zygmunt Bauman, *The individualized society* (Cambridge: Polity, 2002), pp. 26–7. Bauman, like most other writers, ignores the exceptional level of resources, especially oil and the sources of electricity, that makes this lightness anything but 'light'.
25   See, for example, Kwame Anthony Appiah, *Cosmopolitanism: ethics in a world of strangers* (New York: Norton, 2007).
26   See Terry Eagleton, *The idea of culture* (Oxford: Blackwell, 2000).
27   Bronislaw Szerszynski and John Urry, 'Visuality, mobility and the cosmo-politan: inhabiting the world from afar', *British Journal of Sociology*, 2006, 57(1): pp. 113–31.
28   Adam Phillips, *Houdini's box: on the arts of escape* (London: Faber and Faber, 2001), pp. 26–7.
29   Social science research concerned with wealth and power has, for the most part, been preoccupied with the descriptive or objective description of elitism. See, for example, E. Carlton, *The few and the many: a typology of elites* (Aldershot: Scolar Press, 1996); and M. Dogan, *Elite configurations at the apex of power* (Leiden: Brill, 2003).
30   Scott Lash and John Urry, *Economies of signs and spaces* (London: Sage, 1994).
31   See Paul du Gay and Mike Pryke (eds.), *Cultural economy* (London: Sage, 2002).
32   C. Thurlow and A. Jaworski, 'The alchemy of the upwardly mobile: symbolic capital and the stylization of elites in frequent-flyer programmes', *Discourse and Society*, 2006, 17(1): pp. 99–135, 131.
33   Indeed, to take one example, Céline Dion used around 25 million litres of water in a single year at only one of her multiple residences. This is the equivalent of 250 average residents in a neighbourhood in the rich north. Available at: www.justnews.com/news/16400162/detail.html.

5 Mobile relationships: intimacy at-a-distance

1   See, among other contributions, N.R. Gerstal and H. Gross, *Commuter marriage: a study of work and family* (London: Guildford Press, 1984); Sasha Roseneil and Sheeley Budgeon, 'Cultures of intimacy and care beyond "the family": personal life and social change in the early 21st century', *Current Sociology*, 2004, 52(2): pp. 135–59; Raelene Wilding, 'Virtual intimacies? Families communicating across transnational contexts', *Global Networks*, 2006, 6(2): pp. 125–42; and Mary Holmes, 'Love lives at a distance: distance

relationships over the lifecourse', *Sociological Research Online*, 11(3), available at: www.socresonline.org.uk/11/3/holmes.html.

2 Generally, here, see Russell King and Nicola Mai, 'Love, sexuality and migration', a special issue of *Mobilities*, 2009, 4(3): pp. 295–448.

3 This case study derives from a project conducted under a research grant from the British Academy, in 2003, at the University of the West of England, Bristol. All names and socio-economic circumstances have been changed to protect the anonymity of the interviewees. Particular thanks are due to Elizabeth Wood at the Centre for Critical Theory at UWE, who worked diligently on this research project.

4 Aaron Ben-Ze'ev, *Love online: emotions on the internet* (Cambridge: Cambridge University Press, 2004).

5 See David Held, Anthony McGrew, David Goldblatt and Jonathan Perraton, *Global transformations: politics, economics and culture* (Cambridge: Polity Press, 1999); John Urry, *Global complexity* (Cambridge: Polity, 2003); and Sylvia Walby, *Globalization and inequalities* (London: Sage, 2009).

6 Frances Cairncross, *The death of distance* (London: Orion, 1997).

7 See Charles Lemert, Anthony Elliott, Daniel Chaffee and Eric Hsu (eds.), *Globalization: a reader*, Parts V and VI (London: Routledge, 2010).

8 Peter Berger and Brigitte Berger, *The war over the family* (New York: Anchor Press/Doubleday, 1983); Paul Amato and Alan Booth, *A generation at risk: growing up in an era of family upheaval* (Cambridge, MA: Harvard University Press, 2000).

9 See L. Rosenmayr, '*Showdown zwischen Alt und Jung?*', *Wiener Zweitung*, 1992, 26: p. 1.

10 Jeffrey Weeks, *Sexuality* (London and New York: Routledge, 1986), p. 100.

11 Gilles Lipovetsky, *Hypermodern individualism* (Cambridge: Polity, 2000), p. 16.

12 Anthony Giddens, *Modernity and self-identity* (Cambridge: Polity Press, 1991), p. 81.

13 Aaron Ben-Ze'ev, *Love online: emotions on the internet* (Cambridge: Cambridge University Press, 2004).

14 See David Conradson and Alan Latham, 'Friendship, networks and trans-nationality in a world city: Antipodean transmigrants in London', *Journal of Ethnic and Migration Studies*, 2005, 31(2): pp. 287–305.

15 See Michaela Benson and Karen O'Reilly, 'Migration and the search for a better way of life: a critical exploration of lifestyle migration', *The Sociological Review*, 2009, 57(4): pp. 608–25.

16 Anthony Giddens, *The consequences of modernity* (Cambridge: Polity Press, 1990), p. 38.

17 Anthony Giddens, *Modernity and self-identity* (Cambridge: Polity Press, 1991), p. 13.

18 Ulrich Beck and Elisabeth Beck-Gernsheim, *Individualization* (London: Thousand Oaks, 2002), p. 3.

19 Luce Irigaray, *An ethics of sexual difference* (Ithaca: Cornell University Press, 1993), p. 7.

20 Luce Irigaray, *Elemental passions* (London: Routledge, 1992), p. 54.
21 Elizabeth Grosz, *Space, time and perversion* (London: Routledge, 1995), p. 121.
22 The extensive if unequal character of these is elaborated in Sylvia Walby, *Globalization and inequalities* (London: Sage, 2009).
23 Ulrich Beck and Elizabeth Beck-Gernsheim, *Individualization* (London: Sage, 2000), p. 72.
24 Jennifer Mason, 'Personal narratives, relational selves: residential histories in the living and telling', *Sociological Review,* 2004, 52(2): pp. 162–79, 163.
25 Jennifer Mason, 'Personal narratives, relational selves: residential histories in the living and telling', *Sociological Review*, 2004, 52(2): pp. 162–79, 166–7.
26 James Hammerton, 'The quest for family and the mobility of modernity in narratives of postwar British emigration', *Global Networks*, 2004, 4(4): pp. 271–84.
27 UNDP, *Human Development Report 2004* (New York: United Nations Development Programme, UN, 2004), p. 87.
28 Russell King, 'Towards a new map of European migration', *International Journal of Population Geography*, 2002, 8(2): pp. 89–106.
29 Jennifer Mason, 'Managing kinship over long distances: the significance of "the visit"', *Social Policy & Society*, 2004, 3(4): pp. 421–9, 421.
30 Ethan Watters, *Urban tribes: are friends the new family?* (London: Bloomsbury, 2004); Katie Walsh, 'Discourses of love amongst British migrants in Dubai', *Mobilities*, 2009, 4(3): pp. 427–46, 431; Jonas Larsen, John Urry and Kay Axhausen, *Mobilities, networks, geographies* (Aldershot: Ashgate, 2006).
31 Katie Walsh, 'Discourses of love amongst British migrants in Dubai', *Mobilities*, 2009, 4(3): pp. 427–46.
32 Adam Phillips, *On flirtation* (London: Faber, 1994), p. 16.
33 See, on online relationships, Aaron Ben-Ze'ev, *Love online: emotions on the internet* (Cambridge: Cambridge University Press, 2004).
34 Christina Bachen, 'The family in the networked society: a summary of research on the American family', Center for Science Technology Society, Santa Clara University, CA, 2001. Available at: www.scu.edu/sts/nexus/winter2001/BachenArticle.cfm (accessed 2 November 2009).
35 See John Urry, *Mobilities* (Cambridge: Polity, 2007), p. 225.
36 See Cornelius Castoriadis, *The imaginary institution of society* (Cambridge: Polity Press, 1987). See also Anthony Elliott, *Social theory since Freud* (London and New York: Routledge, 2004).
37 Annette Lawson, *Adultery. An analysis of love and betrayal* (Oxford: Oxford University Press, 1990).
38 See N.R. Gerstel and H. Gross, *Commuter marriage: a study of work and family* (London: Guilford Press, 1984); Mary Holmes, 'Love lives at a distance: distance relationships over the lifecourse', *Sociological Research Online*, 2006, 11(3), available at: www.socresonline.org.uk/11/3/holmes.html.
39 Sylvia Walby, *Gender transformations* (London and New York: Routledge, 1997).

40 Simon Duncan, Rosalind Edwards, Tracey Reynolds, and Pam Alldred, 'Motherhood, paid work and partnering: values and theories', *Work, Employment and Society*, 2003, 17(2): 309–30; Lynne Segal, *Why feminism?* (Cambridge: Polity Press, 2000).

41 Mary Holmes, 'An equal distance? Individualisation, gender and intimacy in distance relationships', *The Sociological Review*, 2004, 52(2): pp. 180–200.

42 Arlie Hochschild, 'Global care chains and emotional surplus value', in Will Hutton and Anthony Giddens (eds.), *On the edge: living with global capitalism* (London: Jonathan Cape, 2000), p. 131; and see Barbara Ehrenreich and Arlie Hochschild (eds.), *Global woman: nannies, maids, and sex workers in the new economy* (New York: Metropolitan Books, 2002).

43 Nayla Moukarbel, 'Not allowed to love? Sri Lankan maids in Lebanon', *Mobilities*, 2009, 4(3): pp. 329–48; and see Nicola Yeates, 'Global care chains: a critical introduction', *Global Migration Perspectives No. 44*, (Geneva: Global Commission on International Migration, 2005).

44 See Mary Holmes, 'An equal distance? Individualisation, gender and intimacy in distance relationships', *The Sociological Review*, 2004, 52(2): pp. 180–200, 197.

45 Sietske Altink, *Stolen lives: trading women into sex and slavery* (London: Scarlet Press, 1995).

46 See www.guardian.co.uk/business/2009/oct/14/banking-prostitution (accessed 9 November 2009).

47 Jeremy Seabrook, *Travels in the skin trade* (London: Pluto, 1996), pp. 169–70.

48 Laura Maria Agustin, *Sex at the margins: migration, labour markets and the rescue industry* (London: Zed Books, 1988), p. 43.

49 Laura Maria Agustin, *Sex at the margins: migration, labour markets and the rescue industry* (London: Zed Books, 1988), p. 30.

50 Dennis Altman, *Global sex* (Chicago, IL: Chicago University Press, 2001).

51 Mary Holmes, 'Love lives at a distance: distance relationships over the lifecourse', *Sociological Research Online*, 2006, 11(3), available at: www.socresonline.org.uk/11/3/holmes.html.

6 Consuming to excess

1 Mike Davis and Daniel Bertrand Monk, 'Introduction', in *Evil paradises* (New York: The New Press, 2007), p. xv.

2 See www.burj-al-arab.com/. On Dubai, see Mattias Junemo, '"Let's build a palm island"; playfulness in complex times', in Mimi Sheller and John Urry (eds.), *Tourism mobilities* (London: Routledge, 2004); Mike Davis, 'Sand, fear, and money in Dubai', in Mike Davis and Daniel Bertrand Monk (eds.), *Evil paradises* (New York: The New Press, 2007); and Heiko Schmid, 'Economy of fascination: Dubai and Las Vegas as examples of a thematic production of urban landscapes', *Erdkunde*, 2006, 60: pp. 346–61.

3 Mike Davis, 'Sand, fear, and money in Dubai', in Mike Davis and Daniel Bertrand Monk (eds.), *Evil paradises* (New York: The New Press, 2007), p. 52.

4 See Bülent Diken and Carsten Bagge Laustsen, *The culture of exception* (London: Routledge, 2005).

5 Mike Davis, 'Sand, fear, and money in Dubai', in Mike Davis and Daniel Bertrand Monk (eds.), *Evil paradises* (New York: The New Press, 2007), pp. 64–6.

6 David Harvey, *The new imperialism* (Oxford: Oxford University Press, 2005).

7 Mike Davis, 'Sand, fear, and money in Dubai', in Mike Davis and Daniel Bertrand Monk (eds.), *Evil paradises* (New York: The New Press, 2007), p. 60.

8 Mike Davis and Daniel Bertrand Monk, 'Introduction', in *Evil paradises* (New York: The New Press, 2007), p. ix.

9 Mattias Junemo, ' "Let's build a palm island": playfulness in complex times', in Mimi Sheller and John Urry (eds.), *Tourism mobilities* (London: Routledge, 2004), p. 184.

10 Apart from Davis and Monk, see Scott A. Lukas, *The themed space* (Maryland: Lexington Books, 2007); and Anne Cronin and Kevin Hetherington (eds.), *Consuming the entrepreneurial city* (London: Routledge, 2008).

11 See Celia Lury, *Brands: the logos of the global economy* (London: Routledge, 2004), more generally on the brand as a medium of exchange between the company and consumers.

12 See Erving Goffman, *The presentation of self in everyday life* (Harmondsworth: Penguin, 1971).

13 See Anthony Elliott and Charles Lemert, *The new individualism: the emotional costs of globalization* (London and New York: Routledge, 2009).

14 Anthony Elliott, *Making the cut* (London: Reaktion, 2008), p. 13.

15 See John Urry, *The tourist gaze* (London: Sage, 2002); and John Walton, *Riding on rainbows* (St Albans: Skelter, 2007) on 'riding on rainbows' at Blackpool.

16 Rob Shields, *Places on the margin* (London: Routledge, 1991).

17 See Daniel Miller, *A theory of shopping* (Cornell: Cornell University Press, 1998).

18 Jean Baudrillard, *Simulacra and simulation* (Michigan: University of Michigan Press, 1994).

19 Paul Gilroy, 'Driving while black', in Daniel Miller (ed.), *Car cultures* (Oxford: Berg, 2000).

20 Mimi Sheller, 'Automotive emotions: feeling the car', *Theory, Culture and Society,* 2004, 21: pp. 221–42.

21 Roland Barthes, *Mythologies* (London: Vintage, 1972), p. 88. See Kingsley Dennis and John Urry, *After the car* (Cambridge: Polity, 2009), chapter 2.

22 Maria Isabel Mendes de Almeida, 'Consuming the night', in Anne Cronin and Kevin Hetherington (eds.), *Consuming the entrepreneurial city* (London: Routledge, 2008).

23 See Anthony Elliott, *Making the cut* (London: Reaktion, 2008), as well as Andreas Wittel, 'Toward a network sociality', *Theory, Culture & Society,* 2001, 18: pp. 51–76.

24 David Blackbourn, 'Fashionable spa towns in nineteenth century Europe', in Susan Anderson and Bruce Tabb (eds.), *Water, leisure and culture* (Oxford: Berg, 2002).

25 See examples in Mimi Sheller and John Urry (eds.), *Tourism mobilities* (London: Routledge, 2004).

26 Scott A. Lukas (ed.), *The themed space* (Maryland: Lexington Books, 2007), p. 2.

27 Antonio Luna-Garcia, 'Just another coffee! Milking the Barcelona model, marketing a global image, and the resistance of local identities', in Anne Cronin and Kevin Hetherington (eds.) *Consuming the entrepreneurial city* (London: Routledge, 2008).

28 Michel Foucault, 'Governmentality', in Graham Burchell, Colin Gordon and Peter Miller (eds.), *The Foucault effect: studies in governmentality* (London: Harvester Wheatsheaf, 1991); Erving Goffman, *Asylums* (Harmondsworth: Penguin, 1968).

29 Gilles Deleuze and Felix Guattari, *Nomadology* (New York: Semiotext(e), 1986); Gilles Deleuze, 'Postscript on control societies', in *Negotiations, 1972–1990* (New York: Columbia University Press, 1995).

30 See Chapter 3 above, and Barry Wellman, 'Physical place and cyberplace: the rise of personalised networking', *International Journal of Urban and Regional Research,* 2001, 25: pp. 227–52; Jonas Larsen, John Urry and Kay Axhausen, *Mobilities, networks, geographies* (Aldershot: Ashgate, 2006).

31 See John Urry, *Mobilities* (Cambridge: Polity, 2007), chapter 12, where the distinction between land and landscape is used to capture the import of such connoisseurship.

32 Mimi Sheller and John Urry (eds.), *Tourism mobilities* (London: Routledge, 2004); Machiel Lamers, *The future of tourism in Antartica* (Maastricht: Universitaire Pers Maastricht, 2009); Mike Robinson and Marina Novelli (eds.), *Niche tourism* (Oxford: Elsevier, 2005).

33 Alex Garland, *The beach* (Harmondsworth: Penguin, 1997); and see Colin Campbell, *The romantic ethic and the spirit of modern consumerism* (Oxford: Basil Blackwell, 1987).

34 See Mimi Sheller and John Urry (eds.), *Tourism mobilities* (London: Routledge, 2004).

35 See Barry Schwartz, *The paradox of choice* (New York: Harper, 2004), p. 172.

36 B. Joseph Pine and James Gilmore, *The experience economy* (Cambridge, MA: Harvard Business School Press, 1999).

37 Anthony Elliott, *Making the cut* (London: Reaktion, 2007), p. 145.

38 Available at: http://news.bbc.co.uk/1/hi/health/7043639.stm (accessed 15 October 2007).

39 See David Harvey, *The new imperialism* (Oxford: Oxford University Press, 2005), and *A brief history of neo-liberalism* (Oxford: Oxford University Press, 2005); and Naomi Klein, *The shock doctrine* (London: Penguin Allen Lane, 2007). See Sylvia Walby, *Globalisation and inequalities* (London: Sage, 2009), on the differences between neo-liberalism and social democracy.

40   John Perkins, *Confessions of an economic hit man* (London: Ebury Press, 2005), p. xiii.
41   Mike Davis and Daniel Bertrand Monk (eds.), *Evil paradises* (New York: The New Press, 2007); Tim Simpson, 'Macao, capital of the 21st century', *Environment and Planning D: Society and Space*, 2008, 26: pp. 1053–79.
42   Available at: http://granscalablog.com/gran-scala/ (accessed 8 June 2009).
43   As is well demonstrated in Bülent Diken and Carsten Bagge Laustsen, *The culture of exception* (London: Routledge, 2005), p. 110.
44   Rachel Carson, *The sea around us* (New York: Oxford University Press, 1961), p. 2.
45   Jørgen Ole Bærenholdt, Michael Haldrup, Jonas Larsen and John Urry, *Performing tourist places* (Aldershot: Ashgate, 2004), p. 50.
46   Mimi Sheller, *Consuming the Caribbean* (London: Routledge, 2003).
47   Mimi Sheller, 'Infrastructures of the imagined island: software, mobilities, and the new architecture of cyberspatial paradise', *Environment and Planning A*, 2008, 41: pp. 1386–1403, 1396.
48   Mimi Sheller, 'The new Caribbean complexity: mobility systems and the rescaling of development', *Singapore Journal of Tropical Geography*, 2008, 14: pp. 373–84.
49   Available at: www.royalcaribbean.com (accessed 29 May 2008).
50   Mimi Sheller, 'Infrastructures of the imagined island: software, mobilities, and the new architecture of cyberspatial paradise', *Environment and Planning A*, 2008, 41: pp. 1386–403. Davis and Monk state that the scale of global offshore tax havens is ten times greater than the UK's GDP: 'Introduction', in *Evil paradises* (New York: The New Press, 2007), p. ix. More generally, see Ronen Palan, *The offshore world* (New York: Cornell University Press, 2003).
51   Mimi Sheller, 'Always turned on', in Anne Cronin and Kevin Hetherington (eds.), *Consuming the entrepreneurial city* (London: Routledge, 2008), p. 123.
52   Available at: www.guardian.co.uk/business/2009/feb/02/tax-gap-avoidance (accessed 8 June 2009).
53   See Steve Graham and Simon Marvin, *Splintering urbanism* (London: Routledge, 2001).
54   Barry Schwartz, *The paradox of choice* (New York: Harper, 2004), pp. 109–10.
55   Barry Schwartz, *The paradox of choice* (New York: Harper, 2004), p. 167.
56   Mike Davis and Daniel Bertrand Monk, 'Introduction', in *Evil paradises* (New York: The New Press, 2007), p. xv.
57   Barry Schwartz, *The paradox of choice* (New York: Harper, 2004), p. 191. And see John Urry, *Reference groups and the theory of revolution* (London: Routledge, 1973), on the neglected concept of reference groups.
58   Thorsten Veblen, *The theory of the leisure class* (New York: Macmillan, 1912), pp. 85, 96.
59   Bas Amelung, Sarah Nicholls and David Viner, 'Implications of global climate change for tourism flows and seasonality', *Journal of Travel Research*, 2007, 45: pp. 285–96.

60 Paul Lewis, 'Too high, too fast: the party's over for Dubai', *The Guardian*, 14 February 2009, pp. 28–9.

7 Contested futures

1 John DeCicco and Freda Fung, *Global warming on the road* (Washington: Environmental Defense, 2006), p. 1.
2 Karl Marx and Friedrich Engels, *The manifesto of the Communist Party* (Moscow: Foreign Languages, (1848) 1888), p. 58; see Max Weber, *The Protestant ethic and the spirit of capitalism* (London: Unwin, 1939), p. 181, on the implications of the finitude of the world's fossil resources.
3 Terry Leahy, 'Discussion of "global warming and sociology"', *Current Sociology*, 2008, 56: pp. 475–84, 481; we are not suggesting that other modern economic systems have a 'better' environmental record.
4 Graham Harris, *Seeking sustainability in an age of complexity* (Cambridge: Cambridge University Press, 2007); David Nye, *Consuming power* (Cambridge, MA: MIT Press, 1999).
5 See Stephen Burman, *The state of the American Empire. How the USA shapes the world* (London: Earthscan, 2007).
6 Stephen Burman, *The State of the American Empire. How the USA shapes the world* (London: Earthscan, 2007), pp. 16–26.
7 Julian Borger, 'Half of global car exhaust produced by US vehicles', *The Guardian*, 29 June 2008 (car exhaust in no way makes up all the transport related carbon: see www.guardian.co.uk/environment/2009/apr/09/shipping-pollution); John DeCicco and Freda Fung, *Global warming on the road* (Washington: Environmental Defense, 2006).
8 See Anthony Giddens, *The consequences of modernity* (Cambridge: Polity, 1990).
9 On the idea of borderlessness, see Kenichi Ohmae, *The borderless world* (London: Collins, 1990), a book published in 1990 at the beginning of the decade of 'free world' optimism that ended on September 11, 2001.
10 See David Harvey, *A brief history of neo-liberalism* (Oxford: Oxford University Press, 2005). Naomi Klein, in *The shock doctrine* (London: Penguin Allen Lane, 2007), notes that, even by 1999, Chicago School alumni included twenty-five government ministers and more than a dozen central-bank presidents (p. 166)!
11 Naomi Klein, *The shock doctrine* (London: Penguin Allen Lane, 2007), pp. 3–21.
12 IPCC (2007), available at: www.ipcc.ch/ (accessed 2 June 2008); Nicholas Stern, *The economics of climate change* (Cambridge: Cambridge University Press, 2007).
13 Nicholas Stern, *The Economics of Climate Change* (Cambridge: Cambridge University Press, 2007), p. 3.
14 See James Lovelock, *The revenge of Gaia* (London: Allen Lane, 2006); Elizabeth Kolbert, *Field notes from a catastrophe. A frontline report on climate change* (London: Bloomsbury, 2007); Eugene Linden, *Winds of change.*

Climate, weather and the destruction of civilizations (New York: Simon and Schuster, 2007); Mark Lynas, *Six degrees: our future on a hotter planet* (London: Fourth Estate, 2007); Fred Pearce, *With speed and violence: why scientists fear tipping points in climate change* (Boston: Beacon Press, 2007); George Monbiot, *Heat: how to stop the planet burning* (London: Allen Lane, 2007).

15 And see www.opendemocracy.net/globalization-climate_change_debate/ article_2508.jsp (accessed 9 November 2009).

16 See Constance Lever-Tracy, 'Global warming and sociology', *Current Sociology*, 2008, 56: pp. 445–66, 448–50. Generally, see Kingsley Dennis and John Urry, *After the car* (Cambridge: Polity, 2008), chapter 1.

17 Ulrich Beck, *World at risk* (Cambridge: Polity, 2009), p. 53.

18 José Rial, Roger Pielbe, Martin Beniston, Martin Clavssen, Josep Canadell, Peter Cox, Hermann Held, Nathalie de Noblet-Ducoudré, Ronald Prinn, James Reynolds and José Salas, 'Nonlinearities, feedbacks and critical thresholds within the Earth's climate system', *Climate Change*, 2004, 65: pp. 11–38; James Lovelock, *The revenge of Gaia* (London: Allen Lane, 2006); Fred Pearce, *With speed and violence: why scientists fear tipping points in climate change* (Boston: Beacon Press, 2007).

19 Available at: www.guardian.co.uk/environment/2005/aug/11/science.climate change1 (accessed 17 December 2008).

20 James Lovelock, *The revenge of Gaia* (London: Allen Lane, 2006), p. 35.

21 Fred Pearce, *With speed and violence: why scientists fear tipping points in climate change* (Boston: Beacon Press, 2007), p. 21.

22 Available at: www.who.int/globalchange/news/fsclimandhealth/en/index. html (accessed 13 July 09).

23 Thomas Homer-Dixon, *The upside of down* (London: Souvenir, 2006), p. 81.

24 David Strahan, *The last oil shock* (London: John Murray, 2007), p. 85.

25 See David Strahan, *The last oil shock* (London: John Murray, 2007), chapter 2.

26 Stephen Burman, *The state of the American Empire: how the USA shapes the world* (London: Earthscan, 2007), pp. 26–9.

27 David Strahan, *The last oil shock* (London: John Murray, 2007), pp. 62–3.

28 Jeremy Leggett, *Half gone: oil, gas, hot air and global energy crisis* (London: Portobello Books, 2005); Richard Heinberg, *The party's over: oil, war and the fate of industrial society* (New York: Clearview Books, 2005); Thomas Homer-Dixon, *The upside of down* (London: Souvenir, 2006); Julian Darley, *High noon for natural gas* (Vermont: Chelsea Green, 2004); David Strahan, *The last oil shock* (London: John Murray, 2007); Thomas Homer-Dixon (ed.) *Carbon shift* (Random House, Canada, 2009). But, see P. Jackson, *Why the peak oil theory falls down: myths, legends, and the future of oil resources.* Available at: www.cera.com/aspx/cda/public1/news/pressReleases/press ReleaseDetails.aspx?CID = 8444 (2006; accessed 21 November 2006). The 'official' view is found in the International Energy Agency's *World Energy Report 2008*. This paints an increasingly pessimistic picture as to future oil

supplies, with the strong likelihood of much higher prices (David Strahan, 'Pipe dreams', *The Guardian/Environment*, 3 December 2008, p. 7).

29 Jeremy Leggett, *Half gone: oil, gas, hot air and global energy crisis* (London: Portobello Books, 2005), pp. 12, 15.

30 This is clearly documented in David Strahan, *The last oil shock* (London: John Murray, 2007), chapter 1.

31 David Strahan, 'Pipe dreams', *The Guardian/Environment*, 3 December 2008, p. 7.

32 Thomas Homer-Dixon, *The upside of down* (London: Souvenir, 2006), p. 174. On the significance of oil for food, see the excellently titled work by Dale Pfeiffer, *Eating fossil foods* (Gabriola Island, BC: New Society Publishers, 2006).

33 Available at: www.guardian.co.uk/business/2008/jun/10/oil.france (accessed 12 June 2008).

34 Rob Hopkins, *The transition handbook* (Totnes: Green Books, 2008), pp. 20–1. Rifkin claims that the oil age is 'winding down as fast as it revved up': Jeremy Rifkin, *The hydrogen economy* (New York: Penguin Putnam, 2002), p. 174.

35 James Kunstler, *The long emergency: surviving the converging catastrophes of the 21st Century* (London: Atlantic Books, 2006), p. 65; Thomas Homer-Dixon, *The upside of down* (London: Souvenir, 2006).

36 Available at: http://news.ncsu.edu/releases/2007/may/104.html (accessed 28 May 2008).

37 See Mike Davis, *Planet of slums* (London: Verso, 2007), on how there are probably 200,000 contemporary slums, mostly located on the edge of major cities.

38 Mike Davis, *Planet of slums* (London: Verso, 2007), p. 133.

39 Gilberto Gallopin, Al Hammond, Paul Raskin and Rob Swart, *Branch points: global scenarios and human choice* (Stockholm: Stockholm Environment Institute – Global Scenario Group, 1997), p. 17.

40 J. Timmons Roberts and Bradley Parks, *A climate of injustice* (Cambridge, MA: MIT Press, 2007).

41 Chris Abbott, *An uncertain future: law enforcement, national security and climate change* (Oxford: Oxford Research Group, 2008), available at: www. oxfordresearchgroup.org.uk/publications/briefing–papers/pdf/uncertainfuture. pdf (accessed 18 February 2008).

42 See Randeep Ramesh, 'Paradise almost lost: Maldives seek a new homeland', *The Guardian*, 10 November 2008.

43 Available at TimesOnline: www.timesonline.co.uk/tol/news/world/asia/article 2994650.ece (accessed 11 December 2007).

44 David Pfeiffer, *Eating fossil fuels* (Gabriola Island, BC: New Society Publishers, 2006), p. 15.

45 David Pfeiffer, *Eating fossil fuels* (Gabriola Island, BC: New Society Publishers, 2006), p. 25.

46 David Pfeiffer, *Eating fossil fuels* (Gabriola Island, BC: New Society Publishers, 2006), p. 2.

47   See David Strahan, *The last oil shock* (London: John Murray, 2007), p. 123; Thomas Homer-Dixon (ed.) *Carbon Shift* (Toronto: Random House, 2009), p. 13.

48   Terry Leahy, 'Discussion of "Global warming and sociology"', *Current Sociology*, 2008, 56: pp. 475–84, 480.

49   Ulrich Beck, *World at risk* (Cambridge: Polity, 2009), pp. 52–3.

50   See Foresight, *Intelligent infrastructure futures: the scenarios – towards 2055* (London: Office of Science and Technology, Department for Trade and Industry, 2006). John Urry was one of four science experts. And see Kevin Anderson, Alice Bowes, Sarah Mander, Simon Shackley, Paolo Agnolucci and Paul Ekins, *Decarbonising modern societies: integrated scenario process and workshops* (London and Manchester: Tyndall Centre, 2006); Forum for the Future, *Climate futures* (London: Forum for the Future, 2008); National Intelligence Council, *Global trends 2025* (Washington, DC: National Intelligence Council, 2008); Kingsley Dennis and John Urry, *After the car* (Cambridge: Polity, 2009).

51   See, for fascinating examples, Frank Geels and Wim Smit, 'Lessons from failed technology futures: potholes in the road to the future', in Nik Brown, Brian Rappert and Andrew Webster (eds.), *Contested futures* (Aldershot: Ashgate, 2000).

52   Available at: www.youtube.com/watch?v=wa2DUe2vJew (accessed 16 December 2008).

53   See Marina Benjamin, *Rocket dreams* (London: Vintage, 2003).

54   Robert Costanza, 'Four visions of the century ahead', *The Futurist*, February 1999: pp. 23–8.

55   Gilberto Gallopin, Al Hammond, Paul Raskin and Rob Swart, *Branch points: global scenarios and human choice* (Stockholm: Stockholm Environment Institute – Global Scenario Group, 1997), pp. 35–6; Robert Costanza, 'Four visions of the century ahead', *The Futurist*, February 1999: pp. 23–8.

56   A recent suggestion on rebuilding market towns in the UK captures something of this future; each town would have to have some really special characteristic in order to attract *and* to keep residents there and not to keep travelling elsewhere.

57   David Harvey, *Spaces of hope* (Edinburgh: Edinburgh University Press, 2000).

58   James Kunstler, *The long emergency: surviving the converging catastrophes of the 21st century* (London: Atlantic Books, 2006).

59   James Kunstler, *The long emergency: surviving the converging catastrophes of the 21st century* (London: Atlantic Books, 2006), p. 270.

60   Available at: www.happyplanetindex.org/news/archive/news-2.html (accessed 12 July 2009).

61   Gilberto Gallopin, Al Hammond, Paul Raskin and Rob Swart, *Branch points: global scenarios and human choice* (Stockholm: Stockholm Environment Institute – Global Scenario Group, 1997), p. 29.

62   Various literary post-oil 'warlord' dystopias are now appearing. See Sarah Hall, *The Carhullan Army* (London: Faber and Faber, 2007); and Marcel Theroux, *Far north* (London: Faber and Faber, 2009).

63 Gilberto Gallopin, Al Hammond, Paul Raskin and Rob Swart, *Branch points: global scenarios and human choice* (Stockholm: Stockholm Environment Institute – Global Scenario Group, 1997), p. 34.

64 Kevin Hannam, Mimi Sheller and John Urry, 'Editorial: mobilities, immobilities and moorings', *Mobilities*, 2006, 1: pp. 1–22; Henry Giroux, 'Violence, Katrina, and the biopolitics of disposability', *Theory, Culture and Society*, 24: pp. 305–9.

65 See David Strahan, *The last oil shock* (London: John Murray, 2007), pp. 58–9.

66 J. Timmons Roberts and Bradley Parks, *A climate of injustice* (Cambridge, MA: MIT Press, 2007).

67 See essays in Daniel Miller (ed.), *Car cultures* (Oxford: Berg, 2000).

68 See the 1982 movie *Mad Max 2*. This scenario is termed the Mad Max scenario in Robert Costanza, 'Four visions of the century ahead', *The Futurist*, February 1999: pp. 23–8.

69 Naomi Klein, *The shock doctrine* (London: Penguin Allen Lane, 2007), p. 21.

70 John Tiffin and Christopher Kissling, *Transport communications* (London: Kogan Paul, 2007), p. 204.

71 On rationing air miles, see George Monbiot, *Heat: how to stop the planet burning* (London: Allen Lane, 2006), p. 173. On carbon rationing generally, see David Strahan, *The last oil shock* (London: John Murray, 2007), chapter 10.

72 Available at: www.hp.com/halo/introducing.html (accessed 8 December 2008).

73 Available at: www.advanced.org/teleimmersion.html (accessed 8 December 2008).

74 For details, see Bill Sharpe and Tony Hodgson, *Towards a cyber-urban ecology* (London: Foresight Project on Intelligent Infrastructure Systems, 2006), pp. 1–44.

75 Eric Beinhocker, *The origin of wealth* (London: Random House, 2006), pp. 333, 374.

76 See Information Commissioner, *A report on the surveillance society* (London: The Surveillance Network, 2006).

77 See the BBC Report, available at: http://news.bbc.co.uk/1/hi/uk/6108496.stm (accessed 5 November 2006). There are up to 5 million CCTV cameras in Britain. For a recent examination of the politics of contemporary surveillance, see the 2008 BBC drama *The last enemy*, available at: www.bbc.co.uk/drama/lastenemy/ (accessed 4 April 2008).

78 Nicholas Stern, *Stern Review: the economics of climate change* (London: House of Commons, 2006), p. 1. Significantly, this review ignores the other market failure, namely the using up and probable extinction of oil. Strahan more generally critiques economics for its failure to examine the impact of energy upon rates of economic growth: David Strahan, *The last oil shock* (London: John Murray, 2007), chapter 5.

79 Joseph Stiglitz, *Making globalization work* (London: Penguin, 2007); Stephen Haseler, *Meltdown* (London: Forumpress, 2008).

80 Doug Guthrie, *China and globalisation* (New York: Routledge, 2009).

81   Saskia Sassen, 'Too big to save: the end of financial capitalism', *Open Democracy News Analysis*, 1 April 2009.
82   Nicholas Stern, *The economics of climate change* (Cambridge: Cambridge University Press, 2007), p. 644.
83   Joseph Stiglitz, *Making globalization work* (London: Penguin, 2007).
84   Paul Krugman, *The return of depression economics* (London: Penguin, 2008).
85   Anthony Giddens, *The politics of climate change* (Cambridge: Polity, 2009), chapter 5.
86   Jared Diamond, *Collapse: how societies choose to fail or survive* (London: Allen Lane, 2005).
87   See Thomas Homer-Dixon, *The upside of down* (London: Souvenir, 2006), chapter 2.
88   Joseph Tainter, *The collapse of complex societies* (Cambridge: Cambridge University Press, 1988), p. 216. And see Martin Rees, *Our final century* (London: Arrow Books, 2003); Thomas Homer-Dixon, 'Prepare for tomorrow's breakdown', *The Globe and Mail*, 14 May 2006; Thomas Homer-Dixon, *The upside of down* (London: Souvenir, 2006); and David Strahan, *The last oil shock* (London: John Murray, 2007).

Afterword

1   Anthony Giddens, *The politics of climate change* (Cambridge: Polity Press, 2009), p. 228.
2   See Herbert Marcuse, *Eros and civilization* (London: Routledge, 2nd edition, 1987). See also Fredric Jameson, *The prison-house of language* (Princeton, NJ: Princeton University Press, 1975).
3   Rob Hopkins, *The transition handbook* (Totnes: Green Books, 2008). And see the 2006 film, *The power of community: how Cuba survived peak oil*, an American documentary that explores the economic collapse and eventual recovery of Cuba following the fall of the Soviet Union in 1991. Following the dramatic steps taken by both the Cuban government and citizens, its major themes include urban agriculture, energy dependence and sustainability.
4   Available at: www.romow.com/news-blog/virtual-meetings-gain-popularity-as-travel-costs-increase/ (accessed 11 August 2009).
5   On Cisco Systems' videoconferencing, see: www.nytimes.com/2009/10/02/technology/companies/02cisco.html?hp.
6   See www.eweek.com/c/a/Search-Engines/Greenminded-Google-Gets-Redfaced-Over-Search-Energy-Consumption-Claims/ (accessed 4 November 2009).
7   Paul Voosen, 'Industry lines up behind bold African, Mideast solar project in hopes politicians will follow', *New York Times*, 22 July 2009, available at: www.nytimes.com/gwire/2009/07/22/22greenwire-industry-lines-up-behind-bold-african-mideast-67746.html (accessed 9 October 2009).
8   Todd Woody, 'Alternative energy projects stumble on a need for water', *New York Times*, 29 September 2009. Available at: www.nytimes.com/2009/09/30/business/energy-environment/30water.html (accessed 09 November 2009).

Index

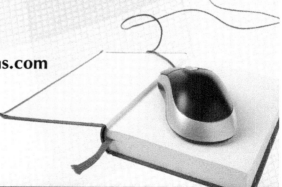

Lightning Source UK Ltd.
Milton Keynes UK
UKOW05f0827250517
301981UK00004B/54/P